MW01608998

The staffe of Christian faith profitable to all Christians, for to arme themselues agaynst the enimies of the Gospell. Translated out of Frenche into English, by Iohn Brooke of Ashe next Sandvviche. (1577)

John Brooke

The staffe of Christian faith profitable to all Christians, for to arme themselues agaynst the enimies of the Gospell: and also for to knowe the antiquitie of our holy fayth, and of the true Church.
Baston de la foy chrestienne.
Brès, Guy de, 1522-1567.
Brooke, John, d. 1582.
A translation of: Le baston de la foy chrestienne.
At foot of title: Cum priuilegio.
Includes index.
[48], 382, [8] p.
Imprinted at London : By Iohn Daye, dwelling ouer Aldersgate, Anno. 1577.
STC (2nd ed.) / 12476
English
Reproduction of the original in the Henry E. Huntington Library and Art Gallery

Early English Books Online (EEBO) Editions

Imagine holding history in your hands.

Now you can. Digitally preserved and previously accessible only through libraries as Early English Books Online, this rare material is now available in single print editions. Thousands of books written between 1475 and 1700 and ranging from religion to astronomy, medicine to music, can be delivered to your doorstep in individual volumes of high-quality historical reproductions.

We have been compiling these historic treasures for more than 70 years. Long before such a thing as "digital" even existed, ProQuest founder Eugene Power began the noble task of preserving the British Museum's collection on microfilm. He then sought out other rare and endangered titles, providing unparalleled access to these works and collaborating with the world's top academic institutions to make them widely available for the first time. This project furthers that original vision.

These texts have now made the full journey -- from their original printing-press versions available only in rare-book rooms to online library access to new single volumes made possible by the partnership between artifact preservation and modern printing technology. A portion of the proceeds from every book sold supports the libraries and institutions that made this collection possible, and that still work to preserve these invaluable treasures passed down through time.

This is history, traveling through time since the dawn of printing to your own personal library.

Initial Proquest EEBO Print Editions collections include:

Early Literature

This comprehensive collection begins with the famous Elizabethan Era that saw such literary giants as Chaucer, Shakespeare and Marlowe, as well as the introduction of the sonnet. Traveling through Jacobean and Restoration literature, the highlight of this series is the Pollard and Redgrave 1475-1640 selection of the rarest works from the English Renaissance.

Early Documents of World History

This collection combines early English perspectives on world history with documentation of Parliament records, royal decrees and military documents that reveal the delicate balance of Church and State in early English government. For social historians, almanacs and calendars offer insight into daily life of common citizens. This exhaustively complete series presents a thorough picture of history through the English Civil War.

Historical Almanacs

Historically, almanacs served a variety of purposes from the more practical, such as planting and harvesting crops and plotting nautical routes, to predicting the future through the movements of the stars. This collection provides a wide range of consecutive years of "almanacks" and calendars that depict a vast array of everyday life as it was several hundred years ago.

Early History of Astronomy & Space

Humankind has studied the skies for centuries, seeking to find our place in the universe. Some of the most important discoveries in the field of astronomy were made in these texts recorded by ancient stargazers, but almost as impactful were the perspectives of those who considered their discoveries to be heresy. Any independent astronomer will find this an invaluable collection of titles arguing the truth of the cosmic system.

Early History of Industry & Science

Acting as a kind of historical Wall Street, this collection of industry manuals and records explores the thriving industries of construction; textile, especially wool and linen; salt; livestock; and many more.

Early English Wit, Poetry & Satire

The power of literary device was never more in its prime than during this period of history, where a wide array of political and religious satire mocked the status quo and poetry called humankind to transcend the rigors of daily life through love, God or principle. This series comments on historical patterns of the human condition that are still visible today.

Early English Drama & Theatre

This collection needs no introduction, combining the works of some of the greatest canonical writers of all time, including many plays composed for royalty such as Queen Elizabeth I and King Edward VI. In addition, this series includes history and criticism of drama, as well as examinations of technique.

Early History of Travel & Geography

Offering a fascinating view into the perception of the world during the sixteenth and seventeenth centuries, this collection includes accounts of Columbus's discovery of the Americas and encompasses most of the Age of Discovery, during which Europeans and their descendants intensively explored and mapped the world. This series is a wealth of information from some the most groundbreaking explorers.

Early Fables & Fairy Tales

This series includes many translations, some illustrated, of some of the most well-known mythologies of today, including Aesop's Fables and English fairy tales, as well as many Greek, Latin and even Oriental parables and criticism and interpretation on the subject.

Early Documents of Language & Linguistics

The evolution of English and foreign languages is documented in these original texts studying and recording early philology from the study of a variety of languages including Greek, Latin and Chinese, as well as multilingual volumes, to current slang and obscure words. Translations from Latin, Hebrew and Aramaic, grammar treatises and even dictionaries and guides to translation make this collection rich in cultures from around the world.

Early History of the Law

With extensive collections of land tenure and business law "forms" in Great Britain, this is a comprehensive resource for all kinds of early English legal precedents from feudal to constitutional law, Jewish and Jesuit law, laws about public finance to food supply and forestry, and even "immoral conditions." An abundance of law dictionaries, philosophy and history and criticism completes this series.

Early History of Kings, Queens and Royalty

This collection includes debates on the divine right of kings, royal statutes and proclamations, and political ballads and songs as related to a number of English kings and queens, with notable concentrations on foreign rulers King Louis IX and King Louis XIV of France, and King Philip II of Spain. Writings on ancient rulers and royal tradition focus on Scottish and Roman kings, Cleopatra and the Biblical kings Nebuchadnezzar and Solomon.

Early History of Love, Marriage & Sex

Human relationships intrigued and baffled thinkers and writers well before the postmodern age of psychology and self-help. Now readers can access the insights and intricacies of Anglo-Saxon interactions in sex and love, marriage and politics, and the truth that lies somewhere in between action and thought.

Early History of Medicine, Health & Disease

This series includes fascinating studies on the human brain from as early as the 16th century, as well as early studies on the physiological effects of tobacco use. Anatomy texts, medical treatises and wound treatment are also discussed, revealing the exponential development of medical theory and practice over more than two hundred years.

Early History of Logic, Science and Math

The "hard sciences" developed exponentially during the 16th and 17th centuries, both relying upon centuries of tradition and adding to the foundation of modern application, as is evidenced by this extensive collection. This is a rich collection of practical mathematics as applied to business, carpentry and geography as well as explorations of mathematical instruments and arithmetic; logic and logicians such as Aristotle and Socrates; and a number of scientific disciplines from natural history to physics.

Early History of Military, War and Weaponry

Any professional or amateur student of war will thrill at the untold riches in this collection of war theory and practice in the early Western World. The Age of Discovery and Enlightenment was also a time of great political and religious unrest, revealed in accounts of conflicts such as the Wars of the Roses.

Early History of Food

This collection combines the commercial aspects of food handling, preservation and supply to the more specific aspects of canning and preserving, meat carving, brewing beer and even candy-making with fruits and flowers, with a large resource of cookery and recipe books. Not to be forgotten is a "the great eater of Kent," a study in food habits.

Early History of Religion

From the beginning of recorded history we have looked to the heavens for inspiration and guidance. In these early religious documents, sermons, and pamphlets, we see the spiritual impact on the lives of both royalty and the commoner. We also get insights into a clergy that was growing ever more powerful as a political force. This is one of the world's largest collections of religious works of this type, revealing much about our interpretation of the modern church and spirituality.

Early Social Customs

Social customs, human interaction and leisure are the driving force of any culture. These unique and quirky works give us a glimpse of interesting aspects of day-to-day life as it existed in an earlier time. With books on games, sports, traditions, festivals, and hobbies it is one of the most fascinating collections in the series.

bibliolife
old books. new life.

The BiblioLife Network

This project was made possible in part by the BiblioLife Network (BLN), a project aimed at addressing some of the huge challenges facing book preservationists around the world. The BLN includes libraries, library networks, archives, subject matter experts, online communities and library service providers. We believe every book ever published should be available as a high-quality print reproduction; printed on-demand anywhere in the world. This insures the ongoing accessibility of the content and helps generate sustainable revenue for the libraries and organizations that work to preserve these important materials.
The following book is in the "public domain" and represents an authentic reproduction of the text as printed by the original publisher. While we have attempted to accurately maintain the integrity of the original work, there are sometimes problems with the original work or the micro-film from which the books were digitized. This can result in minor errors in reproduction. Possible imperfections include missing and blurred pages, poor pictures, markings and other reproduction issues beyond our control. Because this work is culturally important, we have made it available as part of our commitment to protecting, preserving, and promoting the world's literature.

GUIDE TO FOLD-OUTS MAPS and OVERSIZED IMAGES

The book you are reading was digitized from microfilm captured over the past thirty to forty years. Years after the creation of the original microfilm, the book was converted to digital files and made available in an online database.
In an online database, page images do not need to conform to the size restrictions found in a printed book. When converting these images back into a printed bound book, the page sizes are standardized in ways that maintain the detail of the original. For large images, such as fold-out maps, the original page image is split into two or more pages

Guidelines used to determine how to split the page image follows:

• Some images are split vertically; large images require vertical and horizontal splits.
• For horizontal splits, the content is split left to right.
• For vertical splits, the content is split from top to bottom.
• For both vertical and horizontal splits, the image is processed from top left to bottom right.

1595

¶ THE STAFFE of Christian Faith, profitable to all Christians, for to arme themselues agaynst the enimies of the Gospell: and also for to knowe the antiquitie of our holy faith, and of the true Church.

Gathered out of the vvorks of the ancient Doctors of the Church, and of the Councels, and many other Doctors, vvhose names you shall see here follovving. Translated out of Frenche into English, by Iohn Brooke of Ashe next Sandvviche.

With a Table to finde out all that which is contayned in the booke.

EPHES. 6.

Put on the vvhole armour of God, that ye maye stande stedfast agaynst the craftie assaultes of the Deuill.

Imprinted at London by Iohn Daye, dwelling ouer Aldersgate.

ANNO. 1577.

Cum Priuilegio.

Sr. Richard Newdigate of
Arbury in the County of Warwick
Baronet 1709

To the Right honourable and his singular good Lorde and maister, *Edwarde de Vere, Lorde d'Escales, and Badlesmere,* Vicount Bulbecke, Earle of Oxenforde, and Lorde great Chamberlayne of Englande, Iohn Brooke vvisheth long lyfe, vvith the increase of honor.&c.

ALTHOVGH VERtue the roote of well doing (Right honorable Lorde) hath of it selfe, sufficient force to withstande, repell, and ouerthrowe, both the open malice, and secrete slaunders of euill tongues, yet notwithstanding considering howe daungerous, yea howe vnpossible a thing it is to escape that poysoned sting of Zoilus, and also that nothing hath euer ben so well done, but that this Scorpion hath eyther openly or priuily stong, I nede not to doubt, nay I may be right sure, that these my labors shal come into the hands of some, more curious than wyse, more ready to nippe and taunte (yea euen withoute fault) then frendly to admonishe or amende. By occasi-

on whereof (right honorable and my singular good Lorde) I haue not only thought it expedient for hope of your honours fauourable patronage, towardes these also my laboures bestowed in translation: But also for respect of my particular duetie towardes your honor, to offer and dedicate the same likewyse to your fauorable allowance and well liking. For if in the opinion of all men, there can be found no one more fitte, for patronage and defence of learning, then the skilfull: for that he is both wyse and able to iudge and discerne truly thereof. I vnderstanding righte well that your honor hathe continually, euen from your tender yeares, bestowed your time and trauayle towardes the attayning of the same, as also the vniuersitie of Cambridge hath acknowledged in graunting and giuing vnto you such commendation and prayse thereof, as verily by righte was due vnto your excellent vertue and rare learning. Wherin verily Cambridge the mother of learning, and learned men hath openly confessed: and in this hir confessing made knowen vnto al men, that your honor being learned and able to iudge as a

safe

safe harbor and defence of learning, and therefore one most fitte to whose honorable patronage I might safely commit this my poore and simple labours. Likewyse remembring howe much and many wayes I am by dutye bounde vnto your honor, as also howe vnable I am to discharge the same: I haue thought it in respecte also of my behalfe and duty, most meete to offer and exhibite, such trauelles as my abilitie and skill can reache vnto, to your Lordship as pledge and token of my dutifull and vnfained good wil: To the ende that such profyt as by this my trauels may growe to my countrey and common wealthes, may be receiued vnder your Lordshyppes approbation and defence: that all men which doe reape benefyte thereby, should owe thankes vnto you in whose duety and good will I am. Wherefore hartely requiring and humbly beseeching your Lordeshippe to take on you the patronage and defence of these my labors by translation that by your approbation and well liking, others may also the rather like thereof. Crauing pardon for this my symple boldnesse or rather bolde symplicitie hoping also of the continuance of your honors accustomed goodnesse towardes mee, and instantlye praying to God for your prosperous estate, I cease further at this time to sollicite you.

Your honors obedient seruant, Iohn Brooke.

Vnto the Church and congregation of God which is in L. Guido deſireth grace and peace, and the mercie of God, through Ieſus Chriſt our Lorde: And perpetually to perſeuere in the knovvledge of the holy Goſpell of the ſonne of God. Amen.

KNOVVING AND CONſidering the vvarre and combat that yee daylye ſuffer to mayntaine and keepe the true and pure Chriſtian doctrine of the ancient and true Church of God, agaynſt a ſort and heape of glorious deceiuers, vvhich hyde and boaſt themſelues vvith falſe enſignes, of the name and title of the auncient Church, and of the auncient Doctors: I haue dedicated vnto you (my vvelbeloued frendes) this preſent booke, entituled: The Staffe of the Faith, gathered out of the vvorkes of the auncient doctors of the churche, and of the counſelles, and out of many authors: to the ende that thereby you may learne vvholy, to fight againſt your ennemies, vvith the ſame ſtaffe vvith vvhich they doe fight agaynſt you, that is to ſay, the aunciente s. I doe not tell you hovv this ſtaffe, shall keepe you from the danger of your ennemies only, I vvill content my ſelfe in ſpeaking but one vvorde, touching the ſame, (that is to ſay) that you shall not only obtayne and get victory of your ennemies, but alſo ſend them avvay vvith their mouthes ſtopped. Therefore I deſire you in Gods name, that ye be not ſlothfull nor negligent, to ſtudy therein often, and to haue thoſe

ſenten-

sentences therein alledged readily at yovr fingers endes, that thereby the kingdome of Iesus Christe be auaunced, and the dominion of the deuilles and infidels destroyed and abolished.

I doe knovve very vvell that manye people haue accustomed to saye, v vhen it is spoken vnto them of the auncients, speaking vvithout eyther iudgement, or reason, in saying that as touching the Auncientes, they haue nothing to doe vvith them, for they vvvere men as they: but that they content themselues only vvith the vvorde of God. I vvoulde not altogither denie or gainesaye them in that, if they vvould not reiect thereby God and his giftes, by thinking to reiect men and their doctrine. Therefore vve ought to take good heede vnto men vvhen they speake of them selues, and also v vhen God speaketh by them. The same vve may knovve, vvhen their doctrine is confirmable and agreeing to the rule of all right, vvhich is the vvord of God the doctrine of the prophets & Apostles. Furthermore, vve vvould not haue you ignorant, that the auncient fathers haue ordayned and established a great many of ceremonies , and thinges in the churche respecting the time and personnes, and the infirmitie of those that dayly come vnto the knovvledge of the Gospell, asvvell of Ievves as of panims and Idolaters: But they haue done that onely but for a certaine time, to the ende they might dravve to the Gospell all nations, and let and stoppe the vvay of the Heritickes and ennemies of the catholyke faithe, from gayning and vvinning the vveake in faithe. For vve ought not to maruayle, if the auncient fathers haue done many thinges in that time,

vvhich

vvhich novv can not ferue, nor profite vs any thing at all, inasmuch as they haue serued but onely for their time. For the Apostles haue ordayned some thinges vvhich novve ought not to be followed nor kept. As vve doe reade in the actes of the Apostles, that the counsell that vvas celebrated by the Apostles in Ierusalem, decreed that vve should abstaine from bloude, and from the fleshe of beastes that vvere strangled : VVe knovve vvell inough that this ordinance novv hath no more place, and is not in force among the christians, nor ought to haue, bicause that all thinges are cleane and purified through the vvorde and prayer. Then vvee see that that decree, vvhich hath bene decreed by the holy spirite & by the Apostles, to haue bene made, bicause of the personnes, and to serue onely but for that time. *Act.* 15. *Titus.* 1. 1. *Tim.* 1 *Rom.* 14.

Iudge novve, if an ordinance made by the Apostles to support the infirmitie of men hath bene set foorth, and aftervvardes abolished : vvhat oughte vve to iudge of those vvhich are of lesse importance vvhich haue bene ordayned by men, a great deale inferior and of lesse estimation then the Apostles? There is no doubt, that forasmuch as they haue bene ordayned to serue onely for that time, that novve vve may let them alone and forsake them, bicause that there is neyther Ievves nor Turkes among vs, but christians, at the least as they saye.

Also vve ought not vpon this to holde our peace or hide the vnshamelesse malice of many, vvho (neuerthelesse calling them selues christians) vnder colour of antiquitie, and of the auncient doctors, doe forge and inuent of their ovvne vvicked and fil-

thye

thye brayne,naughty and most detestable errors: and aftervvard say that the auncient fathers haue vvritten so, and preached so: and by that meanes make the poore vvorld being seduced to beleeue it. And yet the malice is so great in them,that all they that vvill not receiue and allovve,that vvhich their brayne hath inuented vnder the name of holy men, they crye after them vvith open mouth,to the fire, to the fire vvith the Heritickes. They reiecte the doctrine of the fathers. Alas O my God and Lord thou knovvest our hearts: and the heartes of these lyers, that vve doe not desire but that in all and through all, be it through life or death,that thy son Iesus Christ, and his doctrine, may be onely receiued, loued and vvorshipped: And for this are vve apoynted as sheepe to be slayne: vve are nought set by, mocked, beaten, banished, chased from tovvne to tovvne: To be short vve are esteemed and counted as the most vile & stinking filthynesse of all the vvorld,troden dovvne vnderneth the feete of the vvorldlinges: But for all that vve possesse our soules in patience, looking for the righteous Iudge vvhich vvill iudge all the vvorld, not according to the doctrine of men, but according to hys holy vvorde, for vvhich vve are had novve in suche abhomination to the vvorlde.

Furthermore they vvhich dayly accuse vs vvith so greate rage and furye,against the auncient doctrine of the Apostles and Doctors, shall at the last acknovvledge their malice and liuing,that they haue declared in their bookes, corrupting and marring the bookes of the auncient fathers of the churche: If I durst, I vvould gladly name one vvho in that occupation or science hath serued out his prenty-shyppe, for that cause is called our maister, in his booke that he hath intituled. The bouckler of the faithe: vvherein he declareth the subtiltie of his intent and craft, alledging the auncient Doctors in Latine, after translating them into Frenche, and at euery place vvhere he found Sacrificium, or the like manner of speaking, in steade to put in sacrifice, or holy mysterie, he hath translated them alvvayes the holy mysterie of the Masse, and so by that meanes they finde that vvorde Masse in the bookes of those good fathers, vvhich they neuer thought nor did. I beleeue he thought that his booke should not come but only in the handes of yong children, or else he thought that he had to doe but vvith beastes like vnto himselfe. There is no man though he haue but small iudgement and vnderstanding, vvhich reading that booke, but that he may see at the first dashe hovv he lyeth, and vnsayeth and reuoketh it agayne, and neuerthelesse he is heard and accounted as halfe a God: not only of the poorest sort, but of the greatest in the vvorlde. In the meane time vve ought not to maruayle at this, that such gallants haue bene so hardy and ouerbolde, forasmuch as they vvere supported and maintayned of Kings, Emperors, Princes, and Magistrates, and that they vvere the best vvelcome to their Court.

I remember that I haue reade in the Ecclesiasticall histories, that in the time of the auncient Doctors, there vvere abusers and seducers of the people, that sovved their pestilent venim amongst the doctrine of the auncients: Of that Denise bishop *Euseb. lib. 4. cap. 22.*

of

of Corinth complayned very much, saying, that many haue sovvn in his Epistles much vvicked doctrine. Therefore thinke, that if they haue bene so hardy and bolde that they durst corrupt the vvrytinges of the auncientes, yea vvhilest they vvere yet aliue. VVhat vvill they doe novve? at the least they vvill doe asmuch, as their auncient fathers, that is to saye those Apostates ennemies of the fathers.

Novv notvvithstanding their shamelesse malyce they rebuke and checke vs vvith a vvhores face, that vve are ennemies of the fathers, despisers and contemners of their doctrine, and disturbers of the vvorld. I vvould to God that they vvould permitte and suffer vs to compare our doctrine openly, and before all the vvorld vvith theirs, to the end that all men might knovve vvho be the contemners and ennemies of the fathers: somuch it vvantith that vve should be found condemners and ennemies of those good fathers, that altogither it vvoulde be seene that the same doctrine that vve hold & keepe at this day, is the very same for vvhiche manye of those good fathers haue shead their bloud: and vvould shead it, if they vvere novve aliue.

It seemeth that the same is not true that I haue spoken, that if the fathers vvere yet aliue, that men vvould put them cruelly to death, as most vvicked Heritickes. Yea they vvhich at this daye doe boste and brag them selues to be their obedient children, and make bucklers of their bookes.

Vnderstand and hold fast in minde (dearely beloued) behold this present booke may serue vs for a certayne argument, of that vvhich is composed and faithfully gathered togither, out of the very bookes

of

of the auncient Doctors: That if I vvould present this present booke (vvherein there is nothing in it of mine, but altogither of the auncientes) for confession of my faith to those enemies of the fathers, I doubt not but presently I should be as a moste vvicked Heretick, condemned to be burned quicke into ashes. Novve see (dearely beloued) and iudge iustly before God according to your ovvn conscience, vvhether vve be the enmmies of the fathers or they.

The auncient fathers haue sayde that the breade of the supper abideth alvvayes breade, not being transubstantiated or chaunged: I doe demaund of you in good faith, vvherefore or vvhat is the cause that they shead dayly so abundantly the bloude of the poore children of God? Is it not vpon this onely poynte, or for this cause, that the fathers haue beleeued and mayntayned vvith a common consent, as you shall see in that booke vpon the artycle of the Lordes supper? I leaue it to your ovvne iudgement. Furthermore vve doe reade that the ancient fathers, of vvhom these here doe aduance, and bost them selues to keepe and mayntayne their doctrine, haue broken in peeces the images of Iesus Christe, and of the Saintes, that haue bene set vp in the temple of the christians, saying that it is againſt the Christian doctrine to haue Images in the Church.

VVhat is he that doubteth, that if the good fathers vvere yet liuing, and that they shoulde so breake the Images as they did in that time, but that they shoulde be out of hande, or vvith all speede condemned as heretickes, to be burned, yea if they

escaped

escaped so. For vve do see many dayly vvhich doe not escape so good cheape, but they haue done vnto them all the torments and paynes that these vvorshippers of the fathers can inuent or imagin.

Then vvhen you shall reade the doctrine of the fathers contayned in this present booke, iudge vvhether it may be confessed and maintayned openly before these vvorshippers of the fathers vvithout daunger of lyfe. In the meane time, I desire you (my deare brethren) that ye feare not to abandon your bodie and lyfe, for a doctrine so iust, holy, and good: and let vs reioyce in this, that vve holde the true auncient doctrine of the Prophets, Apostles and Doctors of the Church.

And as touching you, O ye Princes, Iudges, and Magistrates, betvveene vvhose handes this present booke shall happen to fall: I desire and require you, in the name of the liuing God, and of his sonne Iesus Christ our Lorde vvhich hath shed out all his bloud vpon the crosse for the loue of vs, that you doe giue right iudgement vpon the poore faithfull people, of vvhome your prisons are at this time full, through the furor and madnesse of those vvorshippers of the fathers, and bee no more the hangmen of that vvicked Vermine: for it is not counted a thing honest nor meete among men, that the Kings, Emperours, Princes, and Magistrates shoulde bee made the hangmen of beggers.

Be ye then more ashamed than euer you vvere, bicause that you beare the name of God, and the povver to gouerne the people is giuen you from God, not for to abuse it in punishing the good, and

defen-

defending the vvicked, but to maintayne and ayde the good, and to punish the vvicked (as the Apostles haue taught vs.) But alas my God, into vvhat blindenesse is the vvorlde fallen into, to esteeme and thinke that they vvhich holde and keepe the true auncient doctrine are heretikes.

O you Iudges and Magistrates, doe you not see dayly in your prisons, the poore children of God, to eate and drinke very scarsly bread and vvater, and to be cast most vilely and filthily into a lovve dungeon vvith the venimous beastes, lying as the poore beastes vpon a little stravve hauing their armes and legges broken vvith the racke?

Doe you not see (I say) on the other side those goodly masters vvhich beare such great zeale to the auncient fathers, to haue their bellye altogither stuffed vvith vvine and delicate fare, coming forth from their bankets and feastes vvith a face as red as fire, or like to a Butchers boule, comming forth to passe avvaye the time, for to examine the poore faythfull people, vvhich are not sought for at the table vvhere good cheare is, but in a most filthie and darke dungeon: they are poore children of God tyed and bounde vvith chaynes, vvith a pale face and thinne cheekes, brought before those fat bellies and firie faces through their ouermuche drinking and quaffing of vvine, and the first vvords they speake is, come hither thou vvicked heretick, avvay thou dāned seducer of the people, thou hast the deuil vvithin thee. And assone as the pore children of God did thinke to haue spoken for their defence, the fatte bellies quicklye put their hands to their Bible, but it is another Bible than the olde

olde or nevve testament: For they can do nothing but prouide faggots, and crie to the fire, to the fire vvith those vvicked heretickes, I knovve not vvhere they haue learned to doe so. Haue they learned that of the Prophetes and Apostles? It appeareth no. Neyther haue they learned it of the auncient fathers. For they shall finde vvithin this present booke, that they haue spoken and done altogither othervvise: therefore they declare that it is a rage and a madnesse that they haue conceyued against the truth for to extinguishe and abolishe it vtterly, and all those that maintaine it: For libertie to speake is taken from vs. Those that vvould speake, their tongues are cut out of their heades? and aftervvardes are burned.

In the meane time O ye Iudges and Magistrates, vvhich haue the publicke charge, haue regard from henceforth vvhat you doe in condemning them to death. You cannot condemne them to death except ye condemne all the good and auncient fathers to death vvith them. VVhat order doe you call this to condemne to death as Heretickes the Saintes and their doctrine, vnto vvhom they crye and dayly pray vnto in their Letanie, saying, O Sancte Augustine, O Sancte Cypriane, O Sancte Hieronime. &c. Ora pro nobis, that is to say, O Saint Augustine, O Saint Cyprian, O Saint Ierome, and so consequently of the other, pray for vs. And in the meane time they condemne them, and their vvritinges, and all those that follovve theyr doctrine to be burned, as the experience dothe dayly teach vs.

Therefore ye that Iudge the people haue a good

respect

respect vnto that that you haue to doe: for it is not onely vnto vs that you doe adresse your selues, but also to the sonne of God, vvhich hath sayd vnto vs, he that toucheth you, toucheth the apple or sight of mine eye. The same hath bene vvell shevved to Paule, VVhen he persecuted the poore faythfull, crying from heauen after him, Saule Saule vvhy persecutest thou me? he did not persecute him in his ovvne person, but he persecuted him in his members, vvhich are all the faithfull that beleue in him. *Act.9*

Euen so (my deare brethren) vve shall rest in patience, and shall not be ashamed to be condemned vvith all those good and auncient fathers of the church, and not onely vvith them, but also vvith all the Prophets and Apostles. Then vvhen you see your selues bound and brought before the Iudges, to receiue sentence of death and condemnation against you, behold vvith you the Prophets, Apostles and the auncient doctors bound vvith you to be condemned in the same torment. Be ye ioyfull and reioyce to be enrovvled in their bande, for to beare vvith them, the yoke of Iesus Christ? perseuere valiantly in the doctrine that you haue already receiued, for no man can hurt you. Ought vve not greatly to reioyce of this, that the persecuting tyrantes can doe our bodyes no more hurt, then a vvolfe or theefe of the vvoods, vvhich can but murther or kill vs. Let vs reioyce, for our names are vvritten in heauen. VVe haue yet this good turne (thankes be vnto our good God therefore) that the persecutors can do vnto vs no vvorse then to to put and place vs vvith our good God in the company of Angelles and all the blessed soules in heauen.

VVhat is he that vvould not desire to goe playe
1.Cor.2. vvith so happy a company eternally and vvithout ende? Yea to be in glory vvhich the eye hath not seene, and eare hath not heard, neyther hath entred into mans minde, the thinges vvhich God hath prepared to such as loue him.

Againe, forasmuch as they esteeme and count vs so vvicked and abhominable, and crye so spitefully after vs, as after the vvickedest people of all the vvorld, to make vs and our doctrine odious vnto the people: They commaund them not to heare or harken vnto vs, they make the simple people beleeue, vvhen they haue them vnder confession, that if they doe not accuse vs, they shall be damned.

Their craft, subtiltye and enuye agaynste the truth is to be maruayled at. In the meane time I vvould vvillingly that they vvould accord and agree vvith vs to conferre their doctrine vvith ours, their crosse and persecution vvith ours, their lyfe vvith ours, theyr church vvith ours: By that meanes vve should plainly see vvhether they be the childrē of God or vve. First of all haue not vve the baptisme purely administred, as vve doe reade that the Apostles haue administred it vvithout any inuentions of men, but onely according to the vvord of God? Let one reade the Scriptures, and he shall see vvho it is that hath added to the Sacramentes, eyther vve or they.

Furthermore let men behold the persecutions that they suffer for their doctrine, the number is soone counted, for there is not one vvhich hath

suffred

suffred death for their doctrine: neuerthelesse Iesus Christ hath promised that his church shal haue persecution in the vvorld, saying, ye shall be hated of all men for my name. Hovv can they be hated of all men sith that they be in all places the best vvelcome? Hovv commeth it that one shoulde thinke to doe sacrifice vnto God in putting them to death? I did neuer knovve any. *Mat.10.*

I doe accord and agree in this, that they are often times taken prisoners, but it is in the good feastes and bankettes, and in the best seates of the table: and vvhereas the children of God are burned vvith fire, they here are burned throughe the heate of VVine. Their innocent fleshe is hevven and cut in peeces, but it is at the table vpon their trenchers. They are rotten and consumed vvith the Goute of Naples, insomuch that they fall in peeces.

They are melted and melted againe many times in a yeere. Besides all the dangers they put them selues into both day and night to runne after other mens vvyues, in great danger of their life. And yet some vvill say that they are not persecuted: It appeareth that they be, for one shall see a great many more among them to dye Martyrs, of the paines that vve did speake of euen novv, then of their naturall diseases or sicknesses. They are then Martyres, no man can denie, yea, but it is of the diuell; and vvhat is he that doubteth of it?

And as concerning their life it is knovven vvell inough and manyfested vnto all men: Their good vvorkes and godly fruites vvhat it bringeth in all places, destroying and corrupting all the vvorlde, asvvell spiritually as corporally. This I am sure of, that forasmuch as I haue touched and medled but vvith the doore of their kitchin, they vvill say I am a vvicked Hereticke: But vvhat then? Shoulde I hold my peace for their menaces and iniuries? No, no, God forbid, but rather I vvill crye vvith open mouth after them, bicause they haue so corrupted and destroyed the Lordes Vineyard.

Alas, alas, my God vvhat is he that ought not but to lament and vveepe vvith bloudy teares, seeing all the vvorld to be so led into the bottome of hell, so many poore soules led to perdition. O Lord regard thy poore people, haue some pitie and compassion on them, for vvhom thy sonne our Lorde Iesus Christ hath offred to thee his body and bloud in a sacrifice: and suffer not that thy poore sheepe be so put as a pray for to be deuoured of al beastes.

For vve are dayly assaulted vvith so many ennemyes, that sathan riseth agaynst vs, for to make vs forsake and abandon our Lord Iesus Christ, and to renounce his Gospell: One day vve haue vvarre agaynst the Heretickes Anabaptistes, an other day agaynst Libertines, Epicures, Arians, Dauidistes, and agaynst dissemblers, and consequently, against the vvorshippers of the fathers, through vvhose zeale the children of God are put to death. Haue not vve then great neede of vveapons? It appeareth yea, if vve vvould not be taken in their snares, as many at this day are, through the iust iudgement of God.

Therefore if there be any time to pray, or to vvatch, it is novve: Let vs then vvatch and praye, to the end vve may auoyde all those dangers, and perseuer and continevve to the ende.

You

You haue bene the first of your citie (dearely beloued) I also doe hope in the Lord you shall not be the last: But as you haue bene vntill novv the example and myrror of the poore ignorant people, to dravve them to the true light of the spirite, I doe hope through the grace of God, that nothing shall hinder you to continevve vnto the end on so holy a vvorke.

For the poore ignorant people seeing the peace and vnitie, and the promptnesse and good courage that is in you to receiue the holy doctrine, are constrayned through your holy life and conuersation to come vnto the knovvledge of Iesus Christ, and consequently to saluation. Forasmuch then as the Lord doth vnto you dayly so much good, or shevveth vnto you so much of his grace, shevving vnto you from day to day his maruaylous vvorkes, set to so your handes in the vvorke of the Lord, so long as he giueth you time and life, that you doe not leaue for your children that shall come after you, an euill example of life: but instruct them in that holy doctrine that you haue receiued, to the ende they may knovve after your death, that they had fathers and mothers that feared God, and vvell instructed in his vvord, and that they haue not receyued the gospell in their mouthe onely, but also in their handes. And that they vvere not dissemblers, but true confessors of the name of God.

Dispose and bestovve then vvhilest you haue time so vvell your affayres, and businesse according to the meanes as God hath giuen you, that youre successors may haue none occasion to complayne, that you haue left them an euill example: That they say not after that you are dead, vve haue had parents & ancesters, vvhich haue had great knovv-ledge of God, but they feared more to lose the a-mytie and freendship of the vvorlde then of God.

O hovv much ought you to feare the same, for it vvill turne to your great confusion.

Remember also that vvhich the Apostle spea-keth, saying, if there be any that prouideth not for his ovvne, and namely for them of his housholde, the same denieth the faithe, and is vvorse then an infidel. Therefore all faithfull people ought to take god heede and marke vvell those vvordes, for it is a great euill to denye the fayth. *1. Tim. 5.*

Take good heede you be not an offence to any man, I doe meane in doing euil, be gentle curteous & mercifull the one to the other, not rendring euill for euill, but render good for the euill. Liue so holy that if men vvold punish & persecute you, that they doe not punish any thing in you but righteousnes, and good life. And in that doing you shall declare your selues to be the children of God. VVatch al-vvayes, praying that you be made vvorthy, to a-uoyd al things that are to cõe, & that you may stãd before the son of God, after the end of your dayes. *1. Thes. 5.*

I beseeche our good God and father, which ac-cording to his great goodnesse & mercy hath done so much good for vs, to adopt vs for his children to the eternall inheritance of heauen, that it woulde please him through his goodnes to ioyne and knit you in such sort togither (my dearly beloued bre-thren and sisters) through the bonde of his holy spirite, which by the same will gouerne and leade you to eternall life. Amen.

To the Reader.

HOVV EASIE A THING it is (gentle reader) rashly to discõmend, eche one is vnto himselfe a witnesse: but how hard a thing rightly to commend, few, yet the wyser, can testifie. Therefore to make any great or tedious relation of that, which of it selfe is worthy, I thinke a thing vayne and superfluous: or to commend that which in the very shew is commendable, should be to bereeue thee of thy iudgement. Notwithstanding, least I should be accused and condemned of negligence, which I haue sought to shunne and auoyde, I determined priuatly, to set thy sight openly, that this booke hath bene out of the Doctors and Counselles collected carefully, composed by the authour pithilye, and by the same alledged fitly and aptlye: and not onely out of the Doctors, but out of the Popes owne Canons culled gratiously, whereby he hath not brought a Doctor agaynst a Pope, but a Pope with a Pope conferred learnedlye. This being rightly wayed and considered. I thinke there is nothing left for the more enuious (being the motion godly, the matter their owne, the order fitte and conuenient) as an obiect to worke on theyr insatiable minde, and desire of reprehension, except they wyll seeke and runne to the manners of the author (common practises now a dayes) to search and prye ouer curiouslye, something to animaduert and oppugne, and sore agreeued that he hath beaten them with their owne rodde, say with

Zeuxis contending with Parrhasius, when he had seene all, now vncouer thy sheete Parrhasius, that we may see thy worke. Yet least there shoulde growe in their mindes some vndeserued suspition, being the authour vnknowen, I will endeauour not onely to remoue, but to roote it cleane out of their entendement: and playnely affirme that which is credibly and sincerely referred to me, that he was of manners modest, of life laborious, of countenance sober, and of witte quicke, and willing to profite euery one to his power and abilitie. Therefore as I iudge and esteeme, there is no cause for any one, nor yet for the aduersaryes to bee greeued, seeing to the one it redoundeth to his vtilitie, and the other may not complayne, that in disclosing the veritie, he paynted foorthe that which he hath worthelye deserued. Next to this is the cause of the translatour, whome thou shalte thanke, that for thy further benifite, he hath with good zeale learned the authour to talke in an other tongue, and shewing that which before was well spoken to a fewe, to be better spoken to a great many, rendered it, copied out of the French, into thy Englishe, vulgare and natiue speache. Lastly I admonishe the to view and reade diligently the cataloge of the doctors and counselles, alledged by the authour, which I haue layde downe, to the ende thou mightest see for thy emolument what euery one hath bene, and what he hath suffred and written, and the time he florished, wishing thee to ponder the same, and loke if they haue thought any otherwyse, then truth, or fallen into any inextricable error, not redily to condemne them, as the enuious doe: but to aſcribe it to mans fragilitie, as chriſtians ought: and to marke and imprint the ſame in thy minde, not to fall into the like, nor to ſtay on mans ſayinges, ſeeing as it is vſually ſayde:

- nihil omni parte beatum.

Nothing (meaning mortall thinges) is bleſſed or happy on euery ſide: but to boulſter and truſt wholy to Gods mercyes, who is onely the truthe, and the phiſition for euery ſore. Thus much I thought good to aduertiſe thee (gentle re-der) of this preſent booke, being, as it may be ſayde, in ſight fayre, in matter good, in effect fructuous and godly, wiſhing and willing thee to accepte gratefullye that which for thy pleaſure hath bene penned paynefully.

Farewell.

Concuſsus, ſurgo.

C. A.

The Catalogue of the Doctors, and Councels, out of the which we haue gathered togither this present booke, for the approbation of the Articles of our Faith, and to shewe in what time they flourished and were celebrated.

Dionysius Areopagita, a Grecian borne, and iudge in the causes of weight at Athens: was conuerted by S. Paule, when he disputed with the Stoikes and Epicures in the same Citie: and constituted byshop there of the faythfull: Afterwarde he went into Fraunce, and was made byshop of Paris, where he was also beheaded by the gouernour Fesceninus. in the yeare of our Lorde, as Trithemius reporteth, 96. and Paulus Eberus, Pag. 327. being the ix. daye of October vnder the Emperor Domitian in the seconde persecution. He flourished chiefly vnder the two Vespasians father and the sonne. Hee was called the French mens Apostle, and lieth buried in a place in Fraunce, called after his name S. Denis, a little distant from Paris, verye famous

famous throughe the sepulchres of the Kings of that Countrie, reade *Act.* 17. *Euseb. lib.* 3. *cap.* 4. *and lib.* 4. *cap.* 22. *Martinus Polonus in the life of Domitian. Onuphrius Panuinus* in his Chronologie, *Pag.* 14. *Gregorius Turonicus, pag.* 23. *Roffin. pag.* 365. *Pantaleon. pag.* 4. Of his iudgement of the Eclipse of the sunne in the passion of our Lorde, reade the annales of *Glycas, pag.* 306. and in his owne Epistle to *Polycarpus* the martyr.

Clemens, a Grecian, flourished vnder the two *Vespasians*, *Domitian*, and *Nerua*. He was the Disciple of *Paule*, called his fellow labourer, as he himselfe witnesseth: and as *Dorotheus* sayth, one of the 70. disciples. He first preached the Gospell at *Metz* in Frãce. *Pantaleon, pag.* 7. *Maior*, *Munster*. Afterwards was made Bishop of *Sardis* now called *Triaditza*. *Dorotheus* in the lyues of the 70. Disciples. Lastlye bishop of Rome the 3. in succession, and was martyred vnder *Traian, anno.* 103. in the thirde persecution, by tying an anker about his necke, and throwne into the sea. He obtayned the dignitie of the seate 9. yeares, 2. monethes, 10. dayes. *Marti-*

nus

nus Polonus in his lyfe. *Gregorius Turonicus, pag.*21. *Platyna* in his lyfe.

Ignatius, a Grecian, byshop of *Antioch* the yeare of our Lorde.99.seconde in succession after *Peter* the disciple of *S. Iohn* the Euangelist and Apostle: flourished chieflye vnder *Nerua*, and *Traian*, was martyred, as he testifieth of himselfe at Rome in the thirde persecution: the historie saith, that as *Traian* returned from the victorie of his enimies, the yere 109. and threatened death to the Christians, *Ignatius* came towardes him, and confessed himselfe a Christian, wherefore he was straight apprehended and bounde with fetters, and caried to Rome, and deuoured with wild beasts. *Euseb.lib.*3.*cap.*33. shewing his owne Epistle, howe he was bounde and fettered and garded with a great troupe of souldiers, and inclosed with ten Leopardes. *Gregorie* of *Tours, pag.*21. *Martin* the *Polonian* in the lyfe of *Traian. Pantaleon, pag.*9. *Onuphrius Panuinus, pag.*16.

Irenæus a Latine Doctor, the seconde bishop of *Lyons* in *Fraunce*, and successour of *Pothynus* the disciple of *Polycarpus* the

martyr

martyr bishop of *Smyrna*. Florished vnder *Commodus* the yeare.175. *Pantaleon, pag.* 13. He was sent into *France*, by the sayde *Polycarpus*, and was commended by the martyrs there vnto *Elutherius* the 13. byshop of Rome, and confuted there certaine heretikes. *Euseb. lib.5. cap.4. cap.18.* He reprehended sharplye *Victor* successor of *Elutherius* in the sea of Rome, bicause he had excommunicated the Christians of *Asia* and *Greece*. *Euseb. lib.5. cap.23.* Hee was martyred at *Lyons* vnder *Seuerus* in the v. persecution, or according to *Sulpitius Seuerus*, the sixt in the yeare.184. *Gregorie* of *Tours, pag.22. Martin* the *Polonian*, in the life of *Seuerus*. He was present in the Councel of *Palæstine* with *Polycarpus, Theophilus, Narcissus*, and *Bacchylus* the noble and learned Byshoppes of *Asia*. *Platyna* in the lyfe of *Victor* the first.

Tertullian Priest, a Latine Doctor, byshop of *Carthage* in *Aphrica*, flourished in the yeare 202. vnder *Seuerus* and *Antoninus*. He wrate many learned workes, but at length by reason of a schisme risen of emulation betweene him and the Romane Clergie, he fell from the truth into the

Mon-

Montane heresie. *Hieronymus in catalogo.* *Nicephorus lib.4.cap.34.* He wrote an Apologie for the Christians alledged by *Euseb.lib.2.cap.2.*

Origen Priest, a Grecian Doctor, flourished in the yeare of our Lorde 235. the Disciple of *Clement* of *Alexandria*, whom also he succeeded in the schoole, and instructed many in the fayth, which afterwarde became martyrs. In his youth his father was martyred vnder *Seuerus*, who being in prison, he often visited, and therefore was in great daunger of his person, and woulde haue suffred martyrdome if his mother had not hindered him: being growen in age, he gelded himselfe, to the intent he might the freelyer be at his studie. He wrate many things, of which there are not all extant. *Hieronymus in Catalogo.* He liued till the time of *Gallus* and *Volusianus* Emperors, and died in the *69.* yeare of his age, and lyeth buried at *Tyrus.* *Suydas. Euseb.* in the whole 6. booke.

Cyprianus, a Grecian, Bishop of *Carthage*, flourished in the yeare of our Lord 355. vnder the reigne of *Decius. Pantaleon pag.21.* Hee was a great enimie of the

Arians.

Arians, and other heretikes. His opinion that he helde of rebaptizing the heretikes, was the occasion of falling at square with *Stephan* the first bishop of *Rome*. He was present at the first Councell of *Carthage*. *Euseb.lib.7.cap.3.Pantaleon,pag.22.*

Eusebius, a Grecian, Bishop of *Cæsarea* in *Palæstine*, flourished in the yeare of our Lorde 325. vnder the raigne of *Constantine* the great. *Pantaleon,pag.25.* By his familiaritie with *Pamphilus* the martyr, he was surnamed *Pamphilus*. Hee wrate manye workes, of which certayne are extant. *Hieronymus in Catalogo.* Hee was highly esteemed of the great *Constantine*, as appeareth by the Epistles which the Emperour wrate vnto him. *Socrates, lib.1.cap.6.*

Lactantius Firmianus, a Latine Rhetorician, flourished in the yeare of our Lord 340. vnder the reygne of *Constantine* the great. He wrate against the Gentiles, and confuted their errors. *Hieronym. Pantaleon,pag.27.*

Athanasius the great, a Grecian, Byshop of *Alexandria*, successor of *Alexander*, flourished in the yeare of our Lorde

340.

340. vnder *Constantine* the great. He had much adoe with the *Arians*, and was thorow them twyce expelled his Bishopricke: once by *Constantine*. *Socrates lib*.2.*cap*.13. Another time by *Iulianus*: *Theodoret*, *lib*. 4.*cap*.9. At length he died vnder the reign of *Valens* Emperour of the East.

Hilarius a Latine, Bishop of *Poictiers* in *Fraunce*, flourished in the yeare of our Lorde 345. vnder the reigne of the sonnes of *Constantine* the great. He was driuen in exyle by the Gouernour. *Socrat*. *lib*.3. *cap*.8. He wrate many goodly workes, of the which many are extant. He liued vntill the time of *Augustine*. *Hieronym*. *Augustin*. *Epistol*.89.64.

Basile, a Grecian, Bishop of *Cæsarea* in *Cappadocia*, very familiar with *Gregory Nazianzene*, flourished in the yere of our Lord 370. vnder the reign of *Valentinian* and *Valens*. He was a great enimie of the heretikes, and confuted them in manye workes. *Valens* after he banished all the true Christians of the East, for his renoume spared him, yet he went of his own accorde into exile. *Camerar*. *in Catalogo*. *Pantaleon*, *pag*.26.

Gregorie,

Gregorie, a Grecian, Bishop of *Nazanzum*, called the diuine, flourished in the yeare 371. vnder *Valentinian* and *Valens*, although he was elder thā *Basil*. *Camerar. in catalogo*. He wrate many goodly works and was a great Oratour. He liued 90. yeares, a long and quiet lyfe. More of his vertues looke in the aforenamed author.

Epiphanius, a Grecian, Byshop of *Cyprus*, flourished in the yeare 375. vnder the reygne of *Valens*. He wrate eyght bookes against the heresies, in the Greke tongue. He was great enimie of *Origen* and *Chrysostome*. He excited the people of *Constantinople* agaynst the sayde *Chrysostome*. More, looke *Socrates lib.6. cap.11. Sozomen. lib.7. cap.26.*

Ambrose, a Latine, Bishop of *Millaine*, flourished in the yeare 376. vnder the reygnes of *Valens* in the East, and *Gratian* and *Valentinian* sonnes of *Valentinian* in the West. *Pantaleon, pag.31.* He was a noble man, and gouernour of the whole prouince of *Millaine*, and made Bishop after the death of *Auxentius*. After exiled by *Iustina* mother of *Valentinian*, infected with the heresie of *Arius*. He sustayned great troubles, and wrate many learned workes for the defence of religion. *Socrates lib.4.cap.25.lib.5.cap.11.Sozomen.lib.7.cap.13.*

Gregorie, a Grecian, Bishop of *Nyssa*, brother of *Basile* before named, flourished in the yeare of our Lorde. 381. vnder the reygne of *Gratianus* in the West. Hee wrate certayne works, and especially one very learned, *De anima*, agaynst the Philosophers of the Gentiles. Of *Basile* his Epistle to him, *De differentia essentiæ & substantiæ*, reade the *Tripartite* in the ende of *Theodoret*.

Ierome Priest, a Latine, borne at *Stridonium* in *Dalmatia*, flourished the yeare 390. vnder the reygne of *Valentinian* the younger. He liued in *Bethlehem* in *Syria*, and was verye famous for his workes. *Pantaleon, pag.31.* He dyed the yere 422. the 30. of Septēber. *Paulus Eberus. pag. 317.* Reade his owne workes.

Augustine, a Latine, disciple of *Ierome* Bishop of *Hippo*, now called *Bona*, within the realme of *Tunes* in *Aphrick*, flourished in the yeare 395. vnder *Theodosius* the elder. He is so famous by his workes, that

the

the reader may plainely see him in them. He died the yeare 433. in the 40. yeare of his Bishops sea, the 28. of August.

Chrysostome, a Grecian, called *Iohn* of *Antioch*, but so surnamed of his eloquent speach (that is to say, golden mouth) Bishop of *Constantinople*, flourished in the yeare 405. under the reygne of *Arcadius* & *Honorius*. He was the scholer of *Libanius* the Sophister, afterwardes left him, and was christened by *Meletius*. Lastly made Bishop of *Constantinople*, whence he was twyce banished by *Eudoxia* the Empresse, wyfe of *Arcadius*, by the meanes of *Epiphanius*. In ỹ last time of his exile, being at *Cucussa* in *Armenia*, he sickened, and was caried to *Potij*, and there dyed the yere 410. the 14. of September. His workes are extant, being large and learned. *Tripartit.pag.*422.*Glycas.*359. *Eberus,pag.*301.

Cyrillus, a Grecian, Bishop of *Alexandria*, flourished the yere 432. under *Theodosius* the seconde. *Theodorit.lib.*5.*pag.*35. *Socrates lib.*7.*cap.*7. He was a great enimie of the Jewes, and threw them out at *Alexandria*. *Socrates.lib.*7.*cap.*13. Reade of him the whole *Tripartite*.

Primasius, a Latin, a bishop of *Aphrick*, and disciple of S. *Augustine*, flourished the yeare 435. *Pantaleon, pag*. 35. Reade more of him in *Gesner*.

Fulgentius. a Latine, Bishop of *Ruspa* in *Aphricke*, florished the yeare 456. under the reygne of *Martian*. He wrate certaine workes now extant. But of his actes read his lyfe prefixed to his works. Read *Gesn*.

Prosper, a Frenchman, flourished in the yeare 456. under the reigne of Martianus, read *Gennadius in catalogo*. He wrate certayne sentences, and a Chronography, read *Gesner. Simlerus in catalogo scriptor*.

Gelasius, a Latine, borne in *Aphricke*, first of that name bishop of Rome, flourished in the time of *Zeno* and *Anastasius* Emperors of the East. He wrate manye learned bookes. Read *Platyna* in his life.

Iustinian the 57. Emperor of *Constantinople*, sonne of the sister of *Iustinus* the Emperor, flourished the yeare 527. Hee collected the *Codices* of the lawe into a short volume for the beginners, and called them his Institutions. He reygned 38. yeares. Reade *Iornandes*, *Pomponius*. *Lætus*,

Lætus, Ignatius, Constantinus Manasses, *pag*.83.*Annales Glycæ*,*pag*.371.

Cassiodorus, a senatour of *Constantinople*. afterwardes made a Monke, flourished the yeare 575. under *Iustinianus* the Emperor. But as *Pantaleon* accounteth 497, before the reygne of *Iustinian* under *Anastasius*. He wrate being as yet extant, an Historie, and abridged the Tripartite, Reade *Diaconus, lib*. 1.*cap*.11.

Gregorie the first Bishop of *Rome*, called *Gregorie* the great, flourished in the yere 605. But according to *Pantaleon*, 586. under *Mauritius* the Emperour. He wrate diverse things, but especiallye his Moralles are most excellent. Reade *Bedæ histor. Anglosaxon. Platyna* in his lyfe.

Theophylactus, a Grecian, constituted Bishop of *Antioch*, by *Marua*, chiefe of the Saracenes, flourished the peare 608. But according to *Pantaleon*, 761. under *Constantine*. 6. He wrate certayne workes being extant in the Greeke tongue. *Gesn. Simlerus*.*Pantaleon*,*pag*.61.

Beda, a Latine, borne in Englande, and as it seemeth, about Cambridge. For he calleth himselfe *Beda Giruinus*, which *Gir-*

vi or *Giruij* were Cambridge shyre men, as appeareth by the towne of Cambridge, called of olde *Granta Giruiorum. Leland in Cycnæa cantione.* Flourished in the yere 732. But as ẏ truer with *Pantaleon*, 704. vnder *Leo* the 2. and *Iustinian* Emperors. His workes extant testifie what the man hath bene. He wrate an historie of the Saxones. *Platyna* in the lyfe of *Iohn* the sixt.

Druthmarus, a Latine, Monke of the order of Saint *Bennet*, flourished the yere 800. vnder *Irene* the Empresse. He wrate certayne Commentaries vpon the Euangelistes.

The Abbot of *Augspurg* in *Germanie*, a Latine, called Saint *Vlrike*, or *Vldarike*, flourished the yeare 860. vnder the reygne of *Michael* the 3. of the East, and *Lotharius* the first in the West.

Barnard, a Latin, borne in Burgoigne, & the first Abbot of *Clarenaux* in France, flourished in the yeare 1111. vnder *Henrie* the Emperour of the West, and *Alexius* the first Emperour of the East. He wrate moste flourishingly and learnedly. His works are extant in one volume. *Irenicus.*

lib.

lib. 30. *cap*. 106. *Volater*. *Gulielmus Abbas* in his lyfe.

Abbot of *Vrsperg* in *Germanie*, a Latin, by name vnknowne, flourished the yeare of our Lorde 1200. vnder *Alexius* the first Emperour of the East, and *Philip* Emperour of the West. He wrate an historie which is extant, of the Emperors, and other things most notable, from the beginning of the world to his time, to the which there are added *Paraleipomena* (or Chronicles not touched) vnto our time. *Pantaleon*, *pag*. 95. *Gesner*. *Pantaleon* in his *Posopographie*, *lib*. 2.

Thomas Aquinas, a Latine, borne in Italie, Frier of the order of Preachers, and descended of a noble house, of the Lordes of *Aquino*. He flourished the yere 1271. vnder *Michael Palæologus* the 7. Emperour of the East, and *Rodolphus* the first Earle of *Augspurge* of the West. He made Commentaries vpon all *Aristotle*, and likewise in Diuinitie. His works are extant in 14. volumes in *Fol*. newly imprinted at *Rome*. Reade his owne life set forth in a priuate booke.

Xystus the 4. Bishop of Rome, borne at

Cellæ in the territorie of *Genoa* in *Italie*, named Frier *Francis de Rouere*, of the order of *Minores*. He was created Pope the yeare 1414. He lyued vnder *Sigismond* the Emperor. *Onuphrius Panuinus* in hys lyfe.

Bishop of *Panormus* in *Sicilie*, a great Lawyer, called commonly of his Bishopricke, *Panormitan*. Flourished the yeare 1415. vnder *Sigismunde* the Emperor of the West. He wrate very large volumes of the lawe.

Iohn Gerson, a Diuine of France, one of ye Chancellors of the Vniuersitie of *Paris*, flourished in the same time with the former Byshop, and stoutlye resisted the decrees of the Counsell of *Constance*. *Peucer. in synodo Constantiensi.*

Platyna, an Italian, Secretarie of the sea of Rome, flourished the yeare 1470. vnder *Fredericke* the first, Emperour. He wrate of the liues of the Popes from *Linus* vnto *Xystus* the 4. *Sabell. Gesner. Simler.*

Sanazarius, an Italian Poet, flourished in the time of *Maximilian* the first, and *Alexander* the. 6. Pope.

Marcus Antonius Coccius Sabellicus, borne in the dominion of *Venice*, a bishop, flourished the yere 1501. under *Maximilian* Emperour, and *Pius* the 3. Pope. He wrate a large historie from the creation of the worlde to the yeare 1504. whiche is augmented by *Gaspar Hedio*. *Gesner*. *Simler*.

The order of the Councelles according to Pantaleon.

AT *Carthage*, once very famous, now ruinous and cleane destroyed, a Citie in the kingdome of *Tunes*, under the Turkes dominion, were celebrated sixe Councelles. The first, in the yeare, 360. *Galienus* being Emperor, 32. in succession, and *Stephen* the first, Pope. The seconde, the yere 413. *Honorius* being Emperor. The thirde, in the yeare 429. under *Theodosius* the 2. The fourth, fifth, in the yeare 437. under the same Emperor. The sixt, by 217. Byshops in the yeare 459. under *Martianus*.

At *Anticyra* in *Galatia*, was celebrated a Councell by *Vitalis* Bishop of *Antioche* the

the yeare 295. *Diocletian* being Emperour.

At *Nice* a Citie in *Bithynia* nowe called *Nicbea* in *Asia* the lesse, vnder the Turke, were celebrated two Councels. The first against the *Arians*, the yeare 326. vnder *Constantine* the great, where was esta-blished the *Nicene* Creede. The seconde, the yeare 781. vnder *Constantine* the sixt.

The Councell of *Gangra*, nowe called *Cangri* in *Asia* the lesse, was celebrated the yeare 333. vnder *Constantine* the great.

At *Elyberis*, or *Illyberis*, nowe called *Granado* in *Spayne*, was celebrated a Coũ-sell in the yere 337. vnder *Constantine* the great, by xix. Bishops.

At *Ariminum* now called *Rimino* in the territorie of *Flaminia* nowe *Romandiola* in *Italie*, was celebrated a Councell the yere 362. vnder *Iulian* the *Apostata*.

The Councell of *Laodicea* in *Syria*, was celebrated the yeare 368. vnder *Iulian* the *Apostata*.

At *Constantinople* in *Thrace*, sometime called *Byzantium*, builded by *Constantine* the great, nowe the chiefe seate of the

Turke,

Turke, and called in his language *Stambola*, were celebrated eyght Councelles. The first, the yeare 383. by 180. Bishops vnder *Gratian* the Emperour. The seconde, the yeare 448. vnder *Theodosius* the seconde. The thirde, in the yere 546. vnder *Iustinian* the first. The fourth, the yeare 576. vnder *Iustine* the seconde. The fift, the yeare 681. by 289. Bishops vnder *Constantine* the v. The sixt, the yeare 695. vnder *Iustinian* the seconde. The seuenth, the yeare 726. by 330. Byshoppes, vnder *Leo* the thirde, Emperor. The eyght, the yeare 870. vnder *Basilius Macedo* Emperor of the East, and *Lewes* the seconde, of the West.

At *Toledo* in Spayne, were celebrated 13. Councelles. The first, the yeare 393. vnder *Arcadius* and *Honorius*, by 18. Byshops. The seconde, the yeare 470. vnder *Leo* the first. The thirde, the yeare 615. vnder *Heraclius*, by 62. Byshoppes. The fourth, the yeare 632. vnder *Heraclius*. The fifth and sixt, the yeare 639. vnder *Constantine* the thirde. The seauenth, the yere 680. But according to *Phrygio*, 640. by 30. Bishoppes vnder *Constantine* the fourth.

fourth. The eyght, the yeare 666. by 59. Bishoppes vnder *Constantine* the fourth. The ninth and tenth, the yeare 675. by 16. Bishoppes vnder *Constantine* the fourth. The xi. xii. xiii. the yeare 692. vnder *Constantine* the fourth.

The Councell *Mileuitan*, was celebrated at *Mileuita* in *Aphrica* against the *Pelagians*, the yeare 418. vnder *Honorius*.

The Councell of *Ephesus*, nowe called *Epheso* in *Ionia* in *Asia* the lesse, was celebrated, the yeare 430. by 200. Bishops, agaynst the *Pelagians* and *Nestorians* vnder *Theodosius* the 2.

At *Orenge* in France, but excepted from the dominion of the Frenche Kings, hauing a seuerall Prince, were helde two Councelles. The first, the yeare 451. vnder *Theodosius* the seconde, and *Valentinian*. The seconde, the same yere, vnder the sayde Emperors.

The Councell of *Chalcedon* in *Bythinia*, nowe called by the Turkes *Scutari*, situated right ouer against *Constantinople*, was helde, the yeare 453. agaynst the *Eutychians*, *Manichees*, and *Dioscorus*, by 600. Byshops, vnder the reygne of *Theodosius*

the

the 2. and *Valentinian* the 3.

At *Orleans* in Fraunce were helde fiue Councelles. The first, the yeare 518. under *Iustinus* the first, by 33. Bishops. The seconde, the yeare 550. under *Iustinian* the great. The thirde, the same yeare under the same Emperor. The fourth, the yeare 567. under *Iustinus* the second. The 5. the yeare 572. under the sayde Emperour.

At *Bracara*, now called *Braga* in Spain, were helde three Councelles. The first, the yeare 555. under *Iustinian* the great. The seconde and thirde, the yeare 583. *Martianus* being Emperor.

The *Laterane* Councelles were seauen. The first, by *Stephan* the 3. the yere 767. under *Leo*. The seconde, by *Nicolaus* the seconde, the yeare 1058. under *Constantine* the 12. of the East, and *Henrie* the 4. of the West. The thirde, by *Innocentius* the 2. the yeare 1138. under *Caloioannes* of the East, and *Lotharius* the 2. of the West, Emperors. The fourth, the yeare 1167. by *Alexander* the 3. under *Emanuel* of the East, and *Frederike* of the West. The fift, the yeare 1205. by *Innocentius* the thirde,

in

in the presence of 7. Archbishoppes, 412. Bishops. 1300. Prelates, vnder *Henrie* the 6. of the West, and *Balduine* the first, of the East. The sixt, the yeare, 1446. by *Eugenius* the 4. vnder *Frederike* the 3. The seauenth, the yeare 1510. by *Iulius* the 3. vnder *Maximilian* the first.

At *Chalons* in Fraunce, were helde two Councelles. The first, the yeare 670. vnder *Constantine* the 4. The seconde, the yeare 805. vnder *Charles* the first, Emperour of the West, and *Nicephorus* of the East.

At *Wormes* in Germany, were 5. Councelles. The first, the yeare 868. vnder *Lewes* the seconde of the West, and *Basilius* of the East, Emperours. The second, the yere 1067. vnder *Romanus* the second, of the East, and *Henrie* the fourth, of the West. The thirde, the yeare 1494. vnder *Maximilian* the first. The fourth, the yere 1520. vnder the sayde Emperour. The fift, the yeare 1536. vnder *Charles* the fifte.

FINIS.

The summe of the common places contayned in this Booke.

Finis.

The Staffe of the Christian Faith.

Of the holy Supper of our Lorde Iesus Christ.

I Am that liuing breade, which came downe from heauen: If any man eate of this breade, hee shall liue for euer: & the breade that I will giue, is my fleshe, which I will giue for the life of the worlde, &c. Iohn.6.

That which I deliuered vnto you, I receyued of the Lorde, to wit: That the Lorde Iesus the same night in whiche he was betrayed, tooke breade, and when he had giuen thankes, he brake it, and sayd: Take ye, eate ye, this is my bodie which is broken for you: this doe ye in remembrance of me. After the same maner also he tooke the Cup when he had supped, saying: This Cup is the newe testament in my bloude: this doe as ofte as ye drinke it, in remembrance of me. For as often as 1.Cor.11. Math.26 Marc.14. Luke.22. Or the nevv alliance.

ye shall eate this breade, and drinke this Cuppe, yee shewe the Lordes death till he come. Wherefore, whosoeuer shall eate this breade, and drinke this Cuppe of the Lorde vnworthily, shall be guiltie of the bodie and bloude of the Lorde. Let a man therefore examine himselfe: and so let him eate of this breade, and drinke of this Cup.

1.Cor.10. Is not the Cup of blessing whiche we blesse, the Communion of the bloude of Christe? Is not the Breade which wee breake, the Communion of the bodie of Christ? Bicause that we whiche are manye, are one breade and one bodie, in as muche as wee are all partakers of one breade.

1.Cor.10. Our fathers haue all eaten the same spi-
Exod.17. rituall meate, and did all drinke the same
Num.20. spirituall drinke: for they dranke of the spirituall rocke that followed them: and that rocke was Christ.

Iohn.6. I am the breade of life, he that commeth to me, shall not hunger, and he that beleeueth on me shal neuer thurst. &c. This is that breade which commeth downe from heauen, that he whiche eateth of it, shoulde

shoulde not die.

Augustine in his 2. Quinqua. vpon the 96. Psalme.

When the Lorde commaunded this, he spake of his fleshe, and sayde: He that eateth not my fleshe, shall not haue eternall lyfe. And sayd: The wordes that I speake vnto you, are spirite and life. Vnderstand spiritually that which I haue sayde vnto you: you shall not eate that bodie whiche you do see, & you shall not drinke the bloud which shall be shedde by them which will crucifie me. *Iohn. 6.* VVe eate not Christes bodie carnally.

Augustine vpon Saint Iohn, in the 27. treatise vpon the 6 Chapter.

If ye shoulde see the sonne of man ascend vp where he was before. *Iohn. 6.*

What is this? By that he resolueth those whom he hath knowen: of that he manyfested the thing whereby they haue ben offended. For they did thinke that he would giue vnto them his body: but hee sayth, that hee will ascend vp into heauen all whole, saying: when yee shall see the sonne of man ascend vp where he was before: at the least you shall see then that he doth not giue his bodie in the same ma- Christ not eaten by morsels.

ner as ye thinke and iudge: at the least you shal then understand that his grace is not consumed by morsels. &c.

Augustine in his Sermon of the Sacramentes of the faithfull, in the 2. ferie of Easter.

And for this cause (as also the men of God haue understoode it before us) our Lorde Jesus Christ hath recommended his body and his blood to the thinges, which of many are reduced and brought into one thing. For also, the one of many Graynes is confecte and made into one, and the other of many Grapes is reduced into one: he that eateth my flesh and drinketh my blood, dwelleth in me and I in him. Then to eate this meate, and to drink this drinke, is to dwell in Christ, and to haue our dwelling in him. And so hee that dwelleth not in Christ, and in whome Christ doth not dwell: without doubt hee eateth not the flesh, and drinketh not the bloud: although that he eate and drinke the Sacrament of so great a thing, to his iudgement.

The sinner eateth nothing in the supper but the outeward signe.

Au-

Augustine in his.3.booke of the christian doctrine.

If you eate not (sayth he) the fleshe of the sonne of man, and drinke not his blood you shall haue no life in you. It seemeth that he doth commaund an vnlawful thing, or a fault.

That is then a fygure: commaunding that it must be communicated to the passion of our Lorde, and gentlye and profitablye to put in memorye that his fleshe hath bene wounded and crucified for vs.

Augustine of the words of the Apostle in his.2.sermon

Saith: If ye eate not my flesh, and drinke not my blood, ye shall haue no life in you. &c. The disciples were offended, not all truly, but many of them saying within themselues: This is an harde saying, who can abide ÿ hearing of it? What doth this signifie? Doth this offende you? Did you thinke, that of this bodie here whiche you doe see, I ought to make peeces: and that I shoulde deuyde in peeces my members for to giue them vnto you? What and if you shoulde see the sonne of man ascende

Iohn.6.

Christ maketh not peeces of his bodie.

cende vp where he was before? Truly he which is ascended vp all whole, cannot be consumed, &c. What is it to drinke this thing, but to liue? Eate the lyfe, drinke the lyfe: thou shalte haue lyfe, and thou shalt be the whole lyfe. And then this shall be (that is to saye) that the bodie and bloude of Christ shall be the lyfe of euerye one: if that which they do take visibly in ỹ sacrament, be in dede spiritually eaten and drunke. For we haue hearde the Lorde himselfe saying: It is the spirite that quickeneth, the fleshe profiteth nothing. The wordes that I speake vnto you, are spirite and life.

Augustine in his Decrees of penance, in the 2. distinction. Chapiter of Charitie.

To eate the breade, and drinke the wyne, that is to beleeue in Christ, and in louing him, to giue our selues vnto him.

Bede in his Collection: These are also the wordes of Saint Augustine in his sermon made to the children at the aultar of the Sacrament.

The Cuppe of blessing. &c. That which ye

ye see in the Aulter, ye haue also seene it the night past. But you haue not yet vnderstoode what it doth signifie, and howe it conteyneth a Sacrament of a greate thing. That then whiche ye haue seene, is bread, and wine, the which your eyes doo demonstrate vnto you. But that which your faith desireth to be instructed in: the bread is the body of Christ: and the wine the blood. And that truly is breefly sayde, in asmuch peraduenture that it suffiseth the fayth: but the fayth desireth to be instructed: for the Prophet sayth: If ye beleeue not, you shall not vnderstand. Yee may then say vnto me: thou hast commanded that we should beleeue: expound it, to the ende that we may vnderstand it. For such cogitacion and thought may enter into the mindes and vnderstanding of euery one, we doo know very well from whence our Lord Jesus Christ hath taken his flesh: that is to say of the Virgin Mary, he was nourished vp in his infancie, he was brought vp, he became great, and came to the age of a young man. He suffered persecution by the Jewes. He hath ben hanged on the tree, and dyed on the

That vvhich vvee see in the supper, is breade.

Esay.7.

Luc.1.

Math.2.

tree, and was buryed, and rose againe the third day, and ascended into heauen the day it pleased him. There he eleuated his body, and from thence he shall come to iudge the quicke and the dead, there he sitteth now at the right hand of the father. How then is the bread his body? And the cuppe or that which the cuppe conteineth, how is that his blood? My bretheren, therefore are these thinges here called Sacramentes: because that in them, one thing is seene, and an other thing is vnderstoode. That which we see in a corporall likenesse: but that which we vnderstand, to a spirituall fruite. He that receaueth the mistery of vnity, and keepeth not the bond of peace, he receiueth not by him the mistery, but receaueth a witnesse agaynst him selfe. And no man ought in any thing to doubt, but that then euery faithfull man is partaker of the body and of the blood of the Lorde: As to baptisme he is made a member of Christ: and is not depryued from the company of that bread and of that cuppe, also when hee which is constituted in the vnitie of the body of Christ, shall depart out of this

worlde,

world, before he doo eate that bread, and drinke the cuppe: for also he is not depryued from the participation and from the benefite of that Sacrament, whiche hath found that which the Sacrament dooth signifie.

Prosper in his booke of sentences.

He that abydeth in Christ, and in whom Christ dwelleth, hath taken the meate of lyfe, and hath drunke the drinke of the eternitie. For he whiche discordeth from Christ, doth not eate the fleshe of Christ, nor drinketh his bloud: Although that he doe take euery daye indifferently the Sacrament of so great a thing, according to his iudgement.

Innocent in his thirde booke of the holy Aultar. 4. 13. 14. Chapter.

Iudas (sayth he) hath eaten the Lordes breade, but he hath not eaten the breade, which was the Lorde.

Saint Hilarie in his 8. booke of the Trinitie.

The breade which descended from heauen, is not receiued, but of him which hath the Lorde, and which is the true member of him.

Augustine in his 49. treatise vpon Saint Iohn the 11. Chapter.

If fayth be in vs, Christ is in vs. For what other thing, sayeth the Apostle, Christ dwelleth in your heartes through fayth, but that through the fayth whiche thou hast of Christ, Christ is in thy heart.

Augustine vpon Saint Iohn in his 25. treatise and 6 Chapter.

This is then to eate the meate, not that which perisheth, but which abideth vnto eternall lyfe Wherefore make ready thou the teeth, and the belly, beleeue, and thou hast eaten. &c.

Saint Cyprian in his Sermon of the vnction of Christ.

Our Lorde Jesus Christ hath giuen in the table in the whiche he hath made his last banket with his Apostles, the breade and the wyne with his owne hands, but he hath giuen his bodye for to be wounded on the Crosse by the handes of the souldiers. &c.

Augustine vpon Saint Iohn in the 26. Homely.

Sayth: All we haue very well this daye

recey-

receyued the visible meate, but it is another thing of the Sacrament, and of the vertue of the same. From whence commeth it that many doe come vnto the aultar, and take to their condemnation that which they receyue: For the morsell of breade which our Lord gaue vnto Iudas, was poyson vnto him, not for that it was euill, but bicause the man which tooke it, was euill, he tooke it euill. &c. A little after he sayth: the Sacrament of this (that is to saye) the spirituall vnitie whiche we haue with Christ, is presented vnto vs at the Lordes table, to the one to lyfe, to the others to death. A little before hee hath sayde: He which shall eate, shall not die: but I doe vnderstande it of him whiche shall haue the veritie of the Sacrament, and not the visible Sacrament: whiche shall eate him inwardlye, and not outwardly: whiche shall eate him in the heart, and not crashe him with the teeth. *Iohn.6*

In what sense the auncient Doctors of the Church, haue vnderstoode this place: *Hoc est corpus meum*: This is my bodye.

S. Augustine wryting against Adamantius the disciple of Manichæus in the ,12. Epistle.

The breade is the signe of the bodie of Christ.

Saith after this manner: I maye interpret, that this commandement cōsisteth in a signe: for the Lord hath made it no doubt to say: This is my body, when hee gaue the signe of his body. In the same place he sayth these three thinges: The blood is water: Behold my body: And the rocke was Christ. He teacheth these thinges to be sayde, as though he spake by figure in signe and by signification.

Tertullian in his .4. booke against Marcion,

Hoc est corpus meum, hovve to be vnderstode.

Sayth after this sort: Jesus Christ after he toke the bread, and distributed it to his disciples, made it his body, in saying: this is my body. That is to say (saith he) the signe of my body.

Chrisostome vpon S. Mathewe in the .83. homily the .26. chapter, called the symbole of the supper and signe of the body of Christ.

Augustine in his first quinquagesima, in his prologue of the 3. psalm,

Saith: Christ receiued Judas vnto his

supper,

supper, in the which he recommended and gaue the figure of his body, and of his blood to his disciples.

Chrisostome vpon S. Mathew in the .83. homelye,

Saith: When the Heritickes say, how shall it appeare that Christ hath ben offered? We wyll stoppe their mouthes thus, if Iesus Christ be not dead, to what ende shall that sacrifice be a signe.

Saint Ierome vpon the 26. Chapter of S. Mathewe.

After that he acomplished the mysticall Passeouer, or Easter: & had eaten the flesh of the Lambe with his Apostles: He toke the breade which comforteth the heart of man, and passed further to come vnto the Sacrament of the true Easter: That euen as Melchisedech the highe Priest of the souereygne God hath done, in the figure of this, in offering of breade and wyne: Euen so he representeth the veritie of his bodie, and of his bloude.

Iesus Christ representeth his body by the breade.

Saint Ambrose vpon the first Epistle to the Corinthians the 11. Chap.

Forasmuch as we are deliuered by the death of the Lorde, hauing recordation thereof, in eating and drinking, wee doe signifie the fleshe and the bloude, the which haue bene offered for vs. &c.

Chrysostome vpon the 22. psalme.

Christ hath ordeyned the table of his holye Supper, to the ende, that in that sacrament, he doe shewe vnto vs daylye, the breade and the wine, for the similitude of his bodie and of his bloude.

Saint Ambrose in his 6. booke of the Sacramentes, the first Chapter.

The Priest sayth: Make this oblation to bee acceptable vnto vs: the whiche is the figure of the bodie and bloude of oure Lorde. &c.

Chrysostome in the 83. Homelie vpon Saint Mathewe,

If thou haddest bene withoute a bodie, hee woulde haue giuen thee all his signes naked and bare: but bicause that thy soule is ioyned to a body, he hath giuen thee in the sensible thinges, the things which are comprysed by the spirite.

S. Ambrose in his booke of the Sacraments, the 1. Chapter.

Thou doest receiue the Sacrament,

for the similitude of the flesh and of the bloud of Christ: but thou obteynest the grace of his true nature. And in receiuing the bread, in that meate, thou art partaker of his deuine substaunce. &c. And he sayth afterward: Euen as thou hast receiued at baptisme the similitude of death: so likewyse thou hast drunke in that Sacrament the similitude of the precious bloud of Christe. &c.

Bede vpon the .22. chapter of S. Luke.

After he had ended the solemnitie of the ancient Passeouer: the which he made in remembraunce of the auncient deliueraunce out of Egypt: he passed foorth to the newe solemnitye the which the church desireth to celebrate, in remembraunce of her redemption: to the ende that putting the Sacrament of his flesh & of his bloud, vnder the likenesse of bread and wine, in steede of the flesh and of the bloud of the Lambe: he sheweth himself to be him vnto whome the Lord hath swoorne and wyll not repent, thou art a priest for euer. &c. Nota. It followeth after, bicause that the breade doth fortefie the flesh, and that the wine causeth

causeth the bloud in the flesh, the bread is referred mistically to the body of Christ, and the wine to his bloud. &c.

Druthmarus Monke of S. Benet, in his commentary vppon Saint Mathew.

The wine refresheth and augmenteth the bloud, for that cause the bloud of Christ is not vnproperly figured by the same: in asmuch as all that commeth vnto vs from him, doth make vs glad with a true ioye, and increaseth all our goodnesse. &c. A little before he sayth. The Lord gaue vnto his disciples the Sacrament of his body, in remission of theyr sinnes, and for to keepe loue and charitie, to the end that hauing remembraunce of that deede, he would doo alwayes in a figure, that which he ought to doo for them: and shoulde not forget that charytie. This is my body, that is to say, in Sacrament. &c.

Origen vpon Leuiticus in the. 7. homely.

VVe must vnderstande many things in the scriptures spiritually.

Knowe that these are figures which are wrytten in the holy bookes: and therefore they ought to be examined as spiritually and not as carnall: and to vnderstand the

the thinges which are sayd. For if you doo receiue those thinges here as carnall, they doo hurt you and not nourish you: for the letter which killeth is not only found in the old testament: but also in the Gospell, in the new testament. The letter killeth him which considereth not spiritually the thinges which are spoken. For if thou follow according to the letter that whiche is sayd, except that you doo not eate my flesh and drinke my bloud, that letter killeth. Wylt thou that I doo aledge vnto thee an other letter of the Gospell which killeth. He which hath not a sword saith he, let him sell his coate and buy one. Doest thou see, that letter is of the Gospell, but it killeth truely, if thou receiue it spiritually, it kylleth not: but in the same is the quickening spirite, and therefore receiue spiritually the thinges which are spoken, be it in the Lawe, or in the Gospell. For the spirituall man iudgeth all thinges, but he him selfe is iudged of no man. &c. 2.Cor.3 1.Cor.2

Denys in the ecclesiasticall Hierarchia.

Saith: The Byshoppe after that hee shall haue ended by preaching the heauenly giftes, he consecrateth, and blesseth the holy misteryes, and that which he before hath preached, he setteth before euery one couert and hidde by venerable signes and tokens. And after that he hath shewed his heauenly gyftes in all reuerence, he turneth him selfe to the holy communion of them, admonishing all other to communycate: and after that the holy communion is receyued of euery one, rendring thanks unto God, he maketh an end of ẏ mistery.

Mat.26. *Obiec. Hoc est corpus meū*, this is my body.

Aunswere. When God gaue the circumcision to Abraham, he made his couenant before the circumcision, and yet he called the circumcision his couenant, or alliance, *Genes.17.* saying, *Hoc est pactum meum.* This is my couenant. S. Paule expoundeth the same *Rom.4.* saying: Abraham hath receyued the signe of circumcision, as a seale of the righteousnesse of fayth. God sayd to the Prophet *Ezech.4. & .5.* Ezechiel: thou sonne of man, take a tyle stone, and laye it before thee, and describe upon it the citie of Ierusalem: after he saith, this same is Ierusalem.

Hoc est corpus meum.

Augustine vpon Leuiticus 9. & .7.57. also he wryteth agaynst Adamant.

The

The thing whiche signifieth, hath of custome bene called of the name of the thing which is signified. As it is wrytten, the seuen eares, are seuen yeeres: The Scripture sayth not that they signifie seuen yeeres. And the seuen kyne are seuen yeeres, and many such thinges. In lyke manner sayth S. Paule, that the Rocke was christ, and not that it signified Christ, but as if it had ben him in very deede: the which notwithstanding was not Christ by substance, but by figuration. &c.

Genes.41.

1.Cor.10.

Augustine wryting to Boniface. Epistle. 23.

If the Sacraments haue no certayne similitude, or agreeing with the things of which they are sacramentes, they shall be in no maner of wyse Sacramentes. For they take oftentimes the names of the things themselues by reason of that similitude. As the Sacrament of the bodie of Christe is after one fashion or maner, the bodie of Christ, and the sacrament of the bloude of Christ, the bloude of Christ. Also the Sacramente of Fayth, is the fayth.

The sacraments take oftentimes the name of the things that they represent.

Irenæus agaynst the heretike Valens in his 4.booke, & 34. Chapter.

The breade with the which wee render thanks vnto God, although that it be of the earth, yet neuerthelesse when the name of God is inuocated and called vpon, it is not the common breade, but of giuing of thankes, hauing two things in it, the one earthly, and the other heauenly.&c.

Gelasius writing against Eutyches and Nestorius, and also to the Counsell of Rome, in the Chapter Comperimus de consecrat. Distin.2.

The substance of breade and vvine is not chaunged in the supper.

The Sacramentes of the bodie and of the bloude of the Lorde Jesus Christe, which we take, they are heauenly things, whereby we are made partakers by them of the diuine nature. And yet neuerthelesse the substance of the breade and of the wine remayne there still, and trulye the image and the similitude of the bodie and of the bloude of Christ, are celebrated in the doing of the mysteries. Then that is euidently shewed vnto vs which we must fele in Jesus Christ our Lorde: yea, the same

which

which we protest, celebrate, and are in his image, to the ende that euen as the natures are conuerted and chaunged into the diuine substance, by the meanes of the holye spirite, and yet neuerthelesse they abyde in their natures. Also the same principall ministerie (whose efficacie and vertue is trulye represented vnto vs by the things whereof it consisteth, whiche abide properly in their being) doe demonstrate vnto vs, that onely Christ abydeth altogither wholy and in his veritie.

The Councell of Nice.

Let vs not staye here belowe on the breade and wyne, whiche are sette on the Lordes table: but let vs lift vppe our spirites on high through fayth. Let vs consider that the lambe of God whiche taketh away the sinnes of the world, is in that holy table, the whiche is not offered in sacrifice by the Priestes, after the manner of beastes. And in taking his precious bodie and his bloude, let vs beleeue that they are the signes and tokens of our resurrection. And for the same cause we eate not much, but a little, to the ende we may know that the same is not ordeyned for to fill our bel-

Col. 3.

1. Cor. 6.

lye withall, but for to serue to sanctitie and holynesse. &c.

Saint Ambrose in his booke of those which are dedicated to the mysteries.

Consecration is to dedicate a cōmon thing to a holy vse

Before the consecration one kinde, or likenesse is named, but after the consecration the body of Christ is signified. Christe sayth that his bloud before the consecration is called an other thing: but after the consecration is signified the bloud of Christe. &c.

S. Ciprian in his sermon of penitent sinners.

Note that he sayth not the bloude, but the drinke sanctified.

Speaking of the mayd which did vomit out the Sacrament: The drinke sanctified in the bloud of the Lord, issued out of the polluted entrailes.

Chrisostome wryting to Cæsar the Monke.

Before the consecration of the breade, we doo call it bread: but when the grace of God hath sanctified it by the priest, it is deliuered from the name of bread, and is exalted to the name of the body of the Lorde: although that the nature of the bread abydeth alwayes: and is not called

two

two bodyes: but one body of the sonne of GOD.

Augustine vppon S. Iohn in his 80. homelye.

Iesus Christ sayth not that you are cleane bicause of the baptisme, by ye which you haue ben washed: but he sayth it bycause of the word which I haue sayd vnto you. That is for none other cause, but that the word doth wash and clense you in the water. If one doo take away the word, what shall the water be but water? Which if the word be ioyned to the element, it shall be made a Sacrament: and the word it selfe is made as visible: from whence commeth so great vertue to the water, that in touching the body it washeth the hart, but by meanes of the word? Not alwayes, bicause that the word is pronounced, but bicause that one beleeueth. For in the worde it selfe, truly there is a difference betwene the sound passing, and the vertue abyding.

The vvater of baptisme doth not purge sinnes

The Rubrycke wrytten in redde letters, whiche is called cautela Missæ.

If the body of the Lord be found within the armorye or pyxe, to be rotten or mustye, through to great moystnesse of the armorye, or through to great negligence in not changing it. If none can be founde which wyll receiue it, that the sayd body of the Lorde be burned, and the asshes put in a certayne halowed place. Item if the sayd body of the Lorde be found within the sayd armorye to be eaten parte of it with Myce, or Spiders, if none can bee found which wyll receiue it, that it be burned, and the asshes put in a halowed place. Item if any that is sicke, who hauing receiued the sayd body of the Lord, and through the infirmitie of his stomacke is constrayned to vomite it vp agayne, if none can be found which wyll take that refection: that the sayd body of ye Lorde be burned, and the asshes put into an halowed place.

Note vvell and vnderstande.

The bodie of the Lorde cannot stink nor be burned, nor vomited.

S. Peter aunswereth to the same in his sermon.

Psal. 15. *Act.* 2. *Act.* 13.

Thou shalt not suffer thy holy one to see corruption. S. Paule sayth asmuche, in his sermon that he made to the people of Antioche, saying: He whome God raysed agayne, sawe no corruption, also God hath raysed him from death for to returne

no

no more to corruption.

How our Lord Iesus Christ according to his Humanite, cannot be but in one place.

S. Ambrose wryting vpon S. Luke in his 10. booke.

We ought not to seeke thee vpon earth, nor in the earth, nor according to the flesh, if we wyll finde thee. For we may not knowe now Jesus Christ after the fleshe. S. Stephen did not seeke him vpon earth, who did see him at the right hand of God. But Mary which sought him in the earth, had not the power to touche him. Stephen hath touched him, for he sought him in heauen.

Christ vpon the earth, nor in the corruptible elements is not to be sought. *Act.* 7. *Iohn.* 2.

Augustine in his 2. Quinquagesima, psalme. 54.

Untill such time as the heauen shal end, the Lord shall be alwayes on high: but the truth of the Lord is here with vs. For it must nedes be ye body with which he rose agayne, be in one certayne place: but is truth is spread abroad euery where.

The bodie of Christ but in one place.

Augu-

Augustine wryting to Dardanus in the 67. Epistle.

Doubt not that Jesus Christ as touching his manhod, is not there, where we doe looke for him. And doe remember that which we confesse in our crede: That he rose agayne, and ascended into heauen, and that he shall come from thence, and not from any other place, to iudge ẏ quick and the dead. And he shall come according to the witnesse of the Angell, as they haue seene him ascend in that same visible form, and in the same substance to the which he hath giuen immortalitie. But he hath not taken frō him his nature: according to the forme and substance of his body, we must not think that he is dispersed euery where: for we must take heede so to affirme his deytie, that we destroy not his humayne nature. Therefore it followeth not that all which is in God, is God.

Christ shall come as he ascended, that is, in the same forme.

Augustine vpon S. Iohn in his 30. treatyse.

The body of Christ is raysed vp from death, and it must needes be that it is in one place.

2. *Colos.* 3. If ye then be rysen agayne with Christ, seeke

seeke those thinges which are aboue, where Christ sitteth at the righ hand of God. Thinke on the thinges which are aboue, but not on those which are on earth.

Iesus Christ sayth: I am yet a little while with you, and then goe I vnto him that sent me. Iohn.7.

Also the poore ye haue alwayes with you, but me ye shall not haue alwayes. Iohn.12.

My little children, yet a little whyle am I with you, ye shall seeke me, and (as I sayd vnto the Iewes) whither I goe, thither can ye not come. Iohn.13.

Again, I go to prepare a place for you: I wyll returne agayne, and receiue you, euen vnto my selfe: that you may be there, where I am also. Iohn.14.

I tell you the truth, it is expedient for you that I goe away. For yf I goe not away, that comforter wyll not come vnto you: But if I depart I wyll send him vnto you. Iohn.16.

I came out from my father, and came into the world: Againe, I leaue the world, and goe to my father. Iohn.16.

Also the Angell sayde vnto the women, I knowe that ye seeke Iesus whiche Mat.28.

was

was crucified: he is not here, for he is rysen, as he sayd: come and see the place where the Lord was layde.

Luk. 24. Behold my handes and my feete: for it is euen I my selfe: handle me and see: for a spirite hath not flesh and bones, as ye see me haue. And when he had thus spoken, he shewed them his hands & his fete.

Act. 1. And while they looked stedfastly vp to heauen, as he went, behold two men stode before them in white apparell, which also sayd, ye men of Galyle, why stand ye gasing into heauen: This same Iesus which is taken vp from you into heauen, shall so come, euen as ye haue seene him goe into heauen.

Act. 3. Also whom the heauen must contayne vntill the time that all thinges be restored.

That we ought not to take from the lay people the wyne of the supper.

Gelasius Pope of Rome of consecration in the seconde distinction, chapter Comperimus. &c.

We haue vnderstoode that some men receyuing

ceyuing only the bodye of the Lorde, doe abstayne themselues from the Cup, who forasmuch as they sinne by superstition, ought to be constrayned and compelled to receyue the Sacrament wholy: or else to reiect it altogither. For the diuision of this mysterie cannot be without great sacrilege. Jesus Christ commaunded in his supper, and sayde: Drinke ye all of this: For this is my bloude of the newe testament.

The supper to be receyued in tvvo kindes, or else not.

Mat. 26.

The Counsaile of Basile hath ordeined that the laye people shoulde communicate the supper in two kindes.

The Counsell of Basill.

Saint Cyprian in his Sermon of penitent sinners.

Howe shall we exhort the people to shed their bloude for the confession of Christ, if we doe denie unto them the bloude of him when they ought to fight? Or howe can we make our selues capable to drinke the cuppe of Martyrdome, except þ we suffer our selues firste to drinke of the cuppe of the Lorde.

That we ought not to keepe the breade of the supper, nor to carie it here and there.

Saint Clement in his 2. Epistle to Iames. And of the consecration in the 3. Distinction. Chapter tribus. &c.

The vse in the primitiue Church of the supper.

So many hostes ought to be offred at the Aulter, as shall be sufficient for the people. And if any remaine, we ought not to keepe it vntill the next day: but through the diligence of the clarkes, with feare and trembling ought to be receiued, and eaten.

Origen vpon the 7. chapter of Leuiticus.

The breade not caried in processions.

The Lorde hath not ordayned or commaunded, that the bread should be kept, vntill the morrowe, the which he gaue vnto his disciples: but sayd vnto them, take ye and eate. &c. And in this he commaunded not to carry the bread by the wayes, it may be, that by the same is conteyned a mysterye, that is to say, that alwayes thou

thou oughtest to bring forth the newe breade of the worde of God, whiche thou bearest within thee.

Iesus Christ sayth: Take and eate. Mat. 26

In which sense we ought to understand the auncient Doctors: when they haue sayde, we offer, we sacrifice, in calling the supper a sacrifice.

S. Augustine writing against Faustus, the 8. Chapter.

The Hebrues sacrificing the brute beastes, did exercise themselues in the prophecie of the sacrifice which Iesus Christ hath offered: And nowe the Christians in the oblation and communion of the bodie of Iesus Christ, doe celebrate the memorie of the sacrifice already ended.

Chrysostome in his first tome vpon the 8. Chapter of Saint Mathew, in the 16. homily.

For this cause these reuerende and salutarie mysteries, which we celebrate in all the congregation of the Church, are called *Eucharistiæ*, that is to saye: a giuing of thankes: for they are the remembrance of many benefites, and doe shewe the verye eade of the heauenly loue towardes vs, and

VVherefore the sacrament of the supper is called Eucharistia.

and doe make vs alwayes render thankes vnto God.

Psal.50. The Prophet Dauid in the 50. Psalm: Offer vnto God thanks giuing. &c.

Ireneus in his 4. booke against the heresies. Chap. 32. 33. & 34.

He hath willed that we shoulde offer often the gift at the aultar, and without intermission. The aultar then is in heauen, for thither our prayers and oblations are addressed, and directed to the temple (as S. Iohn saith in his Apocalips:) And the

Apoc.11. temple of God was open, and the tabernacle: For beholde (sayth he) the tabernacle of God, in the whiche I doe dwell with men.

S. Cyprian in his 2. boke of Epistles, the 3. Epistle vnto Cecill.

We ought not to follovve custome but Christe, vvhich is the veritie.

We must not, welbeloued brother, that any man thinke, that one ought to followe the custome of some men, whiche haue thought or iudged that we must offer the water only in the Lordes cuppe, we must aske of those, whō they haue for example. For if in the sacrifice which is Christ, we must followe none but Christ: truly then we must heare and doe that which Christ

hath

hath done, and commaunded to be done: *Iohn.15*
Inasmuch as he sayth in his Gospell, if you doe whatsoeuer I commaunde you, I will call you no more seruauntes, but my freyndes. And that Iesus Christ ought to be onely hearde, the father himselfe doth witnesse it from heauen, saying: This is my welbeloued sonne, in whom I am well pleased, heare him. Wherefore if Christe ought to be only hearde, we ought not to regarde that, whiche another before vs shall thinke good to be done: But that he who is before all (that is to saye) Christ, hath done first. For we must not followe the custome of man, but the veritie of god: forasmuche as he sayeth by his Prophete Esay: They worshippe me in vayne, tea- *Esay.29.*
ching doctrines whiche are but mens preceptes. And the Lorde himselfe repeateth the same in the Gospell, saying: ye doe re- *Math.15.*
iect the commaundement of God, for to establishe your owne tradition. But yet he hath sayde in another place: Whosoeuer shall break one of these least comman- *Math.5.*
dements, & teacheth men so to doe, he shall be called the least in the kingdome of heauen. Then if it be not lawfull to breake

the least of all the commaundementes of God: howe much lesse shall it be lawfull, to breake these so greate, so excellent, and so properly appertayning to the Sacramens of the passion of the Lorde, and of our redemption: Or to chaunge it thorow the ordinauce, and tradition of men, to an other thing than to that to ỹ which it hath ben godly instituted? For if Jesus Christ be the very souereygne Priest of God the father: and if he hath bene the first offered sacrifice to God his father: and hath commaunded to doe this in remembraunce of him, he shall doe truly the office of Christ, which shall followe that which Christ hath done. And if he doe begyn to offer in the Church to God the father, according as he shall see that Christ him selfe hath offered: then he shal offer vnto God a full and whole sacrifice. Furthermore, if one kepe not that faithfullye, which is spirituallye commanded, the discipline of all religion and truth is ouerthrowne.

S. Augustine in his booke of fayth vnto Peter. Chap. 16.

In that sacrifice which we doe vse, there is giuing of thankes, and remembrance of of the fleshe of Christ which he offered for vs, and of his bloude which he hath shed.

Augustine in his 10. booke of the Citie of God. Chap. 5.

The visible sacrament is the testament: that is to saye, the holy signe of the inuisible sacrifice.

Chrysostome in the 7. homilye vpon the Epistle to the Hebrues.

We doe offer in deede, but that which we doe offer, we doe it in remembraunce of his death: for that which we doe, is done in remembraunce of that which hath bene done: For he sayth, doe this in remembraunce of me: we doe not make it any other sacrifice, as the priest doth: But wee doe alwayes the very same: and for to tell you better, we doe the remembraunce of the sacrifice which hath ben done. The supper is but a remembrance of the sacrifice.

The Apostle vnto the Hebrues, we doe by him offer, the sacrifice of laude alwayes vnto God: that is to say, the fruite of those lippes which confesse his name. *Heb. 13.*

I beseche you therefore brecheren, by the mercifulnesse of God, that yee make your bodies a quick sacryfice, holy and acceptable vnto God: which is your resona- *Rom. 12.*

ble seruing of God.

Oseas.14. The prophet Oseas, O forgiue vs all our sinnes, receiue vs graciouslye, and then wyll we offer thee bullockes of our lippes vnto thee.

Philip.4. S. Paule sayth, I was filled after that I had receiued of Epaphroditus, the which came from you, an odour that smelleth sweete, a sacrifice acceptable and pleasant to God.

Lactantius Firmianus in his 6. booke the .24.&.25. chapters.

Iesus Christ sayth: I haue pleasure in mercy and not in offring. Math.9. Mat. 12. Oseas.6. and the 1. of Samuel. 15.

Pope Gregory in his .16. decretall the .7. question.

Pope Gregory in his decretals, adiudgeth him culpable of Idolatry, which shall heare the masse of a priest, that is a whoremonger, or which shall communicate at his Sacramentes and Sacrafices.

Francis Maro, in his suffrages for the deade.

He which causeth a masse to be sayde by an vnchast, or whore maister priest, or which is in deadly sinne, it profiteth nothing

thing, neyther to the liuing, nor to the deade.

The Apostle to the Hebrues, the lawe which hath but the shadowe of good things to come, and not things in their owne fashion, can neuer with the sacrifices which they offer yearely, make the commers therevnto perfect. *Heb.10.*

If then the sacrifices commanded of God haue no povver to take avvay sinnes, hovv shall those doe vvhich God hath neuer commanded

Agayne, it is impossible that the bloud of Oxen and of Goates should take away sinnes.

Also, Lo I come to do thy will, O God, &c. By the which will, we are sanctified through the offering of the bodie of Iesus Christ once for all. *Heb.10.*

Moreouer: This man after he had offred one sacrifice for sinnes, sat him downe for euer on the right hand of God. *Heb.10.*

Likewyse, with one offring hath hee perfected for euer those that are sanctified.

Agayne, theyr sinnes and iniquities wyll I remember no more. And where remission of these thinges is, there is no more offring for sinnes. *Heb.10.* *Hebr.9.*

Iesus Christ is no more offred in sacrifice but once for all.

Also he sayth not that Iesus Christ doth offer him selfe often, as the hic priest entred into the holy place euery yeere, with strange bloud, for then must he haue often suffred sence the world began. &c.

That there is but two Sacramentes in the church of Iesus Christe.

Augustine in his .3. booke of the christian doctrine the .9. chapter.

1. Pet. 1. Galat. 3.

The sacraments are tvvo, Baptisme, and the Lordes supper.

But in this time hereafter that the manyfest iudgement of our liberty is reuealed, by the resurrection of the Lorde: wee are not ouermuch charged through heauy operacions, and workinges of signes, which we already doe vnderstand: But the same Lord hath giuen by the doctrine of the Apostles, a certayne little number in steede of many, which are easye to doe, and good to vnderstand, and most chast to keepe: As is the Sacrament of baptisme: and the celebration of the body and bloud of the Lord. And when euery one doth vse them, being instructed to what ende they serue, he shall acknowledge them, not with a carnall seruitude and bondage, but to honor them in the liberty of the spirite.

And

And as it is a seruyle infirmytie to follow the letter, and to take the signes for the thinges, which are signified by them: so is it an euill error, to interprete vnprofitably the signes. &c.

Augustine wryting to Ianuarius in the 118. Epistle.

I would that thou shouldest knowe, that our Lorde Iesus (as he him selfe saith in the Gospell) hath submitted vs to an easie yoke, and light burthen. And therefore he hath ordayned in the christian church, a fewe Sacramentes in number, easie to be kept, excellent in significacion: as the Baptisme, consecrated in the name of the Trinitie: and the communication of the body and bloud of the Lord. And if there be any other thing commaunded in the Scripture. &c.

Saint Augustine nameth but twoo sacraments.

Augustine vpon S. Iohn in the .80. homelye.

The word being adioyned to the Element, it shalbe made a Sacrament.

How we ought to vnderstand this word Sacrament.

Sacrament, Mystery, Secrete, is all one, and is vnderstoode for an hidde and vnknowen thing, the which notwithstanding is reuealed at a certayne time, when it pleaseth the goodnesse of God. Reede Tob.12. Daniell.2. Sapien.2. 1.Cor.4. Ephe.5. Ephes.1. Ephes.3. Collos.1. 1. Timoth.3. Apocal.7.

Of confeßion to God, and of auricular confession.

Psal.32. 1.Par.16. 2.Par.20 David sayth in the.32.psalm: I haue acknowledged my sinne vnto thee: and mine vnrighteousnesse haue I not hydde. I sayd I wyll confesse my sinnes vnto the Lord, and so thou forgauest the wickednesse of my sinne.

Psal.51. Againe, I acknowledge my faultes: and my sinne is euer before me. Agaynst thee only haue I sinned, and done this euill in thy sight.

1.Iohn.1. If we acknowledge our sinnes, he is faythfull and iuste to forgiue vs our sinnes, and to clense vs from all vnrighteousnesse.

Iames.5. Acknowledge your faults one to an other, and pray one for an other. Ecclesi.28. Ephe.4. Collos.3.

If

If thy brother trespasse against thee.&c. *Mat.18.*
Reade Luke.17. Deut.17. 1.Cor.5. 2. Cor.13.

Augustine in his 10. booke of confessions, the 2. chapter.

What haue I to doe then with men, that they should heare my confessions? As though they should heale my griefes. That is a curyous kinde of people, to know another mans life, and slowe to correct and amend their owne, wherefore doe they demaund of me to heare what I am, where they wyll not heare of thee what they are? And how doe they know when they doe heare me, wheather I doe speake true, when in deede no man knoweth that which is done in the man but the spirit of the man which is in him.&c.

Chrysostome in the 12. chapter to the Hebrewes 3. homily, and in the 4. tome 41. homily.

I doe not say unto thee that thou accuse thy selfe openly, nor before others: But I would that thou shouldest obay the *Psal.32.* Prophet which saith, reuele unto ỹ Lorde Confesion thy way: acknowledg then thy sinnes be- to God only. fore God, pronounce thy unrighteousnesse lye.

with

with prayer to the true Iudge, not with the tongue, but by the memory of thy conscience: and then finally haue hope to haue mercie.

And vpon the.51.psalm, in the.2.Tome. Confesse thy sinnes, to the end thou doe put them away: If thou art ashamed to tell vnto an other that thou hast sinned tell it alwayes vnto thy soule. I doe not saye that thou shouldest confesse thy selfe vnto one, like vnto thy selfe, for to rebuke and checke thee of them: tell them to God, which wyll heale them. But when thou wilt not tell them, is God ignorant when thou doest them? He is there present when thou committest them, he knoweth them very well: wyll not he that thou shouldest acknowledg them? Thou wast not ashamed to sinne, and art thou ashamed to confesse them? Confesse them in this worlde, that you may haue rest in the other.

Psal.50.
Mar.2.

Confession to the Priest reiected by Chrisostom.

Chrysostome in his sermon of penance and confession, the .6. Tome.

It is not necessary to confesse it before witnesses: only make the acknowledging in thine heart, this examynation doth not require witnesses, it sufficeth that God only ly doe see and heare thee.

Chrysostome in the 5. homilie of the incomprehensible nature of God, agaynst the Anomians.

I doe not call thee before men, for to discouer thy sinnes, unfolde thine owne conscience before God, shewe thy woundes and strypes unto the Lorde who is the Phisition, and pray him to remedie it: he it is which doth not checke, and whiche gently healeth the poore sicke persons.

In the historie tripartite in the 9. booke and 35. Chapter.

It is sayde that auricular confession was vsed at Constantinople, vntill suche time that a woman making as though she woulde be confessed, was founde that she tooke that cloke, for to lye with one of the Deacons of the same Church. Bicause of which euill fact, Nectarius bishop of the sayd place, a man renoumed in holynesse, and of great learning, abolished that obseruance of confession. Auricular confession abolished in Constantinople.

The hystories doe declare, that there was no lawe or constitution before the time of Innocent the thirde, touching auricular confession. *Ponti.183*

Chry-

Chrysostome in his 4. Tome, of Lazarus.

I would not that thou shouldest confesse thy selfe unto a man, who afterward may rebuke or checke thee, or defame thee in telling thy faultes: but shewe thy griefe unto God, who is the good phisition. Afterwarde he bringeth in God speaking in this maner: I do not compell thee to come in the open assembly, confesse to me onelye thy sinnes, that I maye make thee whole.

The Church of Rome doth commaunde to confesse all our sinnes, not exceptnig any.

Psal. 19. *Answere.* Dauid sayth: Who can tell howe oft he offendeth: O clense thou me from my secret faultes.

Saint Ambrose of the repentance of S. Peter, in his. 46. sermon.

Mat. 26. Peter poured forth teares, not praying in voyce: I doe finde that he did weepe & lament, but I doe not find what he hath sayde: I doe reade of his teares, but I reade not of satisfaction.

Chrysostome in the 12. homilie of the Cananite.

Jesus Christ did heale him that had the Leprosie, and sayde unto him: Go shewe thy selfe unto the Priest, and offer that which Moyses commaunded in the lawe, for thy healing. *Luk.17.* *Leuit.14.*

O thing neuer hearde? the Lorde healed the disease, yet neuerthelesse he did sende them to the lawe of Moyses. Wherefore did he so? For none other cause but that the Jewes might not reproue him as a transgressor of the lawe. How we ought to understand: go & shewe thy selfe to the Priest.

S. Ambrose in his 3. sermon vpon the 119. Psalme.

Go and shewe thy selfe unto the Priest: who is the true Priest, but he which is the euerlasting Priest? *Mar.2.*

S. Cyprian in his 5. sermon of penitent sinners.

The seruant cannot pardon that whiche is committed agaynst the Lorde. Man cannot pardon sins.

Ambrose in his booke of Cain and Abel.

The sinnes are pardoned by the worde of God, of the which the Leuite is the expositor, and as an executor.

Chrysostome in his 7. Tome in the homilie of repentance.

This is the place of healing, not of iudgement: Tell vnto God onely thy sinne, who will giue no punishment, but the remission of sinnes.

Of the power to bynde and vnbynde, or loose.

Augustine in the 50. homilie vpon S. Iohn.

If the figure of the Church had not bene in Saint Peter, the Lorde woulde not haue sayde vnto him, I will giue vnto thee the keyes. For if the same be spoken to Peter only, the Church hath not the keys: if the Church hath them, it was figured in the person of S. Peter.

The keyes giuen to the Church, and not to the person of Peter.

Augustine in the 11. homilie, and in the 124. homilie.

Mat. 16.

Although it be that all were asked, Peter alone aunswered: thou art Christ, and it is sayde vnto him, I will giue vnto thee the keyes, as though the power to bynde

S. Peter receyued the keyes vvith

bynde and loose, had bene giuen vnto him onely. But as he answered for all, so he receyued the keyes with all, as bearing the person of vnitie. He is then named alone for all, forasmuche as there is betweene them vnitie.

all the Apostles.

Augustine vpon S. Iohn in the 124. *treatise. Chapter.* 21.

The rocke is not sayd of that name Peter, but that name Peter is named of the rocke. So Christ is not called Christ of a christian, but the christian is called christian of Christe. And therefore also the Lorde sayde: vpon this rocke I will build my Church, bicause that Peter had sayd, thou arte Christ the sonne of the liuing God: vppon this rocke then (which thou hast confessed) I will builde my churche, and the rocke was Christ, vpon the which foundation also, Peter himselfe hath bene builded. For other foundation can no man laye, than that which is layde, whiche is Jesus Christ. The church then whiche is builded vpon Christ, hath taken the keyes of the kingdome of heauen, of Christ in Peter, (that is to say) the power to bynde and loose.

The rocke giueth name to Peter, & not Peter to the rocke.

Mat. 16.

1. *Cor.* 3.

Theo-

Theophilact vpon Saint Iohn, the 8. Chapter.

Iohn.8. It belongeth to God onely to pardon sinnes: therefore, sayeth he, whosoeuer committeth sinne, is the seruant of sinne, you are then seruãts, for you be all sinners.

Saint Hilarie in his 6. booke of the Trinitie.

The father hath reuealed unto Peter, who sayth, thou art the sonne of GOD: wherefore the building of the congregati- *Mat.16.* on is vpon that rocke of confession: that faith is the foundation of the church: that *Collo.2.* fayth hath the keyes of the kingdome of *1.Iohn.5.* heauen. All that whiche this fayth shall *Philip.1.* bynde and loose in earth, is also bounde *2.Pet.1.* and loosed in heauen. This fayth is the gift of the fatherly reuelation.

Augustine in his first booke of retracta- tion, the 22. Chapter.

S.Augustine recanteth. In the booke where I haue before time affirmed in a certayne place of S. Peter the Apostle, that in him, as in the rocke, the church is builded: The which sense also is song of many in the verses of Saint Ambrose, there where he speaketh of the rocke. But I doe knowe very well, that oftentimes afterwarde I haue thus expounded it: Thou art Peter, and vpon that rocke (that is to say) the rocke, affirming thou art Christ the sonne of the liuing God:

Origen vpon Saint Mathew, the 2. homilie.

Doest thou thinke that the keyes of the kingdome of heauen, are onely giuen vnto Peter, and that none other of the blessed shall receyue them?

Augustine vpon the wordes of the Lord in S. Mathew, in his 13. sermon.

Thou art then Peter, and vppon this rocke which thou hast confessed, vpon this rocke whiche thou hast knowne, saying: thou art Christe the sonne of the liuing God, I will builde my church: Upon me I will buylde thee, and not me vpon thee. For those men which woulde be buylded vpon men, doe saye, I holde of Paule, and I holde of Apollos, and I holde of Cephas, that is to saye, rocke: and the other which will not be builded vpon Peter, but vppon the rocke doe saye: I holde of Christ. &c.

Iesus Christ hath bulded his Church vpon him selfe, and not vpon Saint Peter.

1. *Cor.* 1.

Iesus Christ is the heade of the church,

reade Ephes.4. Colos.1. 2. Reg.22.

Augustine in his 3. booke of Baptisme, the 3. Chap. And they are the wordes of S. Cyprian in the counsell of Carthage.

None of vs truly is establyshed Byshoppe of Byshoppes, or none shall compell his companions by cruell tyranny through necessitie to come thereunto.

Gregory wryting to Eulogius Byshoppe of Alexandria in the 7. booke, .3. Epistle.

Gregorie vvoulde not be called vniuersall Pope.

Beholde how you haue wrytten to me: you haue put this worde of pryde in calling me vniuersall Pope: but I pray your holinesse to call me no more so hereafter. For all that which is giuen vnto an other aboue reason, is taken from you: Concerning my selfe I doe not repute that for honor, wherein I doe see the honor of my bretheren weakened. For my honor is that the estate of the vniuersall Church, and of my bretheren, be mainteyned in theyr strength: If your holynesse doe call me vniuersall Pope, you confesse that you are not in part of that, which you attribute and giue vnto me for the whole.

Of

Of free wyll of the merites of workes, and of iustification by faith.

Iesus Christ sayth, whosoeuer committeth sinne is the seruant of sinne. Rom. 6. 2. Peter. 2. *Iohn. 8.*

All haue sinned and haue neede of Gods mercie. *Rom. 3.*

Also Iesus Christ sayth, without mee ye can doe nothing. *Iohn. 15*

We are not apt to thinke any thing, as it were of our selues: but our abilitie commeth of God. *2. Cor. 3.*

The flesh ryseth agaynst the spirit, and the spirite agaynst the flesh: and these thinges are contrary one to an other, so that ye cannot doe the same thinges that ye woulde. *Galat. 5.*

Also he which beganne a good worke in you, shall goe foorth with it vntill the day of Iesus Christ. *Philip. 1.*

Agayne, it is God which worketh in you both the will and also the deede, according to his pleasure. *Philip. 2.*

Rom.7. Likewyse I doe not that good thing, which I would, but that euill doe I, which I would not.

Augustine in his Enchiridion to Laurence: Chapter .29.

Man cannot be made better by the merit of his vvorkes.

This part of mankinde vnto whome God hath promised deliueraunce, and the euerlasting kingdome can it be made better by his workes? No, no, for what good can he doe which is lost, but asmuch as he shall be deliuered from his perdition? Can he doe by his free wyll the same? the same also he cannot doe. For man ill vsing his free wyll, did lose him selfe, and his free wyll: and as he which killeth him selfe, whiles he is liuing, killeth him selfe: but in putting him selfe to death, he liueth no more, and cannot rayse him selfe vp agayne when he is dead: so when he hath sinned by his free wyll, bicause that sinne hath bene victoryous, hath free wyll ben loste. For of whome soeuer a man is ouercom, vnto the same he is in bondage. This is truly the sentence of S. Peter: And bicause that it is true, I praye you what may be the liberty of a seruant that is in bondage, but when he doth take plea-

Free vvill lost.

2.Pet.2. Iohn.8.

sure

sure to sinne? For he serueth freely which doth willingly the wyll of the Lorde: and therefore he is free to sinne which is the seruant of sinne: and no man shall be free to doe iustly, if first being deliuered from sinne he doe not begin to be the seruant of righteousnesse. This is the true liberty for the bond of the worke that is wel done, and also it is the faithfull bondage, bicause of the obeying of the commaundement. But from whence shall this libertie to doe well come vnto the man which is brought vnder and solde, but by him who hath redeemed him: of whom it is sayd, if the son make you free, then are ye free in deede.

Man is solde vnder sinne.

Iohn.8.

Augustine vnto Paulinus in the .106. Epistle.

Let no man stumble agaynst the stumling stone, as in defending subtelly free wyll and nature: euen as the Philosophers of this world haue done with great force, for to be esteemed, or for to thinke to geat the blessed life, by vertue of theyr owne proper wyll: Let such people then take heede to make through wysedome of wordes, the crosse of Christe vayne: and that the same be not vnto them to

Rom.9.

VVe ought not to defēd free vvill or nature, as the vvise men of this vvorlde doe.

stumble against the stumbling stone. For when humayne nature abydeth in that integryte in the which it hath bene made, yet it cannot in any wise keepe it, if his creator doe not ayde him. Forasmuch then as it cannot keepe the health and saluation that it hath receiued, without the grace of God. How can it receiue that which it hath lost?

S. Augustine in the 107. *Epistle vnto Vitalis.*

If we will in deede defend free wyll, let vs not fight against that whereof it is free: for he which gaynsayeth the grace, by the which our wyll is made free, for to decline from euill, and for to doe good: he would that his free will, be yet bond and captyue.

When man was in honor, he did not
*Psal.*49. vnderstand it: he was compared vnto the beastes, and was made like vnto them.

Augustine in his booke of corrections & grace, the 12. *Chapter.*

Libertie lost thorovv sin. Now then forasmuch as that greate liberty is lost, through the demeryte of sinne, euen so doth remayne and abyde the infirmytie for to be ayded and holpen with

with greater giftes in truth. It hath pleased God so, to the ende cheifely to quenche the pryde of mans presumption: that all flesh (that is to say euery man) should not gloɼie in himselfe befoɼe him. &c. *Psal.* 148

The Counsell Mileuitan in two Canons.

Free will weakened to the first man, can not be repayɼed and amended, but thoɼow the grace of baptisme, the which after that it is lost, cannot be restoɼed agayne, but by him whiche hath power to giue it: Wherefoɼe the truth sayth, if the sonne make you free, then are you free in dede. *Canon.* 1.

The seconde Canon sayeth: God doth woɼke so in the heartes of men, and to free will, that if there be any godly cogitation, any deliberation tending to the honoɼ of God, and any motion of good will, all the same pɼoceedeth from God. Foɼ by him we may doe some good thing, and without him we can doe nothing. *Canon.* 2. No good cogitation can procede from vs but by the vertue of God in vs.

Augustine writing to Valentine of grace and free will. Chap. 18.

To the end it should not seeme that men should doe any thing by free wyll: It is sayd in the. 95. psalme: harden not your *Psal.* 95.

Ezec.18. hartes: And in Ezechiel: cast away from you all your ungodlynesse, that yee haue done: make you newe hartes and a newe spirite, and obey to all my commaundementes: wherefore wyll ye dye, O ye house of Israel, sayth the Lorde? Seing I haue no pleasure in the death of him that dyeth, sayth the Lorde God. Turne you then, and ye shall liue. Let us remember what God sayth: turne you and you shall lyue: unto whome notwithstanding we do say: O God turne us. Let us remember that God sayth: Caste from you all your ungodlynesse, and yet it is he that iustifieth the wicked. Lette us remember that hee sayth: Make you newe heartes and a new spirite: and yet notwithstanding he himselfe sayth, I will giue unto you a newe heart and a newe spirite. Howe then, that he which sayth, make you, sayth agayne, I will giue unto you? wherefore doth he commaunde it, if he himselfe doe giue it? wherefore doth he giue it, if man ought to doe it? Except he giue that whiche hee commaundeth, and aydeth, to the ende that he to whom he doth commaund it, do it. For the will is alwayes free in us, but

God commaundeth that vvhich man cãnot, and giueth that vvhich hee commaundeth.

it is not alwayes good: for eyther it is free from righteousnesse, when it serueth to sinne, and then it is euill: or it is free from sinne, when it serueth to righteousnesse, and then it is good. But the grace of God is alwayes good, and by the same it commeth to passe, that man is of a good will, who before was of an euill and wicked will: by the same also it is brought to passe, that the same good will which hath already begun to be in vs, doth increase, and is made so great, that it can accomplishe and fulfill the commaundements of God, which it will, and when it wil, greatly and perfectly. For to the same serueth that which is written: If thou wilt, thou shalt keepe the commaundements, in such sort, that the man which woulde, and can not yet knowe that he hath a full desire, and shall pray that so great a will be giuen vnto him, then that sufficeth for to accomplishe the commaundements: for he is in this maner ayded, to doe that whiche is commaunded him. For the will is then profitable when we can: for what profiteth it to will which we cannot: or not to will, that which we can?

Saint Augustine in his booke of the newe canticles. Chap.8.

It is well declared what free will can doe which is not aided: it is sufficient of it selfe to doe euill, but not to doe good, if it be not ayded of God. For the first man receyued free will rightly: he did set before him (as sayth the Scripture) fire and water, vnto which thou wilt (sayth he) put forth thine hande. He chose the fire, and left the water: beholde ŷ righteous iudge: that which man hath chosen, being at his libertie, the same hath he receyued: he desired the euill, and the euill followed him: beholde agayne that righteous Iudge which is mercifull: For when he saw that man thorowe his yll vsing of free will, had damned all his posteritie in himselfe as in the roote, before that anye man did intreate him, came downe from heauen, and hath healed mankinde in destroying the proude through his humilitie. He hath led those ŷ wandred out of their way, into the right way, and hath led the straungers into their countrie. Let not mans nature then glorie in it selfe: but glorie it selfe in him which hath made it.

Adam hath damned all his posteritie in himselfe.

Augu-

Augustine in his booke of correction and grace. Chapter 11.

Without the grace of God Adam could not be good, yea though he had free wyll: wherefore God would not leaue him without his grace, although he left him in his free wyll, bicause that free wil is sufficient to doe euill: But to good it is but of small valewe, if it be not ayded with the goodnesse of the Almightie: which ayde if man had not forsaken through his free wyll, he had bene alwayes good: But he did forsake it, wherefore he was also forsaken. Free vvill to doe euil, but not to doe good.

Augustine of the wordes of the Apostle in the 13. sermon.

All those which are leade by the spirite of God, are the children of God: wherefore then wylt thou eleuate thy selfe, when thou hast heard: If you mortify the deedes of the body by the spirite, you shall liue. *Rom. 8.* For thou wast ready to say, my wyll can doe this, my free wyll can doe that: what can will doe? What can free wyll doe? If the holy spirite doe not gouern thee, thou shalt fall, if he doe not gouern thee, thou shalt abide & continew ouerthrowen. How then shall he doe the same? By his

holy

holy spirite, when thou hast heard the Apostle, saying: all those which are conducted with the spirite of God, which if it be absent, thou canst by no manner of meanes doe any good: Thou maist doe some thing by thy free will, although he doth not ayde thee, but that is euill: Unto the same thy will is apte, which is called free, and in doing euill, is made a damnable seruant. When I doe say unto thee, that thou doest nothing without the ayde of God, I speak nothing of goodnesse: for without the ayd of God, thou hast free wyll to doe euill: although that it be not properly free.

Augustine sayde that man hath freevvill, but he doth vnderstande it, to doe euill.

Augustine against the two Epistles of the Pelagians vnto Boniface, 2. booke. Chapter. 8.

But to the ende that the Lord shoulde aunswere unto the Pelagians in time to come, he hath not sayde, without me you can hardly doe any thing: But he hath sayd, without me can ye doe nothing. It appertayneth unto man to purpose a thing in his harte, but the aunswere of the tongue commeth of the Lorde: they are deceiued through euill understanding, and so much as they doe thinke the preparation of the harte

Iohn. 15.
Pro. 16.

harte to appertayne unto man (that is to say) to begin good without the ayde of the grace of God: God forbyd that the sons of the promesse should understand it so. As where they haue heard the Lord saying, without me ye can doe nothing, they doe com as though they would vanquysh, saying, beholde we can without thee, prepare the harte: when they haue heard the Apostle S. Paule, who sayth, not that we are apte of our selues, to thinke any thing, as it were of our selues: but our abilitie commeth of God, as also in ouercomming, vanquishing, and saying: Beholde we are apt of our selues to prepare our harte, and thereby to thinke any good thing: And who is he that can prepare the harte to goodnesse for a good thought? God forbyd that they should understande it so: except it be those which defend their proude free will in destroying the catholike fayth: therefore it is truly wrytten, it appertayneth to man to prepare his heart, but the answere of the tongue commeth of the Lorde, for bicause that man doth prepare himselfe, not alwayes without the ayde of God. In lyke maner it is sayde:

2. Cor. 3

Catholike fayth destroyed by free vvill.

Psal.81. sayde: Open thy mouth wyde, and I shal fill it. And although y we cannot open the mouth, except it be through the ayde of him, without whome we can doe nothing: Neuerthelesse, wee doe open it through his ayde, and through our worke: but the Lorde doth fill it without our worke. By and by after he sayeth, God doth many good things in man, which man doth not: But man doth none, which God doth not, to the ende that man doth them.

Augustine vpon Saint Iohn in the 49. treatise. Chap. 9.

Let no man then flatter himselfe: for of himselfe he is a deuill: but of God he is blessed. And what is that to be of himself, but of sinne? Cast awaye the sinne which is of thee: thy righteousnesse, sayth he, is of me. For what hast thou, that thou hast not receyued?

Man naught of himselfe.

1. Cor. 4.

Augustine in his contemplations of the soule with God. Chap. 18.

O Lorde, I doe confesse, as thou hast taught me, that I am no other thing, but altogither vanitie, and a shadow of death, and but a darke earth, vayne and voyde, the which without thy blessing, doth not

encrease

encrease and bring forth anye fruite, but confusion, sinne, and death. If I haue had any good thing, I had it of thee. All that which I haue receyued is from thee, or I had it of thee. If I doe any thing that is right, that is through thee. But when I am fallen, I am fallen through my selfe, and had alwayes remayned in the myre, if thou hadst not lifted me vp. I had bene alwayes blinde, if thou hadst not illuminated mee. When I did fall downe, I shoulde neuer haue bene raysed vp againe, if thou hadst not giuen me thy hande: And afterwarde also when thou hadst raysed me vp, I shoulde haue fallen agayne, if thou hadst not sustayned mee. I had bene oftentimes lost, if thou hadst not gouerned me. Euen so, O Lorde, euen so thy mercie hath alwayes gone before me, in deliuering me from all euill, keeping me from those that be past, and in keeping me from those that be present, and in defending and preseruing me from those whiche are to come, breaking also in peeces before mee the snares of sinners, in taking awaye the occasions and the causes: for if thou hadst not done vnto me those things, I had done

Genes. 1
Iames. 1

all

all the sinnes of the worlde. For O Lord, I doe knowe verye well, that there is no sinne that euer man hath done, but that an other man dothe the same, if the creator of whome man is made, be absent. But thou hast done it so, to the ende that I doe not that which thou hast forbidden, and hast shed out in me thy grace, to the ende that I may beleeue in thee. &c.

Augustine in his. 2. boke of the remissi- on of sinnes. Chapter. 18.

Men doe take payne to finde in our wyll some goodnesse, which is ours, and not of God: but I doe not knowe howe they can finde it.

Saint Barnarde in the first homily of the Annunciation of the Virgin Mary.

As touching good workes, it is moste certayne that no man hath them of him selfe: for if the humaine nature could not continue in his state, when it was whole and perfect, how much lesse can it rayse it selfe nowe in that it is marred and corrupted? It is most certayne that all thinges drawe to their beginning, asmuch as is possible for them.

Good workes procede not of man.

Augustine vnto Vitalis in the 107. Epistle.

Aunswere I pray thee: how saith the Apostle in giuing thankes to God the father, which hath made vs fitte to be of the company of Saintes in light, if it be not he which doth deliuer our free will, but that the free will doth deliuer it selfe? We doe render then faulsly thankes vnto the father, as if he did that which he doth not: and he hath erred whiche hath sayde that he doth make vs fitte. Aunswere how we haue our free will, for to deliuer vs from euill, and for to doe good, and when free wyll was vnder the power of darkenesse? From which darkenesse if God hath deliuered vs (as saith the Apostle) truely he hath made the wyll free: wherefore it followeth that euen as men are not faythfull but by free wyll: Neuerthelesse they are made faithfull through ẏ grace of God, which hath deliuered free will from the power of darkenesse: And so the grace of God is not denyed, but is declared to be verytable and true, although no meryptes of men preceede it. And free will is so defended, that it is affirmed by hu-

Free vvill deliuereth not.

mylitie, and not ouerthrowen by pryde. Then the grace of God is not geauen in the nature of free will, nor in the lawe, nor in doctryne, as the wicked and peruerse Pelagian hath set foorth. But is geiuen to all the workes through the will of him of whome it is wrytten. O Lord God thou doest seperate from thy wyll the soule that is wylfull: for we haue lost free wyll, for to loue God through the greatnesse of the first sinne. &c. Afterwardes he sayth in that we doe beleeue in God, or in that we doe liue faithfully, it lyeth not then in mans will or running, but in the mercy of God: nor that we ought to wyll nor runne but bicause that he doth in vs both the wyl and the running: Let vs not say then that the grace is the loue: but let vs acknowe-ledge the grace which doth cause the doc-trine and learning to profit, for where that grace is absent: we doe see that the same doth hinder and let the learning.

No grace of God by free vvill, nor by the lavve.

Rom.9.

Augustine in his fyrst booke against Pelagius and Celestine.

Whosoeuer hath heard and learned of the father commeth vnto me. The wyll of mā is so ayded, not only in this that it doth

know

knowe what it must doe, but hauing knowen what it doth: And therefore when the Lorde doth teach through the grace of his spirite, he doth teach in such sorte, that not only euery one doth see that which he hath learned in the knowledge thereof, but of will he doth desire it, and of worke fulfill it.

Augustine in the. 3. booke vpon the wordes of the Apostle. 3. sermō. And in his booke of the spirite and the letter. Chapter. 3.

How are these wicked men proude of free wyll, before they are free, or of their strength if they are already free, they doe not consider, that in this word of free wyll is signified a libertie? For where the spirite of the Lorde is, there is libertie. If then they be the seruantes of sinne, how doe they bragge and bost to haue free wyll? For of whome soeuer a man is ouercome, unto the same is he in bondage: If they are already deliuered how doe they boste them selues, as it were of their proper workes? Are they so free, that they would not be the seruantes of him which sayth, without me ye can doe nothing?

Throughe sinne the freevvill is lost.

2. Pet. 2.

Iohn. 15.

Iohn.6. Jesus sayth: No man can come vnto me, except the father which hath sent me, drawe him.

Iam.1. Saint James: Euery good gift, and euery perfect gift, is from aboue, and cometh downe from the father of lights.

2.Cor.3. Saint Paule also: We are not able of oure selues to thinke anye thing that is good, as it were of our selues: but our abilitie commeth of God.

Rom.7. *Galat.5.* Agayne vnto the Romaynes: I knowe that in me (that is to saye) in my fleshe, dwelleth no good thing. For to will, is present with me: but I finde no meane to performe that which is good: for I doe not that good thing which I woulde, but that euill doe I which I would not.

1.Cor.2. Also the naturall man is not able to perceyue the thinges of the spirite of God, for they are but folishnes vnto him, neyther can he knowe them, bicause they are spiritually discerned.

1.Cor.12. *Esay.26.* And 1.Cor.12. God worketh all things in euery man.

1.Cor.12. Agayne: No man can say, that Jesus is the Lorde but by the holy ghost.

Psal.39. Also Dauid: Euery man liuing is al-

togi-

togither vanitie.

And in the 8. Chapter of Genesis: The heart of man is enclined to euill euen from his youth. Genes.8.

To the Ephesians: We were naturally the children of wrath, euen as well as other. Ephes.2.

Gregorie vpon the 7. psalme, vpon the versicle, Anima mea. &c.

Forasmuch as freewill is corrupted in our first father, we haue not the power to will well, if we bee not ayded with the grace of God.

Saint Hierome in his commentarie vpon Ieremie. Chapter. 23.

Forasmuch as the heretikes haue accustomed to promise felicitie, and to open to sinners the kingdome of heauen, saying: thou mayest imitate the maiestie of God, so that thou be withoute sinne, bicause thou hast receyued the power of free will, and the intelligence and vnderstanding of the lawe, by the which thou mayst obtayne that which thou wouldest: Euen so the sayde heretikes doe abuse the poore simple people through fayre wordes: and chieflye the yong women charged wyth sinnes, who are caryed here and there with euery kynde of doctrine, deceyuing throwe flatterie all those which heare them.

Augustine in the 30. booke of his homilies. Homilie. 41.

We ought not to accorde vvith them vvhich do establish free vvill.

Let vs not consent vnto those which throwe great pride, go about to eleuate and extoll free will: the whiche so doing, doe bring more euill than good, and seeke nothing but to ruinate and destroy man: but let vs consider meekely that which the Apostle speaketh: It is God that worketh in vs, both the will and also the dede, euen of his free beneuolence. Let vs giue thankes vnto the Lorde our redeemer, which without any merite preceding, hath healed vs of our woundes & sores, and hath reconciled vs vnto God, and redeemed vs from captiuitie, and reduced and brought vs from darkenesse into light: and called vs from death to lyfe, &c.

Phil. 2.

Of merite, and of good workes.

2. Ephe. 2. By grace are yee made safe throughe faith, and not of your selues: it is the gift of of God, not of workes, least anye manne shoulde boast himselfe. For we are his workemanship, created in Christ Jesus unto good workes, which God ordeyned, that we shoulde walke in them.

S. Ambrose in the first booke of Cain and Abel. Chap. 7.

It is the deede of a dull and slowe heart, to attribute to his proper vertues, that which is good, or that whiche he doth obtayne of God, and not to the author of grace: but to esteeme himselfe to bee the author of his goodnesse. There is another kinde of sinne, yea lesse, but of equall arrogancie and pryde (that is to say) of those which doe not denie God to be the distributer of goodnesse: but doe thinke the goodnesse which commeth unto them, is bicause of their prudence and wisedome, and that the merites of all other vertues are giuen unto them of right. And for that cause it is sayde agaynst those which haue receyued the heauenly grace, that they doe not esteeme themselues in no wise to bee unworthy to haue suche goodnesse of God: When the Lorde thy God shall begyn to consume his people here in thy presence, say

Nothing done by our vertue.

Deut. 9.

say

saye not in thine heart, the Lorde hath brought me in to possesse this lande for my righteousnesse, &c.

S. Barnard in the fyrst sermon of the Annunciation of the Virgin Mary.

Beleeue not that thou canst throughe any workes merite eternall life, except it be giuen thee freely. For who is that which can make him cleane being conceiued of filthy seede: but only he which is altogeather cleane? And so that which is done, cannot be vndon: But bicause that God doth not impute it, it shall be as though it had neuer bene done. Whiche the Prophet considering speaketh in this sort, blessed is the man, vnto whome the Lord imputeth no sinne. But as concerning good workes it is most certaine that none hath them of him selfe: for if the humayne nature being yet entire and whole, coulde not holde it selfe in his estate: how much lesse can it rayse it selfe, when it is already corrupted? But we doe knowe very well concerning this eternall life, that the afflictions of this life, are not worthy of the glory that shall be shewed vnto vs: Yea when man shall suffer them all

VVee can through no vvorkes merite eternall lyfe.

*Iob.*14.

*Psal.*32.

*Rom.*8.

all togeather. For mans merites, are not suche, as by them eternall life shoulde of right be due unto them, or that God doth iniury and wrong unto some men, if he doe not giue it: For although I should not say that all merites are the giftes of God, in somuch as man is more bound unto God for those merytes, then God is unto man: yet what are all the merites, in respect of so greate glory?

S. Barnarde of free will.

What hast thou that, thou hast not receyued? art thou created? art thou healed? art thou saued? whiche of them hast thou of thy selfe? whiche of them is not impossible for free will? thou couldest not create thy selfe when thou wast not made: nor iustifie thy selfe, when thou waste a sinner. &c. VVe receyued al things of God.

Agayne in the same booke: But if that will upon which all merites doe depende, was not in Saint Paule, by what meanes did he presume, that ye crowne shoulde bee kept for him, which he calleth the crowne of righteousnesse? But it is, bicause that whiche is promised thankfully, is of right demaunded as a thing due. Finallye he

sayth:

sayth: I knowe him in whome I haue beleeued, and am persuaded that he is able to keepe that which I haue committed to his keeping. He doth call the promise of God the thing kept: and therefore he hath beleued him which hath promised it: confidently he doth aske agayne the promise, the promise (I say) done through mercye, but the which ought nowe to bee restored through righteousnesse. The crowne then whiche Saint Paule hath striued for, is the crowne of righteousnesse: but it is of Gods righteousnesse, and not of his. This is trulye a iust thing, that he doth restore that whiche he hath sayde: but he oweth that whiche he hath promised, and that is the righteousnesse of the whiche the Apostle did presume, euen the promise of God.

S. Barnarde vpon the Canticles, sermon. 47.

Wherefore is that? That is to the ende it doe trye and proue it selfe more strong, to be full of grace, when it dooth attrybute all to the grace, that is the beginning and the ende: otherwyse howe shall it be full of grace, if it had any thing which

which was not of the grace? There is no place where grace shall enter, where merypte already hath taken place. Nowe then the full confession of grace, dooth signifie the fulnesse of the same grace in the soule of the confessor: For if there be any thing of it selfe, forasmuch as it is there, it is necessary that grace doth giue place vnto it: All that which thou imputest vnto merypte, is taken away from grace: I wyll none of the merite which putteth out grace, I am afrayd of all that which is of my selfe, which doth make me to be to my selfe, if it be not that peraduẽture rather it should be I which causeth me to be to my selfe. Grace doth make me iustified freely, & so doth deliuer me from the seruitude & bondage of sinne. Ye haue not chosen mee, but I haue chosen you, and I haue not founde thy merytes for to chose thee: but I haue preuented thee: euen so then I haue espoused and marryed thee in fayth, and not by the workes of the lawe. I haue ioyned thee in righteousnesse, but in the righteousnesse wich is through fayth, and not of the lawe: It resteth that you iudge right iudgement, betwene thee and mee, that

Grace cannot bee vvhere merite hath taken place.

Grace doth iustifie vs freely.

Iohn. 15.

Oseas. 2.

that is to say, the iudgement in the which I haue fianced thee, where it is manifested that thy merite hath not bene the meane, but only my pleasure. For beholde the iudgement, that thou doe not exalt thy merit, that thou do not preferre the works of the lawe: that thou doe not preferre the charge of the heate of the daye: But that thou doe knowe rather to haue all thy hope and trust in fayth, in mercye, and kyndenesse.

Augustine of the predestination of Saintes.

Mans merites shall keepe silence here, which were lost in Adam, and the grace of God shall reygne as it reygned by Iesus Christ.

Saint Augustine vpon the 139. Psalme.

The Saintes doe attribute nothing to their merites, but all to the mercie of God.

Augustine in the 2. Quinquagesima. Psal. 88.

When man doth see and perceyue that all ye goodnes that he hath he hath it not of himselfe, but of his God: he doth see yt all

that

that which is prayſed in him, is not of his merites, but of the mercy of God.

Chryſostome vpon Geneſis. Homilie.33.

All our workes whiche doe followe the thankefull calling of God, are as debtes which we doe render vnto him: but his benefites are of grace, beneuolence, and pure liberalitie.

VVe are indebted vnto God vvith all oure vvorkes.

S.Hilarie vpon S.Mathew, in the 20. Canon, vpon this place, called the labourers.

Truly no hyre is not of gift, for it is due for the worke. But God hath giuen vnto all men grace freelye, in iuſtification of faith.

Auguſtine in his Quinquageſima pſalm.137.

I doe not ſay vnto the Lorde that he ſhoulde deſpiſe the worke of my handes: It is very true, that I doe ſeeke the Lord with my handes, and am not deceyued: but I doe not eſteeme the workes of my handes, for I doe feare that if God behold them, that he ſhould finde more ſinne then meryte. This onely doe I ſay, pray, and deſire that he doe not deſpiſe the worke of

VVe ought not to eſteme our vvorkes.

his

his handes. O Lorde then see and beholde thy worke in me, and not mine: for if thou doest see mine, thou wylt condemne it, if thou seest thine thou wylt rewarde and crowne it, and in deede all the good works which I haue, are come from thee.

S. Barnard vpon the canticles sermon.61.

Safetie in the vvounds of our Lord.

Where shall those that are weake find true rest and saftye but in the woundes of our sauiour? I doe dwell there so much the more safely, for that he is puyssant to saue. The worlde is nigh vnto me, to trouble me, my body doth molest and griue me, the deuill also lyeth in wayght to catche me: I wyll not fall bicause that I am stayed vpon a sure rocke. If I haue greuously sinned, my conscience is troubled, but it shall not be confounded, when I shal remember the woundes of the Lorde. &c. Afterwarde he concludeth, saying, my meryte is the mercye of the Lorde, I am not poore of merytes, whilest that the Lorde is ritch in mercye. So muche the more as the mercyes of ye Lord are great: so much the more do I abound in merits. Shall I sing my righteousnesse O Lord? I wyll

Our merite is of the mercie of the Lorde.

I wyll remember thine only righteousnesse, for the same is myne, forasmuche as thou hast bene made for me the righteousnesse of God thy father. 1.Cor.1.

S. Barnarde vpon the psalme: Who so dwelleth. &c. sermon.15. psalm.91.

Behold all the meryte of man, is to put all his hope and trust in him whiche doth saue man wholy.

Augustine vpon the.88. psalm, in his fyrste treatise.

I might despayre bicause of my great sinne, and through my infinite negligences, if the sonne of God had not taken our fleshe. Afterwarde he sayth: all my hope, all the assurance of my confidence, is put in his precious bloud, the which hath bene shedde for vs, and for our saluation. In him my poore hart doth take breath. And trusting altogither in him, I desire to come vnto thee O father, hauing not my righteonsnesse, but that of thy sonne Iesus Christe.

The sonne of God hath taken oure proper flesh, vvherby vve haue firme assurance.

Augustine writing vnto Boniface the.3. booke. Chapter.5.

All the faithfull people which doe sigh and grone vnder the burthen of their corruptible

ruptible fleshe, and inclosed with this present life, haue this only hope, that we haue a mediator (to say Jesus Christe) whiche hath satisfied for our sinnes.

Iesus Christ hath satisfied for our sinnes.

Augustine vpon the. 32. psalm. and the. 109. psalm.

The Lorde is faithfull who made him selfe debter vnto vs, not in taking any thing of vs, but in promising vs all thinges freely.

Augustine in the first Quinquagesima. psalm. 31.

O what are you which secretely doe take pleasure or delight in your owne vertue? O proude infidells which doe reioyce your selues in your strengthes? If you doe beleeue hereafter in him which doth iustifie the wicked, your fayth shall be compted for righteousnesse: Reioyce you righteous in God, and be mery: and wherefore? Bicause you are righteous: and whereof are ye righteous? The same is not through your merytes, but through the grace of God: whereof are you righteous? But for bicause he hath iustified you by fayth, and knowledge, the which without your merytes, he hath giuen vnto you?

The proude reioyce in their ovvne strength.

Also

Also in the same booke.

Unto him sayth the Apostle, whiche doth the workes, the higher is not imputed according to grace, but according to the debt: If thou wilt seperate thy selfe from grace, boste thy selfe of thy merytes: Truly God doth knowe very well what thou art, and what thing he ought to giue vnto euery one. And he whiche dooth not good workes, and which after many euills that he hath done beleeueth in God, who iustifieth the sinner, whiche beleeueth in him his fayth will iustifie him: Euen as Dauid sayth: Blessed is the man whome the Lorde accepteth, and iustifieth without workes: and how is he iustified? But forasmuch as he receiueth of God righteousnesse: and what righteousnesse? the righteousnesse of fayth the which God giueth without any good workes preceeding, but not without good workes following after: for righteousnesse of fayth profiteth not, if after the fayth receiued man doth not exercise him selfe in all good workes.

To boast vpon merits is to be seperate from grace.

Psal. 32.

Iames. 2.

In the same.

I doe not account thy workes good, what soeuer they be, if they doe not pro-

Good workes are the fruite of fayth.

ceede from the good roote of fayth.

In the same.

God doth not giue vnto thee the payne and punishment whiche thou hast well deserued: but he doth giue vnto thee the grace not deserued nor due. He oweth vnto thee punishment, and he giueth vnto thee mercie, and doth pardon thee. Begin then to be in fayth through the forgiuenesse of thy sinnes.

Gregorie vpon Ezechiel, the first boke, homilie.7.

Then our iust aduocate doth defende vs for iust at the iudgement, bicause that we shoulde acknowledge our selues, and accuse our selues as vniust: Let vs not then trust in our weepings, nor in our works, but in the allegation of our aduocate.

Augustine in his booke of meditations. Chap.14.

This is lyfe eternall, that they knowe thee to be the only very God, and whome thou hast sent, Jesus Christ, through a right fayth, and through workes worthy of fayth. For thy inestimable loue exceedeth all knowledge, the which thou hast shewed vnto vs throughe thy pietie and good-

goodnesse, vnto vs whiche are vnworthy. For thy sonne our God in no sort toke the Angels: but he tooke the seede of Abraham, being made like in all things vnto vs, without sinne. This is verily all my hope, and all my trust: for the porcion of euery one of vs is to ẏ same Iesus Christ our Lorde, that is to saye, the fleshe and the bloude, and so where my porcion doth reygne, there I doe beleeue that I shall reygne: there where my flesh is glorified, there I doe know my selfe to be glorified: there where my bloude doth beare rule, there I doe knowe that I shall rule. Although I be a sinner, yet I doe not distrust of the communication of this grace: and if my sinnes do hinder or let it, my substance doth require and aske it. And if my offences doe shut me out, the communion of the nature doth not dryue me backe: but our Lord God is meeke and lowly, and loueth his fleshe and his members, and his bowels in himselfe, which is God, and in Iesus Christ our Lorde, most meeke and louing and gentle, in whome we are raysed vp, and are already ascended into heauen, and already sitting in the celestiall place.

Heb. 2.

Our proper flesh and our proper blud is in Iesus Christ, and there vvhere hee doth reygne, vve doe reygne vvith him.

Math. 11.

Our fleshe doth loue vs, and we haue in him the prerogatiue of our bloude: for we are his members and his fleshe, and finally he is our heade, of whome all the bodie doth depende (as it is written) bone of my bones, and fleshe of my flesh, and they shall be two in one fleshe: this mysterie here is great, I saye in Christ and in the congregation, sayth the Apostle.

Ephes.5.

Genes.2.

Augustine in his manuel. Chap. 22.

All my trust and hope is in the death of my Lorde: his death is my merite, my refuge, my helth, my life, & my resurrection: my merite is the mercy of God. I am not poore of merite, so long as the Lorde of mercie shall be in being: & if the mercies of the Lorde are great, I am great in merites: the more puissant he is for to saue, so much the more am I assured.

The death of Iesus Christ is our merite.

Augustine in his manuel. Chap. 23.

I haue committed a great sinne, and do feele my selfe culpable of a great many of sinnes, and yet I will not despayre. For where sinnes haue abounded, grace hath more abounded. He which hopeth not to haue pardon of his sinnes, he denyeth that God is mercifull: he doth great iniurie vnto God, which distrusteth of his mercy, as much as he can, he denyeth that God hath loue, truth, and strength, in whiche things consisteth all my hope, that is, in the loue that he hath towards me, to make me his adoptiue sonne, in the veritie of his promise, and in the puissaunce of his redemption. Let my foolishe thought nowe thinke, and murmure as long as it will, saying: but what art thou? and what is this glorie? and by what merites thinkest thou to haue it? Then I doe aunswere: in good fayth I doe knowe verye well vnto whom I submit my selfe, and that through great loue he hath made me his adoptiue sonne, and is true in his promises, and of power to fulfill them, and it is lawfull for him to doe all that pleaseth him. I cannot then bee afrayde of the multitude of my sinnes, if I doe remember the Lordes death.

S. Ambrose in the booke of Iacob. and of blessed life.

Euen as Iacob hauing not of his meate the eldershippe, hid him selfe vnder the habite of his brother, and apparayled him selfe with his coate, the which did giue a *Genes. 27* most sweete sauour: and in this manner presented him selfe vnto his father, to receiue to his profite the blessing vnder the person of another: so it is necessary that we doe cloth our selues, and put on the righteousnesse of Iesus Christ through fayth, and that we doe hide our selues vnder the deuine purite of our eldest brother, if wee will be accepted and taken for righteous before God: And truly the same is the true verytie: for yf we doe appeare before God, not clothed with the righteousnesse of Iesus Christ, without doubte we shall be iudged worthy of eternall damnation.

S. Ambrose vpon the. 4. chapter of the Epistle to the Romaines.

They are manifestly blessed, vnto whom without laboure, or without any workes iniquities and wickednesse are pardoned and the sinnes couered, not requiring of them any works of penance, but that they doe beleeue onely.

Ambrose vpon the 3. Chapter of the Epistle to the Romaines.

They are iustified freelye through his grace, bicause that not doing anye thing,

thing, and not rendring the lyke, by onely fayth, they are iustified through the gift of God.

Augustine in his boke of 50. homilies. Homilie. 14.

The Lord will giue unto me the crown as a iust and righteous iudge. For hee which beholdeth, after that he hath beheld the worke, cannot deny the reward. I haue fought a good fight, that is a worke: I haue fulfilled my course, that is a worke: I haue kept the fayth, that is a worke: There remayneth for mee the crowne of righteousnesse, that is the rewarde. But thou doest nothing to the rewarde, and in the worke thou hast not wrought alone: thou hast the crowne of him, but the work is of thee: and yet it is not but throughe the ayde of him. I haue fought, I haue ended and fulfilled my course, I haue kepte the fayth. He doth rewarde the goodnesse, but what goodnesse? Such as he hath giuen. Hath not he giuen unto thee to fight a good fight? If he hath not giuen it, what is that that thou sayest in another place: I haue laboured more abundantly than they all: yet not I, but the grace of God

2. Tim. 4.
1. Cor. 15.
2. Tim. 2.

God which is in me: In that then that he hath ayded thee, and that he hath giuen vnto thee, thou hast fought a good fight, and hast fulfilled thy course, and hast kept the fayth. Pardon mee (Apostle) I doe knowe nothing of thine owne, but the euils. Pardon me (Apostle) we doe speake it bicause ŷ thou hast taught it: I do heare him which confesseth himselfe, and I doe not finde that he is vnthankfull. Truly in all that thou art instructed of thy selfe, we can knowe nothing but euill. Then when God doth crowne thy merites, he crowneth nothing but his giftes, to the ende, that none be waxen proude of such fayth, or of such puritie in good workes through his free will.

Augustine vpon the wordes of the Apostle sermon.15.

Thou shalt doe the worke of God, not only bicause thou art a man, but also bicause thou art iust and righteous: for it is better to be righteous then to be a man: if God hath made thee a man, and that thou makest thy selfe righteous, thou doest a better thing then God hath done: But God hath made thee without thy selfe, for thou

He vvhich maketh him selfe righte-

thou hast giuen no consent vnto God for to make thee: how shouldest thou consent, which wast not then borne? He then which hath made thee without thy selfe, doth he not iustifie thee without thy selfe? He hath then made him which giueth not his consent: but he iustifieth him whiche giueth thereunto his wyll and consent, yet he doth iustifie thee, to the ende it shoulde not be thine owne righteousnesse, and that thou shouldest not turne thy selfe to hurt, detryment, and vnto filthynesse: And shouldest be found in him, not hauing thy owne righteousnesse, which is by the law: but that which is of God, through the fayth of Jesus Christ, (that is to say) the righteousnesse of fayth, for to knowe it, and also to knowe the vertue of his resurrection, and the fellowshippe of his afflictions, and that same vertue, shall be the fellowshippe of the afflictions of Christe that shall be thy vertue.

ous, doth more than if he made himselfe a man.

Phil. 3.

Augustine in the first Quinquagesima: in the Prologue of the. 31. psalm.

Who be those that are blessed? Are not those they in whome God did finde no sinne? No, for he did finde it in all men, *Psal. 32.*

for

Rom.3. for all haue sinned and are destitute of the glory of God. If then sinne be found in all, it followeth that none are founde blessed,
Rom.4. but those whose sinnes are pardoned: Therefore hath he euen so prayfed the same. Abraham beleeued God and it was rekened vnto him for righteousnesse: but vnto him which doth the worke, that is to say which doth presume of workes, and which by the merite of the same saith, that the grace of faith is giuen vnto him: The rewarde is not imputed according to the grace, but according to the debt. What is this but that our rewarde is called grace? if that be grace, it is giuen freely? What is this that is giuen freely? It is that thou hast done no good thing, and yet the forgiuenesse of thy sinnes, is giuen vnto thee, if thy workes be considered, they shal be founde all wicked and euill: if God should render that which is due to such workes, truely he shoulde condemne them: God doth not render vnto thee the punishment due, but he doth giue thee grace, which is not due vnto thee.

If GOD should rewarde our workes, he should finde them altogither wicked, & wold condemne vs.

Augustine in the fyrst Quinquagesima, vpon the. 31. psalme: verse: Lorde I haue hoped in thee.

O Lorde deliuer me, and redeeme me through thy righteousnesse. For if thou doe consider my righteousnesse, thou condemnest me, deliuer me through thy righteousnesse: for the righteousnesse of God is ours, when it is giuen vs: but it is called the righteousnesse of God, to the ende that man doe not esteeme or thinke to haue righteousnesse of him selfe. For as the Apostle saith, vnto him which beleeueth in him, which iustifieth the infidell or vnbeleeuing man: What is he that iustifieth the infidell? He which maketh the infidell righteous. What is he that is not saued freely? Is it he vnto whome the sauiour doth finde nothing for to crowne him, but for to condemne him. He doth not finde the merytes of goodnesse, but he findeth the merites of euill: if he doe as moste truly it is purposed and set foorth by the rule of the lawe, the sinner ought to be damned: if he doe after that rule, whome shall he deliuer? For he hath found them all

Gods righteousnesse giuen vs is ours.

Mā hath no righteousnesse.

all sinners: he is come alone without sinne, who hath fou͞d vs sinners. The same the Apostle speaketh, saying: all men haue sinned and are destitute of the glorie of God, he doth deliuer thee and not thou thy selfe, bicause thou canst not deliuer thy selfe: whereof dost thou vaunte and boste thy selfe? Wherefore dost thou presume of the lawe, and of righteousnesse? Dost thou not see that which shall heale thee inwardly, is against thee? Dost thou not heare the rebell and the confesser, and him which desireth ayde and helpe in the battayle, saying: O wreatched man that I am, who shall deliuer me from this body of death, the grace of God through our Lorde Iesus Christe: wherefore ẏ grace bicause that it is giuen freely without merytes preceeding, but the benefites of God haue preuented it.

S. Ambrose vpon the Epistle vnto the Romains chapter. 34.

Bicause that without the workes of the lawe, faith is reputed for righteousnesse, vnto him which beleeueth, that is to say vnto the gentill which beleeueth in Christ, as it was reputed vnto Abraham: how

how then doe the Iewes thinke to be iu-stified by the workes of the lawe, of the iu-stification of Abraham: seeing Abraham to be iustified, not through the workes of the lawe, but only through faith? The lawe then taketh no place, when the infi-dell is iustified only through faith, before God: according to the purpose of the grace of God. Euen so ought it to be or-dayned, to the ende that the lawe doe cease and that we demaund only faith, of the grace of God for our health and saluation. As also Dauid saith, confirming the same, by the example of the Prophet: The bles-sednesse of man, is in him, vnto whome God, imputeth righteousnesse without workes. He calleth those blessed, vnto whome God hath confirmed the same, ỷ without labour and without any obserua-tions, through faith only they are iustified with God: he declareth then the blessed-nesse of the time, in whiche Christe was borne: as also the Lord did, saying: That many Prophetes and iust men haue desi-red to see those thinges which ye see, and haue not seene them: and to heare those things which ye heare, and haue not heard them.

Abraham iustified thorovv fayth only before the lavve.

Onely faith doth saue vs.

Psal. 32.

Mat. 13.

them.

Augustine vpon the words of the Lord in the mountayne. Sermon. 7.

O thou Christian take heede, take heede (I say) of pride: for although that thou be a follower of the Saintes, yet repute alwayes euery thing to the grace of God: for the grace of God hath done it in thee, and not thy merite which hath had anye abyding in thee. &c.

Augustine vpon the Apostles words. Ser. 15.

Ephe. 2. By grace are yee made safe throughe fayth, and not of your selues: but it is the gyft of God, not of workes, least peraduenture thou doe say: I haue deserued it, and therefore I haue receyued it: doe not thinke that thou hast receyued it in deseruing it, thou which shouldst not deserue it, if thou didst not receyue it. Gráce hath gone before thy merite, grace commeth not of merite, but merite commeth of grace: for if thou hast bought grace thorowe thy merite, then thou hast not receiued it freely: thou wilt saue thẽ (sayth he) freely, thou doest find nothing in thẽ, for to saue thẽ, and yet neuerthelesse thou doest saue them. Thou giuest freely, thou sauest freely,

God giueth his grace freely, bicause he can finde nothing for to saue.

frelye, thou precedest all merites, to the ende that merites doe followe thy giftes: thou giuest altogither freely, for thou findest nothing for to saue, but many things to condemne.

Augustine vpon the wordes of the Lorde in the mountaine. Sermon.7.

In this time the remnant haue bene saued through the election of grace. But if it be through grace (sayth he) then it is not through workes: that is to saye, doe not nowe eleuate nor exalt thy selfe vpon thy merite, otherwise grace shall be no more grace. For if thou presumest vppon thy workes, then the rewarde is giuen thee, and grace is not giuen thee: but if it be grace, it is then giuen freely: I doe now demaunde of thee thou sinner, doest thou beleeue in Christ? I doe beleeue. And what doest thou beleeue? that thy sinnes generally maye be pardoned through him freely. Thou hast that that thou hast beleeued. O grace thankfullye giuen: Thou righteous person what doest thou beleeue? That thou canst not keepe without God his righteousnesse. Then impute vnto fayth all that of which thou art righteous, 2.Cor.11 The righteous cannot abyde in righteousnes if he be not holpen.

and

and in ẏ thou art a sinner, impute it to thy infidelitie. Be thou thine own accuser, and he shall be thy forgiuer. But euery crime, all euill, and all sinne commeth of oure negligence, and all vertue and holynesse is of the indulgence of God.

Augustine vpon the 43. psalme, vpon the verse, And redeme vs for thy names sake.

That is to saye freely, bicause of thy name, not for my merite, forasmuche as thou hast vouchsafed to doe it, bicause that it pleased thee to doe it, not that I am worthye that thou doe it. For in as muche as we haue not forgotten thee, & that our hart is not retired and plucked back from thee. And that we haue not stretched out our hands vnto another God: howe haue we power to doe the same? but through thy ayde, but through thy worde, speaking inwardlye and exhorting vs: and thereby also thou doest not leaue of, or cease to helpe and ayde vs: of whome wee haue the power. Then be it that wee are pacient in tribulation, or be it that we be ioyfull in prosperitie, redeme vs not thorowe our merite, but bicause of thy holye name.

name.

S. Hilarie vpon S. Mathew, in the 9. Canon.

The same moued the Scribes that sinne shoulde be pardoned by a man, for they regarded and behelde nothing in Iesus Christ but manhode, and that the law could not release that which was pardoned of him, for only faith iustifieth: and afterwardes the Lorde behelde inwardly their murmuring and sayd that it was easye for the sonne of man to pardon sinnes in earth: but neuerthelesse none can pardon sinnes but God only: wherefore hee which doth pardon them is God, for none doth pardon but God. *Math. 9.* *Rom. 3.* He vvhich doth pardon sinnes is god

Augustine vpon the wordes of the Apostle. Sermon. 2.

By grace are wee made safe through faith and not of our selues, but it is the gifte of God. Truly there are men that are vnthankefull to grace, which doe attrybute much to the poore and wounded nature: It is true that when man was made that he receyued great force of free will, but he lost it in committing sinne, he faynted in death, and was made feeble. &c. *Ephe. 2.* Free vvill lost by sin.

Againe in the same Sermon.

We are very much constrayned to complayne of our bretheren which gainsay and speake against the grace of God, not against the secrete, but against the cleare and manyfest grace, he is to pardon the Jewes: but what shall be done to the christians? Wherfore are they enimies of ỷ grace of Christ? Wherfore do they presume of them selues? Wherefore are they vnthankefull? For wherefore is Christe come? Was not nature here? Was not nature shee which hath deceyued you in praysing? was not shee the lawe? But the Apostle sayth if righteousnesse came by the lawe, it followeth then that Christ dyed in vayne: That whiche the Apostle sayde of the law vnto the Jewes, the same say we of nature vnto those here. Then if righteousnesse is by nature, Christ died in vayne. The same then which was sayde to the Jewes, we see in those here. They haue a feruent mynde to Godwarde, but not according to knowledge. For they, being ignorant of the righteousnes of God, and going about to establishe their owne righteousnesse, haue not bene obedient to the

Gala.2.

If the strẽgth of our nature coulde iustifie vs, then Christ dyed in vain.

Rom.10.

the righteousnesse of God. My brethren beare with me, where you shall finde such, doe not conceale nor hyde them. Let not peruerse and wicked mercie be in you, where you shall finde such, in no case hide them: rebuke those that speake agaynst it, and those that do resist the same, bring them vnto vs.

Augustine vpon the Apostles words. Ser. 11.

He hath made vs, and not wee our selues. The holy spirite hath foreseene that some shall saye, that God hath made them men. But that they shoulde make themselues righteous, he hath foreseene them, he hath admonished and warned them, and hath called them backe agayne from that pryde, saying: That it is he that hath made vs, and not we our selues. For to what purpose hath he added, and not we our selues, in asmuch as it sufficeth to say, that it is he that hath made vs. What is the same? But that hee woulde admonishe vs of that doing, of which men saye, that we are made of our selues (that is to say) that we haue bene righteous, we are made righteous of our free will: when we were created, we receyued free will: then *Psal.* 100

where we are righteous, we doe the same of our free wil. Wherfore do we yet inuocate and call vpon God, þ he doe make vs righteous, in asmuch as we haue ẏ power of our selues to make our selues righteous? Beholde, beholde him that hath made vs both righteous and vnrighteous, and not we our selues. The first man was created of nature without faulte, without vices, he was created right. But that which he did, is most euident, that in falling from the hande of the potter, he was broken. Afterwards he sayth: Then God did shew vnto mã how much worth free wil maye be without God, we haue proued howe auayleable it is without God: therfore haue we bene made miserable, bicause that we haue proued what power we haue without God. Beholde man was made good, and through free will he was made euill. Then when shall the wicked man be a good man, in forsaking God through free will. He being good, coulde not kepe himselfe good. Nowe he being euill, can he make himselfe good? When hee was good, he coulde not keepe himselfe good. And when he is euill, he sayth, I do make my

Gene. 2.

If vve haue povver to iustifie our selues, vve neede not pray vnto God to iustifie and make vs cleane.

my selfe good. What doest thou being euill, when thou art lost being good, except that he which continueth alwayes good, doe not repayre and amende thee?

Augustine writing vnto Paulinus.
106. *Epistle.*

What is he which shal seperate vs from that masse or burthen of perdition, and from that fight, but only he which is come to saue that whiche was lost? Of whome also the Apostle being asked, say: who is he that doth iudge or discerne thee? where if man say, it is my fayth, it is my will, it is my good worke: It may be answered him agayne: and what hast thou that thou hast not receyued? If thou hast receyued it, why reioycest thou as though thou hadst not receiued it? And yet neuerthelesse all this is sayde, not that man shoulde reioyce: but hee that reioyceth, shoulde reioyce in the Lorde, and not of workes, to the ende that none doe exalte himselfe: not that good workes are frustrate throwe that faythfull cogitation. Howe is it that God will rewarde euery man according to his deedes? And y^t vnto euery man which doth good, shall be ren-

Mat.18
Luk.19.
1.Cor.4.
1.Cor.1.
2.Cor.10.
Ierem.9.
Rom.2.
Psal.62.
Mat.16.

Apoca.22. dred prayse, honor and peace: but bicause
Galat.5. that workes are of grace and not grace of
Rom.5. workes: for faith which worketh by loue
is nothing worth, if the loue of God bee
not spreade abroade in our heartes by the
Rom.12. holy Ghoste, which is giuen vnto vs: yea
Ephe.4. we haue not that faith, if God doe not
1.Cor.12. deale to euery man the measure of faith, &c.

Augustine writing to Valentin
46. Epistle.

Iam.1. Euery good gift and euery perfecte is from aboue, and commeth downe from the father of lightes: and let no man say that the grace of God is giuen vnto him eyther by the merites of workes, or by the merite of his prayer, or by the merites of his faith: And that he doe not esteeme that to be true, which the Heritickes say, that the grace of God is giuen vnto vs according to our merites, the which is altogither false: But the grace and mercie of God doth conuerte man, of whom the Psalmist sayeth. The mercie of my God shall goe before me, to the ende that he that is an infidell be iustified, that is to say, that of an infidell he be made a righteous man: and that he doe begin to haue good

The grace of God not giuen vnto vs by our vvorkes.

Psal.59.

good merites, the which God shal crowne when the world shall be iudged.

Augustine in his booke of the true definition of faith.

There is neyther Saint nor righteous man which is without sinne, and yet neuerthelesse he leaueth not of nor ceaseth therefore to be holy and iuste, inasmuche as through affection hee holdeth sanctification: for we are not holy through the force and strength of mans nature: but we doe obtayne sanctification through the grace of God, whiche dooth ayde and helpe our purpose. And therefore all the Saintes truely doe declare them selues to be sinners, for truely they haue inough for to lament and bewayle. And although that their consciences doe not rebuk them, yet they haue to lament, bicause of the nobilitie and unconstancie of nature subiecte to preuarication.

There is no Saint which is without sinne.

Psal. 143.
Iob. 9.

S. Ierome against the Pelagians.

A certayne man of our writers hath very well affirmed, the Philosophers to be the Patriarkes of Heriticks, & to haue defiled the puritie of the Church through peruerse doctrine, insomuch as that they doe not knowe that, which they speake of mans fragilitie or weakenesse. Whereof should earth and ashes bost them selues? In asmuch cheifely as of them the Apostle speaketh, saying: I see another law in my members. &c. And againe, I doe not that good thing, which I would, but that euill doe I, which I would not. If he doe not that which he woulde, how can that be true, whiche is sayde, that man may bee without sinne if he will? By what reason may he be that which he will, when the Apostle affirmeth that he cannot accomplishe and fulfill that which he desireth? When I shall thinke my selfe to be come to the ende of vertues, then shall I but beginne: the onely perfection of men is to acknowledge them selues imperfect.

Rom.7.

The ende of vertue is but a beginning.

Chrysostome in his imperfect worke. Chapter.6.

If euery one doe consider the motions, or mouinges of his flesh, he shall be founde to do no goodnesse: for all goodnesse is accomplished of vs, in gainesaying and speaking against our selues, bicause that the nature of the fleshe is contrary to goodnesse.

Galat.5.

S.Ierome

S. Ierome against the Pelagians firste booke.

Then are we righteous when we doe confesse our selues to be sinners, and our righteousnesse is not of our owne proper mertie, but consisteth in the mercy of God: for the Scripture saith, the righteous man is an accuser of him selfe, in the beginning of the worde.

Our righteousnesse is only of the mercye of God.

S. Barnard in his.5.Sermon of dedication

Who shall be saued? Say the Apostles to the Sauiour? And he saide unto them, things which are unpossible with men, are possible with God. This is all our trust, this is all our consolation, this is all the reason of our hope: but we whiche are already certayne and sure of the possibilitie, what doe we determine of the wil? Who knoweth whither he be worthy of loue or hatred? Who hath knowen the minde of the Lorde? Or who was his counseller? Now it is here necessary for vs that fayth doe helpe vs: It behoueth here that the truth doe ayde vs, insomuche as that which is hid from vs in the heart of the father, be reueled unto vs by his holy

Luk. 18.

Rom. 11. *Esay.* 40. 1. *Cor.* 2. *Sap.* 9.

It behoueth that faith do ayde oure debilitie.

ly spirite: and that his spirite in giuing witnesse, doth perswade our spirites and mindes that we are the children of God, that he doth perswade vs in calling, in iustifying vs freely through faith. &c.

Gregory in his morales. 22. booke. 6. Chapter.

There are also some men, who in doing any good thing, doe forget incontinently their sinnes, and doe fasten the eye of the hart in the consideration of the good works that they doe, & therby doe esteme & thinke themselues already holy: wherefore among ÿ goodnesse that they do, they take away ÿ remembrance of their faults: in the which peraduenture they are yet stil wrapped: who if they did consider diligentlye the rigours of the Iudge, they woulde more feare their euils, then they woulde reioyce of their imperfect goodnesse: They ought to regarde rather that they are debters of thinges ÿ they ought to doe, that they haue not payed by their good workes the parte already due. And so after the manner of the trauayler, we ought by no manner of meanes to regarde or marke what way we haue walked in, but what way we haue yet to walke in: we ought then rather to beholde the goodnesse which we haue not yet done, then those of which we doe reioyce our selues to haue already done: and the elect are often times tempted with such vices, and oftentimes it is rysen in their heartes to bring them in remembraunce of all the goodnesse that they haue done, and to reioyce themselues of the band of assurance. But if they be truly elected, they will turn awaye their eyes from thinking of the same, wherein they doe please themselues, and keepe backe in them all the ioy of the goodnesse which is alreadye done, and be sorie for those which they knowe to be by no maner of meanes done. They doe esteeme themselues vnworthye, and they onely do not see their goodnesse which are of all men seene by good example. &c.

Of iustification of Fayth.

Augustine in the first Quinquagesima, in the prologue of the 31. psal.

TRuly the Apostle Saint Iames in his Epistles hath praised the works *Iam. 2*

of

of Abraham, agaynst those which woulde not do any good, and which presume them selues of faypth: of which Abraham, Saint Paule hath praysed his faypth, and yet the Apostles are not contrarie the one to the other: but he speaketh of the work which is knowne to all men (that is to saye) that Abraham did offer his sonne vnto God, for to doe sacrifice. That is a great worke, but that is of faypth. I doe prayse the buylding of the worke made vpon the foundation, but I doe beholde the foundation of faith. I doe prayse the fruite of the good and iust worke, but I acknowledge the roote in faypth. For if Abraham did those things without right faypth, nothing woulde haue profited him, whatsoeuer worke it hadde bene. Furthermore, if Abraham did keepe so the faypth, that when God commaunded him to offer his sonne for sacrifice, hee thought in himselfe, I will not doe it, and yet neuerthelesse I doe beleeue that God will deliuer me, although that I doe contemne and despise his commaundements. Faypth without workes shoulde be deade, and shoulde abyde as a drie roote, barren, and without fruite. What then? we ought

S.Paule and S.Iames are not contrarie the one to the other.

not

not to preferre workes before fayth: that is to say, nothing is sayde to be well done before fayth: although that they are esteemed of men prayse worthye, yet notwithstanding they are vayne. And me thinketh that they are like vnto great strengths, and vnto the easie course out of the waye. Let none then esteeme his workes. &c. Afterwardes he sayth: Let vs not then obiect the Apostle Saint James to Paule, but the same Paule to himselfe, and let vs say vnto him by this worde: thou doest suffer vs somwhat to sinne without punishment, when thou sayest: wee doe esteeme man to bee iustified thorowe fayth withoute workes: but thou wilt saye to the same, faith worketh by loue. How am I so much assured by the same, if I doe nothing? yea, I shall not bee counted by the same to haue trust in the good fayth, if I doe not worke by loue. O Apostle I doe heare thee, wilt thou here prayse vnto me fayth without workes? But loue is the worke of fayth, which loue cannot be ydle, that it doe forsake all euill, and doe all the good that it can. And what maketh loue? Declyne from euill, and doe good. Prayseſt thou

Rom. 4.
Galat. 5.

Loue cannot be ydle, for it forsaketh euil, and doth good.

1.Cor.13. thou then faythe without works? And thou sayest in another place: If I had all fayth, so that I coulde moue mountaynes out of their places, and yet had not loue, I were nothing: then if fayth doe not profite any without loue, and that there where loue shall be, it behoueth that it work (for faith worketh by loue) howe then is man iustified without workes? The Apostle aunswereth: O thou man, therefore haue I sayde this thing vnto thee, that thou doe not presume of thy workes, and that thou doe not thinke to haue receyued the grace of fayth thorowe the merite of thy works: Presume not then of workes before fayth, acknowledge that fayth hath founde thee a sinner, and if the fayth which hath founde thee a sinner, hath made thee righteous, then it doth finde him an infidell whiche it hath made righteous. The fayth (sayth he)

Rom.4. is counted for righteousnesse vnto him, which beleeueth on him that iustifieth the vngodly.

Augustine in his booke of the 83. questions.76.Chapter.

If any man doe departe out of this life immediatly after ŷ he hath beleued the iustificastification of faith abideth with him: and commeth not to him by any workes precedent, or going before (for it is not giuen through merite but through grace nor through workes following, bicause that he is not permitted to be in this life:) and therefore the two sentences of the two Apostles, Paule and James, are not contrary the one to the other: For the one saith that man is iustified through faith without workes: And the other saith that faith is dead without workes: for Paule speaketh of workes whiche goe before faith, and James speaketh of works which doe followe faith.

Rom.4. *Iame.2.* The meaning of S. Paule, and of S. Iames, and hovve vvee ought to vnderstād them.

Origene vpon the Epistle to the Romans. 3. booke. 3. Chapter.

The onely iustification of God, sufficeth so, that he which beleeueth onely is iustified, when in deede no workes shall be done by him. For the thefe was iustified through faith without the workes of the lawe: and vpon that faith the Lorde did not demaunde what that is that he had done before, and did not tarry after that he had beleeued what worke he shoulde doe, but receiued him as iustified throughe the

the onely faith for to enter with him into paradise. Also that woman which is receited by the Euangelist the which did heare at Iesus feete, thy sins are forgiuen thee:
Luc.7.
And again, thy faith hath saued thee, go in peace: But also in many places of the gospell, Iesus Christ hath vsed such wordes, where he sayth, that the cause of saluation is the faith of him which beleeueth. Man then is iustified through faith, vnto whome the workes of faith serue nothing at all for iustification. But where faith is not, which iustifieth the beleeuing man, when any one shall haue the workes of the law, neuerthelesse bicause they are not buylded vpon the foundation of faith, although that in appearance they are good, yet they cannot iustifie the worke, if it be without faith: the which is the marke and token of those which are iustified of God. And what shall he be which wyll boste him selfe of his righteousnesse, when he heareth God and the Prophet saying: all our righteousnesse are as a menstruous cloth, wherefore the only right glorye is in the fayth of Christ.

The vvorkes of the lavve serue nothing for iustification.

Esay.64.

Augustine in his.50.homilies. homily.17.

Peace be vnto the bretheren, and loue with the faith of God our Father, and of our Lorde Iesus Christ. What hast thou, that thou hast not receiued? If thou hast receiued it, why reioysest thou, as though thou haddest not receiued it? Did Abraham so reioyce? He reioysed of faith, what is the full and perfect faith? The same which beleeueth that all our goodnesse are of God, yea faith it selfe. Againe the Apostle saith, I haue obtayned mercie. O true confession? He doth not say I haue obtayned mercy bicause that I was faithful: but to the ende that I should be faithfull, I haue obtayned mercie. Let vs come vnto the first works of Paule: Let vs behold Saule which did wax madde, let vs behold him in his crueltie: let vs behold him breathing out his threatnings, and thirstie after bloude. This was the way of Paule, Christ was not yet his way: what had he in his heart? What had he but euill? Giue me his merites? Whiche if we doe searche his merites, they shall bee merites of damnation and not of deliuerance.

1. Cor. 4

1. Tim. 1

Gala. 1.
Act. 9.

Augustine vpon the wordes of the Lorde. Sermon. 40.

The medecine of the soule, is the only propitiation for the sinnes of all, that is to beleeue in Christ, &c. Afterwarde he saith: wherefore doe the children of God whiche beleeue in him liue: for they are borne of God, by the adoption of grace, whiche is through the faith of our Lorde Iesus Christ. And therefore, welbeloued, it is not
Iohn. 6. without cause that our Lord and Sauiour
Mat. 9. saith, that same to be the only sinne of
Mat. 5. which the holy Ghost rebuketh the world, to wete because they haue not beleeued in
All sinnes pardoned by fayth. him. He would then that the world should be reproued only of that sinne, that they doe not beleeue only in him, to wete because that in beleeuing in him all sinnes are pardoned: he woulde that to be imputed, by which all the other are assembled. And therefore in beleeuing they are borne of God, and are made the children of God,
Iohn. 1. for he hath giuen vnto them the power (saith he) to be the sonnes of God, euen to them that beleeue in his name. &c.

Chry-

Chrysostome vpon the.25.chapter of Saint Mathewe, 2. Tome.2.homilye.

Come ye blessed of my father inherite ye the kingdome prepared for you from before the beginning of the worlde: bicause that you haue giuen that which you cannot haue: receiue that which you shall possesse eternally: for one graine that you haue sowen vpon earth, you shall haue an hundreth folde asmuch in heauen. For the kingdome of heauen hath not bene created suche as the righteousnesse of man could merite it, but such as the power of God might prepare it: for if he woulde haue created the kingdome of heauen according to the merites of mans righteousnesse: Truely he would haue created it after mans workes: but bicause that nowe he hath not ordayned the reward of Saintes according to the reward of men, but according to his greatnesse: therefore hath he prepared the kingdome of heauen in heauen, before that he created the saints in heauen.

Mat.25.

Mat.19.

The kingdom of heauen not created as man coulde merite, but as God might prepare it.

S. Barnarde vpon the first sermon of the Annunciation of the virgin Marie.

2.Cor.1. The testimonie of our conscience is our
Luk.18. reioycing, sayth the Apostle: not such testimonie as the proud Pharisey had in his wicked thought, and seducing his master which bare witnesse of him selfe, whiche witnesse is true, which the spirite doth witnesse vnto our spirite. For I doe beleeue that this witnesse consisteth in three things. First, and aboue all things, it is necessarie to beleeue that thou canst not haue remission and forgiuenesse of thy sinnes, but throughe the indulgencie of God. Secondly, thou canst not haue any good workes, except he himselfe doe giue them vnto thee. Finallye, that thou canst not merite eternall life for any workes, and it must be giuen thee freely. &c. Afterwardes he sayth: For we doe well know, that as for eternall life, the afflictions of this lyfe are not worthie of the glorie which shall be shewed vpon vs, although that one only man doth abide and suffer al. For mans merites are not suche, that for them eternall life shoulde be due of right,

No remissi-on of sinnes, but of God.

Rom.8.

or that we shoulde saye that God doth vs wrong, if he doe not giue them vs by reason of them. For though I shoulde holde my peace, that all merites are the gifts of God, insomuch that for them man is more indebted to God, than God is to man. What is that that all the merites doe in respect of so great glorie? To conclude what is he that is more excellent than the Prophete, vnto whome the Lorde doth giue so excellent a witnesse, saying: I haue founde a man according to mine owne heart. And yet he had neede to saye vnto God: Enter not into iudgement with thy seruant. &c. Let no man then deceyue himselfe, for if he will thinke well, he shall finde without all doubt that he can not with ten thousande men go to meete him whiche commeth agaynst him wyth xx. thousande. But these things which we haue now spoken of, are not yet altogither sufficient, but wee must the rather holde them for a beginning and foundation of fayth. Therefore if thou beleeue that thy sinnes cannot be put or blotted out but by him agaynst whome onely thou hast sinned, thou doest well. But adde yet one

1. Reg. 16

Psal. 143.

thing more, to wete, that thou beleeue also that thy sinnes by him are pardoned: Beholde the testimonies and witnesses which the holy ghost doth giue into our heartes, saying: thy sinnes are pardoned thee. For euen so doth the Apostle think, that man is iustified freely through fayth.
Luc.7. *Rom.3.* In lyke maner as touching merites, if thou beleeue that one cannot haue them but by him, it sufficeth not vntill such time as the spirite of fayth doth witnesse that thou hast them through him: Euen so it is necessarie that thou haue also witnesse, to wete, that thou doest come thereunto through Gods liberalitie. For it is he which pardoneth sinnes, which giueth merites: and yet neuerthelesse doth giue agayne the rewarde. For all his testimonies are most assured. For as to the remission of sinnes, I doe hold the passion of our Lord for a most strong argument. For the crye

Let vs assure our selues to come to heauen through the gift of God.

Heb.12. of his bloude hath had greater force than the bloude of Abel: in as much as he doth crie in the heartes of the electe, remission of all sinnes. For he was deliuered to death for our sinnes. And there is *Rom.4.* no doubt but that his death is more puis-

sant

sant and of greater force to doe good, than our sinnes are to doe euill. As touching good workes, his resurrection is an argument for me which hath no lesse vertue. For asmuch as he is rysen againe for our iustification: as touching the hope of reward, his ascention serueth for a witnesse, for he is ascended for our glorification. Thou hast these three things in the psalm saying: Blessed is the man vnto whome the Lorde imputeth no sinne. And in another place, blessed are the men whose strength is in thee: Also in an other place: Blessed is the man whom thou hast chosen and receiuest vnto thee, that he maye dwell in thy courte: such is the true glory (I say) which is within, for that doeth departe from him which dwelleth in our heartes through faith. But the sonnes of Adam seeking the glorye which commeth from man, will not haue that whiche commeth from one only God: and therfore in seeking it outwardly, they haue no glory in them selues, but rather in an other.

Remission of sinnes is through the bloude of Christ.

Ephe. 4.

Psal. 32.

Psal. 84.

Psal. 65.

Sixtus Pope of Rome, in his Epistle to the first tome of the Councels.

He that is doubtfull in the faith, is an infidell,

Iames 1.

infidell: wherefore let vs esteeme and iudge those which doe commaund vs to doubt of the fauour of God towardes vs, not only to contende and striue against the sentence of the true Catholicke church, but also to giue euill counsell to the health and saluation of the church.

S Barnard in his .5. Sermon in Quadragesima.

The trusting to vvorkes, auaileth nothing to seke eternall life.

It may be that some doe not seeke, through humilitie euerlasting life, but as in the trust and confidence of their workes and merits, & I do not say this, that grace receiued doth not giue boldnesse to praye, but it must not be therefore that in the same they haue their hope and trust to obtayne it: for that only doth giue the giftes promised, to the ende that of the mercy of God which giueth those thinges, we may hope yet for greater thinges. Let then those thinges which doe belong to our only necessities be restrayned, the prayer which is made for the temporall thinges, and that which is made for the vertues of the soule, sequestred from all impuritie and vncleanenesse, be only attentife towardes the good will of God. And that whiche is made

made bicause of eternall life, let it be made or done in all humilitie, presuming (as he must) of the only deuine mercie.

Grace be with you and peace, from God our father, and from the Lord Jesus Christe. Rom.1. 1.Cor.1. Colos.1.

O wretched man that I am, who shall deliuer me from this body of death? The grace of God through Jesus Christe our Lorde. Rom.7.

Euen so at this time, the remnante is left through the election of grace: if it bee of grace, then it is not of workes: or els were grace no more grace. But if it be of workes, then is it no more grace: or els were workes no longer workes. Rom.11. Rom.9.

By grace are ye made safe throughe fayth: and that not of your selues: it is the gift of God, not of workes, least any man shoulde boast of himselfe. Ephes.2.

Also: That we being iustified by his grace, shoulde be made heyres according to the hope of eternall lyfe. Titus.3.

Saint Peter sayth: why tempt ye God, to laye a yoke on the Disciples neckes, which neyther our fathers, nor we, were able to beare? but we beleue that through Act.15. 2.Par.10

the grace of the Lorde Jesus Christ wee shall be saued, euen as they doe.

God doth not saue vs of the deedes of righteousnesse which we wrought, but of his mercie.

He which began a good worke in you, shall go forth with it vntill the day of Jesus Christ.

Unto you it is giuen for Christe, that not onely ye shoulde beleeue on him, but also suffer for his sake.

He sayth agayne: And as touching the righteousnesse whiche is in the lawe, I was without reproche. But the thinges which were vauntage to me, I counted losse for Christes sake: yea doubtlesse I thinke all things but losse for that excellent knowledge sake of Christ Jesus my Lorde: for whome I haue counted all things losse, and do iudge them but dung, that I might winne Christ, and might be founde in him, that is, not hauing mine owne righteousnesse, which is of the law, but that whiche is throughe the fayth of Christ, I meane the righteousnesse which commeth of God through fayth. &c.

I am nowe ready to be offred, and the

tyme of my departing is at hande: I haue fought a good fight, and haue fulfilled my course, and haue kept the fayth. From henceforth is layde vp for me a crowne of righteousnesse which the Lorde that is a righteous iudge shall giue me at that day: not to me only, but vnto all them also that loue his comming. *Esay.50. Psalm.3. Psal.73. 44.102.*

But nowe in Christe Iesus ye whiche once were farre of, are made nye by the bloude I say of Christ. *Ephe.2. 1.Pet.2.*

It is God which worketh in vs bothe the will, and also the dede, euen of his free beneuolence. *Philip.1.*

To as many as receyued him, to them he gaue power to bee the sonnes of God, euen to them which beleeue in his name, which are borne not of bloude, nor of the lustes of the fleshe, nor of the lust of man, but of God. *Iohn.1.*

In thy light shall we see light. *Psal.36.*

Your eyes haue seene great miracles and wonders: and yet the Lorde hath not giuen you an heart to perceyue, nor eyes to see, nor eares to heare. *Deut.29.*

O Lorde giue me vnderstanding, open myne eyes for to beholde the wonderous things *Psal.119.*

things of thy lawe.

Ezech.36 Ezechiel speaking in the person of God, sayth: A newe heart will I giue you, and a newe spirite will I put into you: as for that stonie heart I will take it out of your bodie, and giue you a fleshie heart. I will giue my spirite among you, and cause you to walke in my commaundements, to kepe my lawes, and to fulfill them.

Psal.62. As for men, they are but vayne: if they be put in the ballaunce, they are lighter than vanitie it selfe.

Ierem.31. Conuert thou me, and I shall be conuerted, for thou art my Lorde God: yea, as soone as thou turnest me, I shall reforme my selfe.

Rom.3. Therefore we gather that a man is iustified by faith, without the deedes of the lawe.

Rom.4. *Genes.15.* *Galat.3.* *Iam.2.* Againe, Abraham beleeued God, and it was counted to him for righteousnesse. To him that worketh, the rewarde is not reckened of fauour but of duety. But to him that worketh not, but beleeueth on him that iustifieth the vngodly, his faith is counted for righteousnesse. Also: for if they

Rom.4. which are of the lawe, bee heires, then

is faith but vaine, and the promise of none effect. &c. Therefore by faith is the inheritance giuen, that it might come of fauour, and the promesse might be sure to all the seede (that is) not to them only which are of the lawe: but also to them which are of the faith of Abraham. Then being iustified by faith, we haue peace with God through our Lord Iesus Christ, by whom also we haue accesse through faith, vnto this grace, wherein we stand, and reioyce in hope of the glorye of God. *Rom. 5.*

Bicause of vnbeleefe they are broken of and thou standest stedfast by faith. *Rom. 11.*

What soeuer is not of faith, is sinne. *Rom. 14.*

We know that a man is not iustified by the deedes of the lawe, but by the faith of Iesus Christ: euen we I say haue beleeued in Iesus Christ, that we might be iustified by the faith of Iesus Christ, and not by the deedes of the lawe: bicause that by the deedes of the lawe, no flesh shal be iustified. *Galat. 2.*

I doe not abrogate the grace of God, for if righteousnesse commeth of the lawe, then Christ dyed without a cause. *Galat. 2.*

So ye knowe, that they which are of *Galat. 3.*

faith, are the children of Abraham: for
Genes.15. the Scripture sawe afore hand, that God
would iustifie the Gentils through fayth:
and therefore preached before hande the
Gospell vnto Abraham, saying, in thee
shall all the Gentiles be blessed: so then
they which be of fayth, are blessed with
faythfull Abraham. For as many as are
vnder the deedes of the law, are vnder the
Deut.27. curse. For it is written: Cursed is euerye
man that continueth not in all things that
are written in the booke of the lawe, to
fulfill them. And that no man is iustified
Abac.2. by the lawe in the sight of God, it is eui-
Rom.1. dent: For the iust shall lyue by fayth: and
Heb.10. the lawe is not of fayth: but the man that
Leuit.18. shall fulfill those things, shall liue in them.
Nowe Christ hath redeemed vs from the
curse of the lawe, when he was made ac-
Deut.21. cursed for vs. For it is written: Cursed
is euery one that hangeth on a tree. That
the blessing of Abraham might come on
the Gentiles through Iesus Christ, and
that we might receyue the promise of the
spirite through fayth.

Galat.3. But the Scripture hath concluded all
things vnder sinne, that the promise by
the

the fayth of Iesus Christ shoulde be giuen to them that beleeue.&c. For ye are all the sonnes of God by fayth in Christ Iesus. Galat.3. *De pœnitentia, Distinction.3.chap.* which beginneth, *Totam.&c.*

And we are iustified freely by his grace, through the redemption that is in Christ Iesus, whome God hath set forth to be a pacification through fayth in his bloude, to declare his righteousnesse, in that hee forgiueth the sinnes that are passed. *Rom.3.*

Without fayth it is impossible to please God. *Heb.11.*

In whome euen nowe, though yee see him not, yet doe ye beleeue, and reioyce with ioye vnspeakable and glorious, receiuing the end of your faith, the saluation of your soules.&c. And God which knoweth the heartes, bare them witnesse, in giuing vnto them the holy Ghost, euen as he did vnto vs: and he put no difference betwene them and vs, seing that with faith he purified their heartes. *1.Pet.1.* *Act.15.*

S. Ierome vpon Sophon. Chapter.3.

They doe seeke the righteousnesse, the which is not but Christ alone.

Iesus Christ sayeth: Daughter bee of *Math.9.*

good comfort, thy fayth hath made thee whole.

Math.9. Agayne: Beleeue ye that I am able to doe this? And they sayde vnto him, yea Lorde. Then touched he their eyes, saying: according to your fayth bee it vnto you.

Luk.8. Also: Daughter, be of good comforte, thy fayth hath made thee whole, goe in peace.

Iohn.6. Also: What shall we doe, that wee might worke the workes of God? Iesus aunswered and sayd vnto them. This is the worke of God, that ye beleeue on him, whom he hath sent.

Mar.9. Likewise: all things are possible to him that beleeueth.

Rom.6. The wages of sinne is death, but the gyft of God, is eternal life through Iesus Christ our Lorde.

Rom.10. If thou shalt confesse with thy mouthe the Lorde Iesus, and shalt beleeue in thine heart, that God raysed him vp from death thou shalt be saued. For the beleefe of the heart iustifieth, and to confesse with the mouth, saueth a man.

Rom.10. Who soeuer beleeueth on him, shal not be

be ashamed. *Esay.28.*

But ye are of him in Iesus Christ, who of God is made vnto vs wisedome, and righteousnesse, and sanctification, and redemption: that according as it is written: He that reioyceth, shoulde reioyce in the Lorde. *1.Cor.1.* *2.Cor.10* *Ierem.9.*

This is the name that they shal call him, euen the Lorde our righteous maker. *Iere.23. and 33.*

To him giue all the Prophets witnesse, that through his name all that beleeue in him, shall receyue remission of sinnes. *Act.10.* *Ierem.31.* *Mich.7.*

For among men there is giuen none other name vnder heauen, whereby wee must be saued. *Act.4.*

Ye are gone quite from Christ as many as are iustified by the lawe, and are fallen from grace. *Galat.5.*

Let no man esteeme of himselfe, more then it becommeth him to esteeme: but that he discretely iudge of himselfe, according as God hath dealt to euery man the measure of fayth. *Rom.12.*

How shoulde I then aunswere him: or what wordes shoulde I finde out agaynst him? yea, though I be righteous, yet will I not giue him one worde agayne, but *Iob.9.*

meekely submit my selfe to my Iudge. If I will iustifie my selfe, myne owne mouth shall condemne me. If I will put forth my selfe for a perfect man, he shall proue mee a wicked doer: for that I shoulde be an innocent, my conscience knoweth it not: yea, I my selfe am weary of my life.

Iob.10. Thou hast graunted me lyfe, and done me good: and the diligent heede that thou tookest vpon me, hath preserued my spirite, &c. If I doe wickedly, wo is me therfore. If I be righteous, yet dare I not lift vp my heade: so full am I of confusion, and see mine owne miserie.

Iob.15. What is man that he shoulde be cleane? What hath he (which is born of a woman) whereby he might be knowen to be righteous? Beholde there is no trust in hys Saintes: yea, the very heauens are not cleare in his sight. Howe much more then an abhominable and vile man, which drinketh wickednesse like water?

Iob.25. But how may a man compared vnto God be iustified? Or how can he be clean that is borne of a woman?

Esay.64. We are all as an vncleane thing, and all our righteousnesse are as the clothes

stayned

stayned or a menstruous cloth.

There is not one iust vpon earth that doth good, and sinneth not. *Eccle.7.* *3.Reg.8.*

Verely in the Lord is my righteousnesse and strength. To him shal men come: but all they that thinke scorne of him, shal be confounded. And the whole seede of Israell shall be iustified, and praysed in the Lorde. *2.Cor.6.* *1.Iohn.1.* *Esay.45.*

The Lorde helpeth me, therefore shall I not be confounded. I haue hardened my face like a flint stone, for I am sure that I shall not come to confusion. Mine aduocate speaketh for me, who will then goe with me to lawe? *Esay.50.*

My righteous seruant shall with his wisedome iustifie and deliuer the multitude, for he shall beare away their sins. &c. *Esay.53.*

We being iustified by his grace should be made heires according to the hope of eternall life. *Titus.3.*

Yet darest thou say, I am giltlesse: Tushe, his wrath cannot come vpon me: behold I wyll reason with thee bicause thou darest say: I haue not offended. O howe euill will it be for thee, to abyde it: when it shall be knowen, how oft thou hast *Ierem.2.*

gone backwarde?

Ierem.14. Doubtlesse our owne wickednesse rewarde vs, but Lorde doe thou according to thy name, thoughe our transgressions and sinnes be many, and haue sinned against thee.

Esay.57. They that put their trust in me, shall inherite the land, and haue my holy hill in possession.

Act.13. Be it knowen vnto you therefore men and brethren, that through this man is preached vnto you the forgiuenesse of sinnes, and that from all sinnes, from which you could not be iustified by the lawe of *Moyses*: by him euery one that beleeueth is iustified.

Iohn.1. And of his fulnesse haue all we receyued, euen grace for grace.

Rom.8. Which he predestinated before, them also he called, and whō he called, them also he iustified, and whome he iustified, them he also gloryfied. What shall wee then say to these thinges, if God be on our side, who can be against vs?

Rom.8. Who shall laye any thing to the charge of Gods chosen? It is God that iustifieth. Who then shall condemne? It is Christe

which

which is dead, yea rather which is rysen againe: which is allso at the right hand of God, and maketh intercession for vs.

O Lorde enter not into iudgemente with thy seruaunte, for in thy sight shall no man liuing be iustified. *Psal.143.*

A iuste man falleth seuen times, and ryseth vp againe. *Prou.24.*

If thou O Lorde wilt be extreme to marke what is done amisse, oh Lord who may abyde it. But there is mercye with thee, that thou mayest be feared. *Psal.130.*

Of the lawe.

The lawe is not giuen vnto a righteous man, but vnto the lawelesse and disobedient. *I.Tim.I.*

Augustine of free will and grace.
Chapter.6.

The Pelagians doe thinke them selues to knowe great thinges, when they say, the Lorde will not commaund that, which he knoweth man cannot doe: who is hee which knoweth not that thing? But therefore he commaundeth some things *VVhat vvee ought to demaunde.*

which we cannot doe, to the ende that wee may knowe that which we ought to demaund of him: and that is faith, which in praying obtayneth that the lawe commandeth. Finally he which hath sayde, if thou wilt thou shalt kepe the commandements.

Psal.141. Set a watch O lord before my mouth. &c. This is a most sure and certaine thing that if we will we may kepe the commandements: But bicause the Lorde prepareth and maketh the will ready, we muste demaund the will which suffiseth to doe it willingly: it is certaine that we wil when we haue the will: but it is he that causeth that we desire and will the good, of whom

Psal.37. it is sayde: The Lorde ordereth a good mans goinges, and hath pleasure in his way: and it is God which worketh in us,

Philip.2. both the will, and also the deede, yea, euen of his free beneuolence. It is certaine that we doe it, when we doe giue the vertue of most greatest efficacie and strength to the will, the which sayth: I will cause you to walke in my iustifications, and that you shall keepe my iudgementes, and doe them.

God giueth vvill, that vve may doe that vvhich hee commaundeth.

Augu-

Augustine vpon the 31. psalme.

Without the grace of God, without the loue of eternitie, the lawe and the commaundements of God are a great and importable charge.

Augustine vpon the wordes of the Apostle. Sermon. 6.

O death where is thy sting? Graue where is thy victorie? The sting of death is sinne: and the strength of sinne is the lawe. For by forbidding, sinne is augmented, and not put out, the lawe hath giuen power to sinne, in commaunding only by the letter, and not in helping by the spirite. For the lawe commaundeth, and doth not accomplishe it, bicause ẏ the flesh doth resist it inuincibly where there is no grace. And the lawe was weakened thorowe the fleshe, bicause that the lawe is spirituall, but I am carnall. Howe then shall the lawe ayde and helpe me, in commaunding by the letter, the which giueth nothing by the spirite? It was made weake through the fleshe. What is that that God hath done, considering that it was a thing vnpossible to the lawe, and that it was weakened through the fleshe?

1. Cor. 15

The lawe weakened thorowe the fleshe. Rom. 7.

God sent his sonne, wherefore was the lawe weakened, and wherefore was that impossible to the lawe? It was weakened through the flesh. What is that then that God hath done, he hath sent the fleshe against the flesh: for he hath killed the sinne of the fleshe, and hath deliuered the substance of the fleshe. God hath sent his son in the similitude and likenesse of the fleshe of sinne: yea verilye in fleshe, but not in fleshe of sinne. That then which was impossible to the lawe, which caused preuarication, bicause the thought being vanquished, hath not yet foūd out the sauiour, wherein it was weakened throughe the fleshe. God hath sent his sonne in the likenesse of the fleshe of sinne, and hath condemned the sinne in the fleshe. Howe then had he no sinne, if sinne hath condemned sinne? The sacrifice for sinne was in the lawe called sinne, the lawe doth remember that thing, not once or twyce, but verye oftentimes. The sacrifices for sinnes were called sinnes, such sinne was Christ, for what shall we say, had he anye sinne? no, no he had no sinne, but he was the sinne, he was (I say) the sinne, according to the intelli-

..45.
..Christ
..thout
..and
..nde
..s
..ne.

intelligence and vnderstanding, bicause that he was the sacrifice for sinnes.

For what the lawe could not doe, in asmuche as it was weake, bicause of the fleshe: God sending his owne sonne in the similitude of sinful fleshe, and that for sinne, condemned sinne in the fleshe: That the righteousnesse of the lawe, might be fulfilled in vs, which walke not after the fleshe, but after the spirite. *Rom. 8.*

Jesus Christ is come to redeme them which were vnder the law, that we might receiue the adoption that belongeth vnto the naturall sonnes. *Galat. 4.*

Jesus Christ is the ende of the law, to iustifie all that beleeue. *Rom. 10.*

They being ignorant of the righteousnesse of God, and going about to establish their owne righteousnesse, haue not bene obedient vnto the righteousnesse of God. *Rom. 10.*

Is the lawe then against the promise of God? God forbide: For if there had bene a law giuen which could haue giuen life, then no doubte righteousnesse shoulde haue come by the lawe. *Galat. 3.*

The lawe was our schole maister to bring vs to Christ, that we might be made *Galat. 3.*

righte-

righteous by faith. But after that faith is come,now are we no longer vnder a schole maister.

Galat.5. Ye are gone quite from Christ as many as are iustified by the lawe, and are fallen from grace.

Galat.3. And this I say: That the law whiche began afterward, foure hundred and thirtye yeeres, cannot disanull the couenant, that was confirmed afore of God in respect of Christ,to make the promise of none effect: for if the inheritance come of the lawe, it commeth not then of promise,but God gaue it vnto Abraham by promise.

Galat.3. *Abac.2.* *Rom.1.* No man is iustified by the lawe in the sight of God, it is euident: For the iuste shall liue by fayth.

Galat.3. And the lawe is not of fayth: But the man that shall fulfill those things, shall liue in them.

Galat.3. *Deut.27.* For as many as are vnder the deedes of the lawe, are vnder the curse. For it is written: Cursed is euery man that continueth not in all things, whiche are written in the booke of the lawe to fulfill them.

Iames.2. Whosoeuer shall keepe the whole lawe, and yet fayleth in one poynt, he is gyltie

in

in all.

The iust man falleth seauen times in a daye. *Pro.24.*

S. Paule propounding the similitude of the infant that is an heire, and the allegorie of the children of Sara and Agar, declareth that the lawe hath ceased. *Gala.4.*

The fulfilling of the lawe, is loue towardes our neighbour. *Rom.13.* *Mat.22*

In abrogating through his flesh the hatred (that is to saye) the lawe of the commaundements which standeth in ceremonies, for to make of twayne, one new man in himselfe, so making peace. *Galat.5.* *Ephe.2.*

Christ hath put out the hande wryting of ceremonies that was agaynst vs, which I say, was contrarie vnto vs: he tooke it out of the way, and hath fastened it on his crosse. *Col.2.*

For by the lawe commeth the knowledge of sinne. *Rom.3.*

Lawe entred in, that offence shoulde increase. *Rom.5.*

I had not knowen what lust had ment, except the lawe had sayde: Thou shalte ot lust. *Rom.7.*

We knowe that the lawe is spirituall, *Rom.7.*

but

but I am carnall, solde vnder sinne.

Augustine in his.9.booke of confessi-ons.Chapter.13.

Woe be vnto mans life, although it be praysed neuer somuch, if the mercy of God drawen from it, thou wilt examine or discusse it.

Augustine in his first booke of Retractions.Chapter.19.

All the commaundemeutes of God are reputed to be done, when that whiche is not done is pardoned.

Augustine in his booke of the spirit and of the letter.Chap.36.

To loue god vvith all our heart, and our neighbour as our selfe, cannot be accomplished in this life.

This first commaundement of righteousnesse, by the which it is commaunded vs to loue God with all our heart, with all our soule, and with all our thought, the which is following the other, which is to loue our neighboure in this life, then wee shal fulfil them when we shall see thee face to face. But therefore it is commanded vs in this world, that we may be admonished and warned of that which we ought to aske through faith: afterwardes and by that same as farre as I can perceiue, hee profiteth much in this life in righteousnesse

nesse which ought to be ended, who in profiting knoweth how much he is farre from the perfection of righteousnesse.

Ambrose vpon the.3.Chapter of the Romaynes.

He that beleeueth in Christ, keepeth the lawe.

The similitude of the creditor: the goodman of the house willing to take account of his seruants, one was brought vnto him which ought him ten thousande talentes, and had not wherewith to paye, and yet notwithstanding woulde be payde.&c. *Mat.18.* It is asked againe of him vvhich hath not vvherevvith to pay, as also God demaundeth that vvhich vve cannot doe.

We are debters, not to the fleshe, to liue after the fleshe, but to the spirite. *Rom.8.*

Ye haue not receyued the spirite of bondage to feare anye more: but ye haue receyued the spirite of adoption, whereby we crye Abba, that is to say, father. *Rom.8.*

There is no feare in loue, but perfecte loue casteth out feare, for feare hath painfulnesse: and hee that feareth is not perfect in loue. We loue him, bicause he loued vs first. *1.Iohn.4.*

Augustine of free will and grace. Chapter.19.

John sayth: God is loue. And the Pe-

The Pelagians say that they haue loue of them selues. lagians also doe saye, that they haue God, not of God, but of themselues. And where they confesse that the lawe is giuen vs of God, they will haue the loue of themselues, and do giue no eare vnto the Apostle, which sayth: Knowledge maketh a man

1.*Cor*.8. swell, but loue edifieth. Also the Scripture sayth, that true fayth and holy doctrine are both of God. For it is written: From his face proceedeth wisedome and vnderstanding. And it is written: Loue

1.*Iohn*.4. commeth of God.

Augustine vpon the exposition to the Galat.3.Chap.

Galat.3. *Leuit*.18. *Rom*.10. *Ezec*.20. The lawe is not of fayth: but the man that shall fulfill those things, shall liue in them. He doth not say: he which shall doe the lawe, shall liue in it: insomuche that thou doe vnderstande, that the lawe in that place is put for the workes themselues. But those who doe liue in their workes, doe feare, that if they had not done them, they had bene stoned, or crucified, or suffred some other kinde of payne. Wherefore he sayeth: he whiche shall doe those things, shall liue in them, that is to saye, he shall haue the rewarde, to the ende not

to

to be punished with such death.

Saint Barnarde vpon the Canticles. Sermon. 50.

He which hath commanded, the commaundementes was not ignorant that the burthen of the commandement exceedeth the strength of men: but by that meanes, hath iudged that it is profitable to admonishe them that they are not able, and that they may plainely know to what ende of righteousnesse they must endeuor them selues with all their vertues: then in commanding impossible thinges, God hath not made men transgressors of the lawe: but hath made them humble, that euerye mouthe might be stopped, and that all the world be made subiect to God. For no flesh shall be iustified before him through the workes of the lawe: Euen so when wee haue receiued the commandement, and that we doe feele our default, we crye vnto heauen, and God hath mercye on vs: and knowe in that time, that he hath saued vs, not of the deedes of righteousnesse whiche we wrought: but of his mercy.

God knovveth verye vvell that vve cannot do that that he commandeth, but to keepe vs in humilitie.

Titus. 3. 2. Tim. 1.

Augustine against the aduersary of the lawe and of the Prophetes 2.booke.7.Chapter.

It was very needefull, that the lawe in the old Testament should be set forth vnto the proud, and vnto those which did truste in the vertue of their owne will: the which lawe doth not giue iustice, but it doth command it: and euen as those being wrapped in, through the death of preuarication, or transgressiõ, ought to haue their refuge to grace, the which only doth not commande, but also helpeth.

The blasphemers, of the heauenly wordes, doe thinke that the lawe whiche was giuen by Moyses was euill, bicause that it was called the administration of death, figured in letters of stone, not regarding that it is sayde, for those whiche doe thinke that the lawe was sufficient for their free will. &c.

The lawe was giuen by Moyses, but grace and truth came by Iesus Christ.

Did not Moyses giue you a lawe, and yet none of you keepeth the lawe?

Augu-

Augustine vpon Saint Iohn.3.Treatise.1. Chapter.

The lawe was giuen by Moyses,which helde them guiltie. For what sayeth the Apostle? The lawe entred in,that offence shoulde encrease. This is heauye vnto the proude, that is, that he sayth, to the ende that sinne may encrease. For they doe attribute muche to themselues, and doe assigne much to their strengths. And cannot accomplish righteousnesse,if he which hath commaunded it,helpe them not. God willing to tame their pride, gaue the law. As if he had sayde: beholde, accomplishe it, to the end that you doe not thinke your selues to be without him which commandeth: you are not without a commaunder, but there is no fulfiller.

The lawe giuen to the ende that sin abounde.

Rom.5.

Augustine of the spirite and the letter. Chapter.14

2.Cor.3.

Doth not S.Paule call that lawe written in his two tables, killing letters? When he sayth: the letter killeth: speaketh he only of the lawe of Circumcision, and of other olde Sacramentes alreadye abolished? Howe shall we esteeme it so, in as much as it is put in this lawe, thou shalt

The lavv by the vvhich vve cannot be iustified, is the lavv of the tvvo tables, and not the ceremoniall lavve.

Deut.5.

shalt not couet? By the which commaundement (although that it be holy, iuste and good) he saith that sinne hath deceiued it, and thereby killed: And what is that the letter killeth and the spirite quickeneth, but that the law cannot iustifie. &c. Immediatly afterwarde he saith, these my commaundementes if they are well kept as they are written, we must thinke that it appertaineth not to the lawe of workes, by the whiche none is iustified: but to the lawe of faith, by which the righteous man liueth. Who shall be of so wicked opinion to thinke that the administration of death figured in the tables of stone, is not saide of all the tenne commaundementes, but only of one, which appertayneth to the saboth? Where shall we put then this place, the lawe ingendreth wrath? For where no lawe is, there is no transgression, and sinne hath bene in the worlde euen untill the lawe, and sinne was not imputed when there was no lawe. &c. Read the chapter all at length. Reade also the same booke the. 31. chapter.

Of purgatory.

It is written in the Hebrewes the first chapter: which sonne being the brightnes of the glorye, and the ingraued forme of his person, bearing up all thinges with the worde of his power, hath by him selfe purged our sinnes, and sitteth at the right hand of that most highe maiestie. Heb.1.

Through Jesus Christ we haue redemption through his bloud, euen the forgiuenesse of sinnes, of his ritch grace. Ephe.1

In whom we haue redemption through his bloud, that is to saye, the forgiuenesse of sinnes, to reconcile all thinges unto him selfe, and to set at peace through the bloud of his crosse, both thinges in earth and thinges in heauen. Col.1.

For asmuch as ye knowe how that ye were not redemed with corruptible things as siluer and golde, from your vaine conuersation, which ye receyued by the traditions of the fathers: but with the precious bloud of Christ, as of a lambe undefiled, and without spot. 1.Pet.1

1. Iohn. 1. And the bloud of Jesus Christ his son clenseth vs from all sinne.

Apoc. 1. Unto him that loued vs and washed vs from our sinnes in his bloud.

Heb. 9. If the bloud of bulles, and of goates and the ashes of an heyfar sprinkled, sanctifieth them that are vncleane, as touching the purifying of the flesh: how much more shall the bloud of Christ which through the eternall spirite offered him selfe without spot to God, purge your conscience from dead workes, for to serue the liuing God?

Esay 43. Esay speaking in the person of God saith, it is I, it is I only that for mine owne selfe sake doe away thine offences and forget thy sinnes.

Rom. 8. For I confirme, that the afflictions of this life are not worthy of the glory which shall be shewed vnto vs.

Titus. 3. After that the kindnesse and loue of our sauiour God to manward appeared, not of the deedes of righteousnesse whiche we wrought: but of his mercy he saued vs, by the fountayne of the newe byrth, and with the renuing of the holy Ghost.

VVe are saued by gods mercie, and not by the fire of purgatorie.

Esay. 1. Nowe goe to (saith the Lorde) we wil talke

talke togither. Is it not so? Though your sinnes be as redde as scarlet, shall they not be whyter then snowe? And thoughe they were like purple shall they not by like white wooll?

And hee put no difference betweene them and vs, seeing that with faith he purified their heartes. *Act.* 15.

There is no condemnation to them which are in Christ Iesus. *Rom.* 8.

Iesus Christ saith, verely verely I say vnto you, he that heareth my wordes, and beleeueth on him that sent me hath euerlasting life, and shall not come into damnation, but is escaped from death vnto life. VVe cannot go into purgatorie vncondemned. *Iohn.* 5.

Againe, he that shall beleeue and bee baptised shall be saued. *Mar.* 16.

Also enter in at the straite gate, for wyde is the gate, and broad is the way that leadeth to destruction: and many there be which goe in there at. *Mat.* 7. There is but tvvo vvayes.

Obiection.

Agree with thine aduersarie quicklye, whiles thou art in the way with him, least thine aduersarie deliuer thee to the iudge, and the iudge deliuer thee to the sergeant, and then thou be cast into prison. Verily *Math.* 5. *Luc.* 12.

I saye vnto thee, thou shalt not come out thence, till thou hast payde the vtmost farthing.

Aunswere.

Saint Ambrose sayth vpon these wordes of Saint Mathewe: When thou shalt go vnto the magistrate, &c. Chrysostome vpon S. Mathewe. 5. Homelie. 10. Doth expounde it of the reconciliation. And Theophilact vpon the same place, sayth as much. Likewise S. Hilarie vnderstandeth it so in his Canons.

Obiection.

Verily I saye vnto thee, thou shalt not come out thence, till thou hast payde the vtmost farthing.

Answere.

Mat. 1. In the first of S. Mathewe it is sayde, that Joseph knewe not his wife, till shee had brought forth hir first borne sonne.

S. Augustine expoundeth that place by the Rauen that Noe did sende forth: and sayth that the Rauen did neuer returne agayne: euen so Joseph neuer knewe the *Psal.* 110. virgin Marie, for she is a virgin.

Act. 2. Also: Sit thou on my right hande vn-
Heb. 1. till I make thine enimies thy footestoole.

Ob-

Obiection.

Whosoeuer shall speake agaynst the sonne of man, it shall be forgiuen him: but whosoeuer shall speake agaynst the holye ghost, it shall not be forgiuen him, neyther in this worlde, neyther in the worlde to come. *Mat.12.* *Mar.3.*

Aunswere.

Chrysostome in the 12. of S. Mathewe, Homely 24. expoundeth it thus: Forasmuche as this sinne is not veniall, you shall be grieuously punished, both in this lyfe, and in the life to come.

Saint Augustine vpon Genesis.
10. baoke.

It is better to doubt of secrete things, than to pleade of incertayne things. I doe not doubt but that we must vnderstande that the riche man was in most cruell torments, and that poore Lazarus in ioy. &c. *Luc.16.*

Secret thinges not to be reuealed.

Thoughe the righteous bee ouertaken with death, yet shall he be in rest. *Sapien.4.*

The soules of the righteous are in the hande of God, and the payne of death shall not touch them. In the sight of the vnwise they appeare to die, and their ende is taken for very destruction. The waye of the *Sapien.3.* *Deut.33.*

righteous is iudged to be vtter destruction, but they are in rest.

Luc.8. Oure Lorde sayde vnto the woman: Daughter be of good comforte, thy fayth hath made thee whole, go in peace.

Luc.23. Agayne vnto the theefe: Uerily I saye vnto thee, to day shalt thou be with me in paradyse.

Eccles.12. Man after his death, goeth to his long home. Also the bodie shall returne agayne vnto the earth from whence it came, and the spirite shall returne vnto God whiche gaue it.

Psal.146. Put not your trust in Princes, nor in any childe of man, for there is no helpe in them. For when the breath of man goeth forth, he shall turne agayne to his earth, and so all his thoughts perishe.

1.Thes.4. S.Paul speaking of the dead, maketh no mention of purgatorie.

I woulde not brethren haue you ignorant concerning them which are fallen a sleepe, that ye sorrowe not as other doe which haue no hope. For if we beleue that Iesus died, and rose agayne: euen so they also which sleepe in Iesus, God will bring with him.

Augu-

Augustine of the Citie of God. 13. boke. 9. Chapter.

The soules of ye good men being seperated from the bodie are at rest, and we must nothing at all doubt of it. But those of the wicked are punished vntil that the bodie of those shall ryse againe to eternall lyfe, and of those here to eternal death, which is called the seconde death.

Irenæus sayth as much, writing against the hereticke Ualentine.

Augustine agaynst the Pelagians. 5. booke.

There is but two wayes, that is, one to damnation, and one to saluation.

Augustine in his Enchiridion. 108. Chapter.

The time then which is betwene ye death of man, and the latter resurrection, the soules are receyued into secrete receptacles, euen as euery one is worthy, eyther of rest, or of miserie, according to that that he hath deserued when it liued in the flesh.

The gloser Gratian vpon those vvords, saith as much.

Augustine of the Citie of God. 10. boke. 24. Chapter.

Speaking vnto *Porphyrius* a Platonist: He hath not known Iesus Christ to be

Iesus Christ is our purgatorie.

be the beginning, throughe whose incarnation we are purged.

In the same booke. Chapter. 22.

We haue then victorie in his name, who hath taken mans fleshe, and hath liued without sinne, to the ende that he being the Priest and the sacrifice, was made the forgiuenesse of sinnes, that is to saye: by the mediator of God and men, the man Iesus Christ, through whom the purgation of our sinnes is made & we are restored agayne with God. For men are not seperated from God but through sinne: of which the purgation is not done in our life through our vertue, but through Gods diuine mercie, through his clemencie, not through our power, for the same vertue which is called ours, whatsoeuer it be, is graunted vnto vs through his goodnesse.

1. Tim. 2.

Men are not seperated from God but through sinne.

Reade Lactantius Firmianus 6. booke 3. Chapter of the institutions agaynst the Gentiles and Idolaters: There is but two wayes, the one of vertue, the other of sinne, which leadeth vnto hell.

Augustine of the Trinitie. 4. booke. 13. Chapter.

By his death, that is to saye, throughe one

one onely and moste true sacrifice whiche hath bene offered for vs, he hath purged, and hath abolished and put out all the faultes, for the whiche the principalities and powers doe detayne vs, for to bee punished: and hath called vs through his resurrection vnto a newe lyfe, we which are predestinated: he hath iustified those whom he called, and hath glorified them whome he iustified. Rom. 8.

Augustine in his Enchiridion vnto Laurence. Chapter. 66.

Some men beleeue, that those also whiche haue not abandoned the name of Christ, and whiche haue bene baptised in his Churche, and haue not bene cut of from the same through any schisme or heresies, that in whatsoeuer sinnes they haue liued, the which they haue not defaced and blotted out through penaunce, nor redeemed through almes, but shall perseuer and continue in them continually vntil the last day of this life, shall be saued through the fire, Although that according to the greatnesse of their sinnes and misdeedes, that fire shall be diuturnall, not eternall. But me thinketh that those which beleeue that,

Sinnes not purged in the fire of purgatorie.

that, and notwithstanding are catholikes, are deceyued through mans beneuolence. For the holy Scripture, if one doe loke in it, answereth an other thing.

S. Ierome vpon the Prophet Esay. 65. Chapter.

He which shall not obtayne pardon of his sinnes whilst that he liueth in this body, and shall so depart out of this life, hee perisheth to God, and leaueth to bee, although ẏ he ryse vnto himselfe in paines.

Augustine writing vnto Macedonius. 54. Epistle.

There is no other place for to correcte the manners then in this life, for after this life euery one shall haue that he hath here gotten.

Againe, in this world the mercye of God helpeth those which doe repent, but in the world to come repentance profiteth not, but we must render and giue account of our workes.

Repentance hath no place but in this life.

Libertie of repentance is only giuen vnto vs in this life: after the death there is no licence of correction, nowe is the time of mercye, afterward shall be the time of iudgement.

Augu-

Augustine vpon S. Iohn.
12.*treatise.*

Expounding the wordes of Christ, hee which beleeueth not is already iudged: Also the iudgement is not yet appeared, but the iudgement is already done. And the Lorde knoweth those which are his: and knoweth those which shall abyde, looking for the crowne of glorye, and those whiche abyde looking for the fire. *2.Tim.2*

S. Chrysostome in the.2.sermon of Lazarus.

Make readye the workes for the ende, and prepare thy selfe to the waye: And if thou hast taken by violence anye thing from anye man restore it and make restitution, and saye with *Zachæus*, if I haue taken any thing from any man by forged cauillation, I restore it him foure double: And if thou art angry with any man, reconcile thy selfe before that thou cummest to iudgemente: paye here all thinges, to the ende that without trouble or molestation thou mayest see that iudgement: All the while that we be here in this life, we haue a most faire and shining hope: but when we shall be departed and deade, *Luk.19.* VVhile vve be here in this life, vve haue good hope, but after there is no place for to vvash & purge sinnes

we

we shall no more repent, nor doe penance, nor washe and clense the sinnes that wee haue committed. Afterwardes he saith, truly he which shall not in this lyfe washe and clense his sinnes, in the other lyfe he shall finde no consolation.

Saint Cyprian agaynst Demetrian.
1. Treatise.

Beleeue, and ye shall liue, and ye which doe persecute vs for a certayne time, bee ioyfull with vs for euer. When one shall depart from hence, he shall haue no more place of repentaunce, nor no more effect of satisfaction: Here is the lyfe lost or wonne. Here is conquered the eternall health, through the veneration of God, and through the fruite of faith: and so long as one shall abyde in this lyfe, no repentance is to late. &c.

S. Ierome in his. 7. Tome vpon Ecclesiastes. 9. Chapter.

Bicause that before he hath sayde, that the heartes of men are full of wickednesse and shame, and after that all these things doe ende when they doe die: nowe he maketh an ende of the same, and repeateth, that

that as long as men doe liue, they may be made righteous, but no occasion of good workes is giuen after death. For the sinner that is alyue, maye be better than the righteous whiche is deade. If he will passe into the vertues of him: or verily he maye be better than he which reioyceth in his wickednesse, and in his strength and shame, the which is deade: and maye be better than he, howe poore or base socuer he be. Wherefore? Bicause that those that be liuing, for feare of death, may doe good workes. But the deade can nothing adde to that that they haue once caried away with them from this life. &c.

As long man liu he may profite, but not after he is deade.

Chrysostome vnto the people homily. 69. and. 70. and vpon S. Iohn. 11. Chap. and vpon the Hebrues. 2. chapter. 4. Homelye.

Let vs not bewayle without reason those that are deade, but let vs bewayle those which are dead in sinne. Those are worthy of sorowe and of teares. For what hope hath he to be gone with his sinnes, where it is not giuen him to put of the sinnes?

There is no hope to bee gone from this life, vvhere it is not giuen to put of sinnes

Ambrose

Ambrose in the first Tome of the goodnesse of the dead. chap. 2.

The holy man Dauid, hasted him selfe to goe out of the place of his pilgrimage, saying I am a stranger and a pilgrimme with thee, as all my forefathers were: and therefore as a pilgrimme he hasteth him to goe to that countrey common to all the Saintes, in asking (bicause of the filthynesse of that tarying) that his sinns should be pardoned him before that he did depart from this life: for he that shall not receiue here forgiuenesse of his sinnes: he shal not haue it in the other life. And he shall not haue it, for he cannot come to eternall life, bicause that eternal life is the forgiuenesse of sinnes: and therefore he saith, pardon me that I may be comforted before that I goe, and that I be no more: wherefore then doe we desire so greatly this life? In the which the longer that any one shall be in it, so much the more is he charged with the more sinnes. &c.

S. Ierome in the Epistle of the Galatians. 6. Chapter.

This little sentence doth declare vnto vs (although that it be somewhat obscure) a newe a newe doctrine and hidde, that is when we be in this world we may helpe our selues togither, aswell through prayers as through counsell, when notwithstanding when we shall come before the consistorye and iudgement of God, neyther Daniell, no nor yet Iob, can praye for any one, for euery one shall beare his burthen.

The Canon of the.3.councell of Toledo. Chapter.22.and.23.2.chap. which beginneth,

Qui diu.

We doe commaund that those whiche depart out of this life, through Gods calling, should be carryed to the earth with psalmes only, and not the song of those which doe sing: for we doe forbyd altogither that prayer of the funeralles which they haue accustomed to sing commonly for the dead. That it suffiseth that they doe giue vnto the bodyes of the christians the seruice of the heauenly songes, in hope of the resurrection.

The counsel of Toledo doth forbid prayer for the deade.

Epiphanius in his.2.booke Tome.1. Heresy.59.

Upon that place of the songes. O my Doue come out of the caues of the rockes, *Canti.2.*

which toucheth the wall, out of the holes of the rocke, in the loue of Christ, and in the mercy of the Lord: These are ẏ caues of the rockes of faith, of hope and veritie, touching the wall. That is to say before that the gate be shut, before that the King being within the wall receiueth no person vnto him, after the departing from hence and death, when the gates are no more, touching the wall, but are shut, and it is no more lawfull to correct. And afterward he saith, there is neither fasting nor almes nor penance nor righteousnesse neyther good nor euill, which doth profite or hurte after that one is dead. For Lazarus did not come vnto the ritch man, nor the riche man vnto Lazarus: And the rich did not receiue that that he demaunded, although that he demaunded it through great prayer of the mercifull Abraham: for the garners and cellers are shut vp, and the time is accomplished, and the combat ended, and those whiche haue fought, doe rest themselues, &c.

Nothing can profite after death.

Luke. 16.

S. Cyprian in his sermon of mortalitie.

We must not thinke that the deathe of the wicked is of such forme and condition

as

as is of the good men. The good men are called to rest and solace, the wicked and uniust to paynes and tormentes: safegarde and defence is sodainlye giuen unto the faythfull, and tormentes unto the unfaythfull. We are verye much unthankfull for the heauenly benefites, not acknowledging that which is giuen unto vs. &c. Afterward he sayth: we ought not to mourne for our brethren deliuered frō this world, through Gods vocation: Forasmuche as I doe knowe very well that they are not vtterly lost, but are onely sent before, preceding those which depart, and that wee ought to desire their companie, and not to bewayle them, euen as those do which go by lande or by sea, and that we must not here take blacke robes, in asmuch as they haue already taken vpon them whyte vestures. &c.

Black vvedes not to bee vvorne in funerals.

Augustine of the Citie of God. 1. *booke*, 12. *&* 13. *Chapters, and in the* 4. *of his sentences*, 45. *Distinction.*

It is also written in the Decretals, and also by the Maister of the sentences. The diligence and labor that some take about funerals, the ornament and decking of burials, the pompe of obsequies and burials, are more for to comforte the liuing, than for to ayde the deade. If the costly burying doth profite any thing vnto the wicked, the vyle and contemptible sepulture shall hurt the good, or if they remayne vnburied. &c.

Gregorie Neocæsarian vpon Eccles. Chapter. 9.

Nothing common vvith the deade.

Those whiche are departed out of this worlde, haue no more any thing common with our affayres.

Luc. 16.

And it was so that the begger dyed, and was caryed by the angels into Abrahams bosome. The riche man also dyed, and was buried. &c.

Chrysostome vpon the Epistle vnto the Hebrues. Chap. 13.

No place for buriall ought to be sought.

In what place soeuer we be buried, the earth is the Lordes, and all that therein is, that which a man ought to doe, let him doe it. But to bewayle, weepe, and lament for those whiche depart oute of this lyfe, commeth of weakenesse, and for lacke of courage, and we cannot vnderstand it, but that it cometh of none other thing, but of a despayre of the resurrection to come. &c.

1. Thes. 4.

Dauid

Dauid prayed for his chylde that was sicke, he fasted lying vpon the grounde: But when they tolde him that he was deade, he rose vp and ceased. Nowe the chylde dyed without Circumcision, the which Circumcision was vnto them, as Baptisme is vnto vs, yet Dauid did not despaire of the saluation of the chylde. 2.Sam.12 1.Cor.7.

Obiection.

The Priestes say that we must offer for the deade.

S. Cyprian in the.4. booke of Epistles. 5.Epistle.

Writing of Celerin which hath had almost all his houshoulde martyred and put to death for ye name of Iesus Christ, sayth thus: It is alreadye a long time sithence that Celerin his grandmother hath bene crowned for a martyr, his vncle by the father, and Laurence his vncle by the mother, & Ignatius which once haue fought, and haue bene men of armes in worldlye affayres: but being true and tryed men of armes to fight in Gods quarrel, hauing vanquished the diuell through the confession of Christ, haue obteyned of the Lorde rewards and crownes through a glorious

The diuell is ouercome through the confession of Christ.

suffering: We doe offer alwayes (as you doe remember well inough) sacrifice for them, as often as we doe celebrate the passions of the martyrs: and that we do make commemorations of their dayes yearely.

To offer is here taken for giuing of thankes.

See diligently the commemoration that the priestes doe make for the dead, which is the.10.part of the Canon.

Memento etiam domine, famulorum, famularumque tuarum, N. qui nos præcesserũt cum signo fidei, & dormiunt in somno pacis: ✠ ipsis domine, & omnibus in Christo quiescentibus, locum refrigerij, lucis & pacis, vt indulgeas deprecamur per eundem dominum nostrum. Amen.

That is to say, remember O Lorde thy menseruauntes and maydseruauntes N. which haue gone before vs with the signe of faith, and do sleepe in peace: ✠ vnto them O Lorde, and vnto all those whiche doe reste in Christe, we desire thee that thou wylt giue them place of comforte, through the same Christe our Lord amen.

The Priests doe here agaynst their doctrine, in praying for the virgin Marie, and for all the Apostles & Martyrs vvhich are departed vvith the signe of fayth.

Aunswere.

In the 4. of the sentences, Distinction 45. and the 13. glose.

Iniuriam facit martyri, qui orat pro martyre

That

That is to say, he which prayeth for a Martyr doth iniury and wrong vnto the Martyr.

S. Cyprian in his. 4. booke of baptisme. and the maister of the sentences 4. distinct. 4. Chapter.

If all the deaths and all the tormentes, that all men the Patryarckes, Prophets, Apostles, Martyrs, and confessors haue euer suffered should be put togither: they shall not be sufficient to put out the leaste sinne of the world.

Knowe ye not that the vnrighteous shal not inherite the kingdome of God: Bee not deceiued: neyther fornicators, neyther idolaters, neyther aduouterers, neyther wantons, neyther abusers of them selues with the mankinde, neyther theeues, neyther couetous, neyther dronkardes, neyther euill speakers, neyther extorcioners shall inherite the kingdome of God. And such were some of you, but ye are washed, but ye are sanctified, but ye are iustified in the name of the Lord Iesus, and by the spirite of our God. *1. Cor. 6*

Christe loued the church, and gaue him selfe for it, to sanctifie it, and clensed it in *Ephe. 5.*

the washing of water through the worde. To make it vnto him selfe a glorious church, without spot or wrincle, or anye such thing: but that it should be holy and without blame.

Iohn.3. Marke vvell he sayth not of fire.

Jesus Christ sayth, verely verely I doe saye vnto you, except that a man be begotten of water and of the spirite, he cannot enter into the kingdome of heauen.

Math.3. Iesus Christ purgeth his, and not the fire.

Saint John Baptist sayde of Jesus Christe, he shall baptise you with the holy Ghoste and with fire, which hath his fanne in his hand, and will make cleane his floure, and gather the wheate into his garner, but will burne the chaffe with vnquencheable fire.

Iohn.15.

Jesus Christ saith, nowe are ye cleane through the wordes which I haue spoken vnto you.

Iohn.13.

Also Peter saide vnto Jesus: thou shalt neuer washe my feete. Jesus sayde vnto him, if I doe not washe thee, thou shalt not haue parte with me: Peter saide vnto him Lord not my feete only, but also my hands and my head. Jesus sayd vnto him, he that is washed, needeth not saue to washe his feete but is cleane euery whit.

He

He shall put downe our wickednesse, and caste all our sinnes into the bottome of the sea. *Mich.7*

Raymonde sayth:

Gratia magna dei veniamnon dimidiabit,
Aut nihil aut totum propitiando dabit.

That is to say, God doth not pardon the moytie or halfe: but his great mercye pardoneth all or nothing.

Moyses and Saint Paule doe say, our God is a consuming fire. *Heb.12. Deut.4.*

The Pope in his Canons in the Glose of Baptisme and of his effect. Chap. which beginneth, maiores Causas.

The Pope sayth that God doth not giue pardon to the moytie, and so there is no purgatorie.

Larga dei pietas veniam non dimidiabit.
Nam nihil aut totũ te lachrymante dabit.

That is to say: the great goodnesse of God wyll not giue pardon for the moyte: for when thou commest unto him with teares and weepings, he will giue thee all or nothing.

Moyses saith, The workes of God are perfect. *Deut.32.*

O Lorde thou forgiuest all our sinnes. *Oseas. 14.*

Chry-

Chrysostome in the.2.homily vpon the 50.psalme.

When one demandeth mercy, that is that he might not be examined of his sinne, to the end he should not be handled according to the rigour of righteousnesse, and to the ende that all punishment may cease: for where there is mercie, there is no more hell fire, neyther rigour nor paine.

VVhere ther is mercie, there is no more hell fire, rigour, nor payne.

Chrysostome in his sermon of penance and confession.

The Lord doth punish vs for our sinnes, not for to take anye recompence of oure sinnes, but for to aduise vs of things to come.

S. Ambrose vpon S. Luke, of repentance. first distinction, Chapter which beginneth Petrus.

Peter was sorowfull and did lament, for he hath transgressed as man. I doe not finde what he sayde, I doe knowe verye well that he hath wept, I doe reade of his teares, and not of his satisfaction.

The Priestes doe sing in the beginning, or prose of those that be deade. such wordes.

Rex tremendæ maiestatis, qui saluandos

saluas

saluas gratis, salua me fons pietatis.

That is to saye: O redoubtable king in maiestie, whiche doest saue freely those which ought to be saued, saue me O fountayne of goodnesse.

The Priests vvoulde be saued thorovve grace according to their song.

Blessed are the deade, which hereafter die in the Lorde, euen so sayth the spirite. For bicause they rest from their labours, and their works followe them. *Apoc.14.*

Of a truth he onely taketh away our infirmitie, and beareth our payne: yet wee shall iudge him as though he were plaged and cast downe of God, where as he (notwithstanding) shall be wondred at for our offences, and smitten for our wickednesse. For the payne of our punishment shall be layde vpon him, and with his wounds shal we be healed. *Esay.53.*

Iesus Christ taketh avvay our infirmities, he pardoneth them the fault & the payne.

As concerning the place of S. Paule, 1.Cor.3. That euery one shall be saued, as it were by the fire, S. Augustine (in his boke of the Citie of God, the 21. booke, Chapter.26. And in his treatise of fayth and of workes, Chapter.16. And in his Enchiridion, Chapter 28.) expoundeth it of the fire of tribulacion, and of the crosse, and persecutions of this worlde, by the which *1.Cor.3.*

Hovve saint Augustine expoundeth this place, the 1. of the Cor.3.

which the Lorde examineth those that be his.

Gregory vpon Iob the.29.Chapter. And in his morals the.28.booke the.17. chap. And in the.16. distinct. Chap. whith beginneth Canones glossæ atque.

Gregorie sayth that the bookes of the Machabees are not canonicall.

As touching the bookes of the Machabees the church doth not hold them for canonicall, saying: we doe nothing vnorderly if we bring in the examples of the bookes, which although that they be not canonicall yet neuerthelesse doe serue for the edification of the churche.

S. Augustine of the citie of God.18.booke. 36.Chapter. And of christian doctrine.2.booke.8.chapter.

Speaking of the number of the times which haue bene sithence the returne from Babilon, vntill the comming of Iesus Christe: the count and computation of them are not found in the holy Scripturs, which are called canonical but in the other among whom are the bookes of the Machabees.

S. Ierome in the Epistle written vnto Chromatius and Heliodorus bishops. And also in the Byble before the booke of the Prouerbes.

The Churche doth reade the bookes of the Machabees: but it doth not receiue them as canonicall. Also, although that the Church doth reade the bookes of Iudith, Tobie, and of the Machabees: yet neuerthelesse the Church doth not receyue them as Canonicall scripture. And so the Church may read these two bokes for the edification of the people, but not for to confirme ecclesiasticall doctrine.

Ierome in his Prologue Galeatus which is set before the booke of the Kings.

Sayth, that he hath neuer founde the seconde booke of the Machabees in the Hebue tongue, but he hath founde it in the Greeke tongue.

And writing against the Pelagians.

The seconde booke of the Machabees is written by Iosephus the Historiographer.

Ierome vnto Chromatius in the 5. Distinct. Chapter which beginneth, Sancta.

The Counsell of Laodicea, the 59. chap. doth not name them in the roll of the canonicall Scriptures, and reciteth that which is of other canonicall bookes amongst his other Decretals.

The author of the boke of ẏ Machabees in the ende of the sayde booke, doth praye that if he haue sayde any thing whiche is not good, to pardon him: Let vs then willingly pardon his faultes.

Of honoring and worshipping of Saintes.

S. Augustine of true religion. The last Chapter.

That our religion be not after our fantasie.

Let vs not loue the outwarde and visible spectacles, for feare that in erring and straying from the truth, and in louing the shadowes, wee bee cast into darkenesse. That our religion be not after our fantasies. For whatsoeuer truth it be, it is better than all that our will can feyne and inuent. That our religion be not the worship-shipping of deade men. For if they haue liued faythfully, they are not suche to demaunde and aske suche honor, but they woulde that wee shoulde honor him, by whom they being illuminated, are gladde that we shall be seruaunts with them, of their holy lyfe. We ought then to honour them bicause of their imitation, and not to adore and worshippe them bicause of their religion. For the same was done through temporall dispensation for our helth, that the vertue of God, and the immutable wysedome of God which is of one substance, which is coeternall to the father, toke on him mans nature, by the which he would teach vs that man ought to honor the thing which ought to be honored of all creatures, hauing vnderstanding and reason. And let vs also beleeue that the verye Angells them selues the most good and excellent administrators of God, woulde it so, to wete that we should honor one onely God with them, through whose contemplation they are blessed. For we are not blessed in seeing and beholding the Angells, but in beholding the verytie, by the which we doe loue the Angells, and doe

Our religion is not the veneration of dead men.

The Aungelles, the Saints vvold not that vve should honour them, but God.

reioyce

reioyce of them: wherefore we doe honor them through loue and charytie and not through seruice.&c. And let vs not buylde any temples for them, for they woulde not be so honoured of vs: for that they doe knowe when wee bee good, wee are the temples of the soueraigne God: And so it is rightly written, that it was forbydden to men by the Angels, that they should not worshippe them, but one only God, vnder whome they all were togither seruauntes.

Apoc.19.

Esther.13 I doe greatly feare least that I shoulde set the honor of a man in the steede of the glory of God, and that I woulde worship none but only thee my God.

Act.10. Cornelius fell downe at Peters feete, and worshipped him: But Peter tooke him vp saying, stand vp, for euen I my selfe am a man.

Act.14. Barnabas and Paule sayde vnto the people whiche would haue done sacrifice vnto them. O men, why doe ye these thinges: we are mortall men like vnto you, and preache vnto you, that ye shoulde turne from these vayne Idoles vnto the liuing God, which made heauen and earth

VVe ought not to doe sacrifice vnto the saints, nor to offer vnto them, for they are but men.

and

and the sea, and all thinges that are in them.

Chrysostome vpon S. Mathewe.45.homilye.23. Chapter.

Howe shoulde ye escape the damnation of hell? shal that be in buylding the sepulchres of Saintes? or rather in making cleane your heartes from malyce? dooth God iudge as man doth? man iudgeth man in workes, but God iudgeth the heart. But what is that righteousnesse to honor the Saintes, and to contemne their holynesse? The first degree of fidelitie is to loue sanctite, afterwardes the Saintes, for the Saintes haue not bene before holynesse, but holynesse hath bene before the Saintes. He then without cause doth honor the righteous, which despiseth righteousnesse. Shall the Saintes whose sepulcres ye decke and beutifie deliuer you? The Saintes cannot be the freendes of those to whome God is an enemye? Can the houshold be in peace and quietnesse, when the Lord is an aduersarye? Howe can ye doe it? will the bare name deliuer you? for asmuch as possible ye thinke, that ye are the people of God? What profiteth

The Saints giue no ayde vvhere God hateth.

it the harlot if shee haue the name of a chast woman? Euen so doth it not profite the sinner, to be called the seruant of God. In the same towardes the ende he sayth howe can ye escape the damnation of hell? In buylding of churches, and not holding the ende of the ecclesiasticall veritie? In reading the Scriptures, and not beleuing them? In naming the Prophets Apostls and Martyrs and not following the works of the Martyrs nor their confession, &c.

The iudgement of god cannot be auoyded in building of Churches.

Augustine vpon Saint Iohn.23. Treatise.5. Chapter.

This is the Christian religion, that one God onely be adored and worshipped, and not many Gods. For nothing maketh the soule blessed, but one onely God. It is made blessed through the participation of God, and the soule being feeble, is not made blessed through the participation of an holy soule, and also the holy soule is not made blessed through the participation of an angel; but if the weake and feble soule requireth to be made blessed, it must demaunde that whereof the holye soule is made blessed. For thou shalt not be made blessed by an angel, but thou shalt be made

VVe cannot bee made blessed by Saints nor by Angels.

blessed by him of whome also the angell is made blessed.

Augustine of the Citie of God. 10.booke.

They which are constituted immortall and blessed in the heauenly places, who togither doe reioyce themselues of the participation of their creator, the which are made strong through his eternitie, by good reason woulde not that wee shoulde make any sacrifice vnto them, but onely vnto him of whom they doe acknowledge themselues with vs to bee the sacrifice. For with them we are togither the Citie of God, of the whiche it is sayde in the Psalme: Very excellent things are spoken of thee, O thou Citie of God.&c. *Psal.87.*

Augustine in his 10.booke of the Citie of God. 16.Chapter.

Then if there be any angels which desire that any shoulde offer vnto them sacrifice, truly we ought to preferre those which doe not desire that one shoulde sacrifice vnto them, but vnto God the creator of all, vnto whom they serue. For therby they shewe how entire the loue is that they doe beare vnto vs: for they pretende

Reade Lactantius Firmianus of his heauenly institutions, 2.booke, 7.chapter.

not to make vs subiecte vnto them tho-rowe sacrifice, but vnto him, throughe whose contemplation they are also blessed, and they do go about to leade vs vnto him from whom they themselues are not turned.

Augustine of the Citie of God.8.booke. Chapter.27.

We doe not ordayne for the Martyrs, temples, neyther sacrifices of diuine seruice: for they are not our God, but their God is ours. Truly we will honor their memorials, as of the holye men of God which haue fought for the truth, euen vnto death, that true religion might bee knowne, and that false religions might be vanquished.

Epiphanius agaynst the Colliridians.

VVe ought not to vvorship the virgin Marie.

The bodie of the virgin Marie was in dede holy, neuerthelesse she was not God. Of truth the virgin was a virgin, and honoured, neuerthelesse she was not put forth to be worshipped, but she hirselfe worshipped him, who according to the fleshe proceeded and was borne of hir.

Augustine in his booke of the care and sorowfulnesse that men ought to haue for the deade.

Chap.13.

If the soules of the deade were present with those of the liuing, when we doe see them in dreames, they woulde speake vnto vs. And without speaking of others, my holy mother, who hath followed me by sea and by lande; for to liue with me, woulde not forsake me one night. God forbydde that through the most blessed life in which she is, it shoulde chaunce that she woulde not comfort hir sorrowfull sonne (when I haue any anguishe in mine heart) whome she loued dearely, whome she would neuer see sorrowfull. But truly that which holye Dauid sayth, is true: My father and mother haue forsaken me, but the Lorde hath taken me vp. If then our fathers haue forsaken vs, howe are they present at our affayres or doings? And if our parents are not present, who are they among the dead which doe knowe what we doe or suffer? The Prophet Esay sayth: Thou art our father, for Abraham knew not vs, neyther is Israell acquainted with vs. If the wor-

The saints vvhich are in heauen, haue no knovvledge of our affaires.

Psal.27.

Esay.63.

thie Patriarkes were ignorant, or knewe not the things whiche the people of the worlde did which were engendred and begotten of them, vnto whome that people were promised, that he wold come of their lyne and stocke, bicause they haue beleeued in God, and was promised that the people themselues shoulde come of their roote or stocke. Howe is it possible that the deade shoulde knowe and helpe the affayres of the liuing? Howe doe we saye that it happened well vnto them which are departed, to die before that the euilles shoulde come which are come after their decease, if it be so that after their death they perceyue all things which shall happen in the calamitie of mans lyfe? Shall it be possible that wee can erre in saying and thinking those to be in rest, which are tormented with the lyfe of the liuing, whiche is full of ingratitude? What is that then that God promised vnto the most holyest king Iosias for a great benefite? That is, that he shoulde die before the euils whiche shoulde happen vnto that place, and vnto that people should come, and that to ye end he shoulde not see them. The words of the Lorde

It is not posśible that the dead can in any thing helpe the liuing.

Lorde are these: Thus sayeth the Lorde God of Israel, as touching the wordes which thou heardest: bicause thine heart did melt, and thou didst humble thy selfe before the Lorde, when thou heardest what I spake agaynst this place, and the inhabiters of the same, howe it shoulde be destroyed and made accursed, and tarest thy clothes and didst weepe before me: of that also I haue hearde, sayth the Lorde. And therefore see I will receyue thee vnto thy fathers, and will fet thee vnto thy graue in peace, thyne eyes shall see none of the euill which I will bring vpon this place. Iosias being afraid of Gods threatnings, did weepe, and rent his clothes, and beleeued all the euilles to come, by the death which shoulde come, bicause that by that meanes he shoulde rest in peace: in suche sort that he shall not see all those things. Then the soules of the deade are in one place, where they see not the thinges which are done or chaunced in the lyfe of men. 2.*Reg*.22

The soules departed, see not the things vvhiche are done in this life.

S. Ierome in his commentary vpon Ezechiel. 16. Chapter.

The righteousnesse of the righteous,

shall be vpon him, and the wickednesse of the wicked shall dwell vpon him: euerye one shall die in his owne sinne, and shal be saued through his righteousnesse. And the Iewes doe saye in vayne, Abraham is our father, forasmuch as they haue not the workes of Abraham: and if there bee any thing whereon we must put our trust, let vs haue our hope and trust in the Lorde onely: for the man is cursed whiche putteth his trust in man, yea though he be holy yea and also a Prophet. We doe reade in the Scripture: put not your truste in Princes nor in the sonnes of men. And againe: It is good to truste in the Lorde rather then in Princes, not only in the Princes of the worlde, but also in the Prelates of the churche, who if they be righteous, will saue only their soules.

VVe ought to put our trust in no Saints, but in God only

Ierem. 17.

Psal. 146.

Genes. 22. God sayde vnto Abraham, in thy seede shall all the nations of the earth be blessed.

Galat. 3. S. Paule saith that the seede is Christ.

Act. 4. Among men there is giuen none other name vnder heauen whereby we must bee saued, but by the name of Christ,

Esay. 55. Seke the Lord, while he may be found, and call vpon him while he is nie.

The

The time shall come: that whosoeuer that calleth on the name of the Lorde shall be saued. *Ioel.2.* *Rom.10.*

He is ritche vnto all that call on him. *Rom.10.*

Augustine in his manuell.22.chapter. And of the wordes of the Lord 40. Sermon.

All my hope is in the death of my Lord, his death is my meryte, my refuge my health, my life and my resurrection.

Epiphanius in his.3.booke the 2. commentarye.

Speaking of the Christians whiche committed Idolatrye with the dead bodyes sayth, many thinges and the like vnto this haue bene done in the world for the seduction of the deceiued, not that the Saintes are a cause of offence to any man. But bicause that the thoughtes of men cannot be kept quiet, but are peruerted and turned into euil. For although that the Virgin Marye be dead and buryed: her sleepe is in honor, and the death in chastitie, and the crowne in Virginitie: or be it that shee hath bene killed (as it is written the sword shall pearce throughe thy soule) among the Martyrs, that is hir

In the olde time there vvere christians vvhich committed idolatrie to the deade bodies, as also novve in our time.

glory

glory and the holy body of her, by whome the light is come into the world in prayses: or be it that shee doe continewe. For it is not impossible to God to doe all that he wyll: for the ende of her is not knowen of any man, we must not honor the Saints besides the deutye, but we must honor the Lorde of them. Then let that error of the seduced cease: for Marye is not God, and hath nother body from heauen, but of conception of man and of woman, disposed neuerthelesse according to the promise, as the body of Isaac.

Chrysostome of the seuen Machabees 2. homilye.

Speaking of the seuen Machabees. Staye not vpon the ashes of the bodyes of Saintes, and of the relikes of their fleshe, and to all the bones which are consumed by the time. But open the eyes of faythe, and beholde the hidden thinges of the heauenly vertue and of the grace of the holye spirite, and shining of the clerenesse of the heauenly light.

Yet Michael the Archangell when he stroue against the deuill, and disputed about the body of Moyses, durst not blame

him

him with cursed speaking, but sayth the Lorde rebuke thee.

Moyses the seruant of the Lorde dyed there in the land of Moab at the commandement of the Lorde. And was buryed in a valley in the land of Moab besides Beth Pheor: but no man wist of his sepulcher unto this daye.

Deut. 34. The sepulchre of Moses is vnknovvne.

John was beheaded of Herode, and after his disciples came, and tooke vp his body, and buryed it. And certayne men fearing God, carryed Stephen among them, to be buryed and made great lamentation ouer him.

Mat. 14. Iohn vvas not put in a reliquarie, bvt in a sepulchre. *Act. 8.*

God saide vnto Adam, earth thou art, and vnto earth shalt thou returne.

Genes. 3.

Eusebius in the ecclesiasticall history 4. booke. 15. Chapter.

The diuell inuyted Niceta the father of Herodes and brother of Alces, to obtayne of the iudge that he would not suffer the body of Saint Policarpe to be buryed, fearing (saith he) least the Christians should leaue and forsake him whiche hath bene crucified, and would beginne to worshippe him here. &c. The faithfull wil aunswere: The miserable men doe not knowe

that

The faithful cannot forsake Iesus Christ and adore saints.

that we can neuer forsake Iesus Christe, who hath suffered death and passion for vs, and that we cannot adore or worshipe any other then he whom we doe knowe to be the true God. And afterwardes they gathered the bones of the Martyr, which were burned, and haue put them in a sepulchre.&c.

Chrysostome in his vnperfect worke vpon Saint Mathewe.

23.Chapter.

Mat.23.

They make their Phylactaries broade.&c. O ignorante priestes (saith he) is not the Gospell reade euery day in the church, that is to say in the congregation, and heard of all? And if the Gospell put into the eares of many doe not profit them any thing at all to saluation, doest thou thinke that it will profite them any thing to hang it about their neckes? Furthermore I doe aske thee, wherein consisteth the truthe of the Gospell, in the figures of the letters, or in the vnderstanding of the same? If the vertue of the Gospell dooth consiste in the figures of letters written, thou doest well to carry them hanging about thy necke: But if the vertue of the

The Gospel profiteth nothing to be hanged aboute our necke, nor vvritten in a booke, but in the heart.

Gospell

Gospel consisteth in the true sense and true understanding (as thou must beleue) thou shalt then doe better to beare and carye them in thy heart than about thy necke. But other which would shewe themselues to be more holye, adde with the letters of the Gospell, one part of the hemme or of the heares, to wete, of Jesus Christ, and doe hang them about their necke. O wickednesse, they woulde shewe that there is greater holynesse in the robes than in the proper bodie of Jesus Christ. And seeing that they are not healed in receyuing the bodie of Jesus Christ, they thinke to bee through the holynesse of the hemmes: they despayre of the mercie of God, and put their trust onely in the robe of man. And thou wilt say unto me: Did not S. Paule giue his partlets and napkins for to heale those that were diseased? I doe confesse the same, but that was before that men had knowledge of the true God, whom he declared and shewed forth. And it was good reason, and to the same had Saint Paule respect, to the end that through the holynesse of the men whiche doe declare the true God, they shoulde acknowledge his

Act.19.

Hovve vve must understande that Paule gaue his partlets for to heale the diseased.

his vertue and power : but nowe it is folie. For sithence that wee haue the power of God, what doth it profite to knowe the puissance and strength of men.

Act.3. Ye men of Israel, why maruayle ye at this? or why looke ye so stedfastly on vs, as though we by our owne power or godlynesse had made this man go? The God of Abraham, and Isaac, and Iacob, the God of our fathers hath glorified his son Iesus.&c.

Esay.42. I my selfe, whose name is the Lorde, which giue my power to none other, neyther myne honor to the Gods.

Epiphanius in the 2.Tome.3.booke, Heresie.79.

God which is the worde, hath taken fleshe of the virgin, neuerthelesse, not to the ende that the virgin shoulde bee worshipped, or that we should make hir God, or to that ende that wee shoulde offer in hir name. And agayne he sayth: that the father, the sonne, and the holy ghost should be worshipped, that none doe worshippe Marie, nor anye woman, nor anye man. That mysterie is due vnto God. The angels themselues are not capable of suche glorie.

God hath taken fleshe of the holye virgin, not to the ende that the virgin shoulde be worshipped.

glorie. Anon after he sayeth: Let not the women saye, we will honour the Queene of heauen. &c.

Of one onely mediator.

S. Augustine vpon the first Epistle of S. Iohn, the first treatise.

This manne here hath not sayde, yee haue an aduocate with the father: but if any man haue sinne, wee haue an aduocate with the father. He hath not sayde, ye haue: nor hath sayde, ye haue me. And also he hath not sayde, ye haue also very Christ: but he hath put Christ, and not himself: and hath sayde, we haue, and not ye haue. He had rather to put himself in the number of sinners, for to haue Christ for an aduocate, than to put himself an aduocate for Christ, & to be found amongst the proude damned creatures. My brethren we haue an aduocate with the father, Iesus Christ the righteous, & he it is ẏ obtayneth grace for our sinnes. He ẏ holdeth this doctrine, holdeth no heresie, nor doth any schisme. For from whence

1. Iohn. 2.

S. Iohn did put himselfe in the number of sinners, that he maye haue Christ for an aduocate.

whence come the schismes or diuisions, but when men saye, wee bee righteous? when men saye we doe sanctifie those that be defiled, we doe iustifie the infidels, we aske and obtayne it. But what is that that John sayth? If any man sinne, wee haue an aduocate with the father, to wete, Jesus Christ the righteous. But some will say, doe not the Sayntes then aske for vs? doe not the Bishoppes then praye for the people? vnderstande the Scriptures, and marke that also the Prelates doe commend themselues vnto the people, in praying also togither for vs.

Prou.17.
Iam.4.

The Apostle prayeth for the people, and the people doe praye for the Apostle. My brethren, we doe pray for you, but pray ye also for vs. Let all the members pray one for another, and the heade shall be the mediator for all. Therefore it is no maruayle that he sayde that which followeth: where he stoppeth the mouth of those which deuyde the Church of God. For he sayeth: we haue Jesus Christ the righteous for an aduocate: he it is that obtayneth grace for our sinne, for those which ought to talk and saye: Lo, here is Christ, or there is

Collo.4.
2.Thes.3.

Some men vvold shevv Iesus Christ by sight, those doe deuide the Church.

Mat.24.

Christe, and for those which will shewe in parte him which hath redeemed all, and possesseth all thinges.

Augustine against Parmenian in his 2. and. 6. booke. 8. Chapter.

The Christians doe commend them selues the one to the other in their praiers, but he which prayeth for all, for whom no man can praye, is the true and onely mediator. Although that Saint Paule were one of the chefest members, neuerthelesse in asmuch as he was a member (knowing that the Lorde Jesus the true hie priest for all the church and congregation was entred into the sanctuary of God, not by figure or image, but in truth) he commendeth him self to ÿ prayers of the faithfull: and maketh not him selfe a mediator betwene God and man, but requireth that all the members of the body doe praye also for him, as he also prayeth for other, according as all men ought to haue mutuall care and compassion. In this manner the mutuall prayers of all the members which doe trauaile yet vpon the earthe, ought to mount and ascend vnto the heade which is gone before to heauen, in whome

Iesus Chist is the true and onely mediator.

If Paule vvere a mediator, the other Apostles shoulde be alſo, and ſo there vvere many mediators.
1.*Tim*.2.

we haue remiſſion and forgiueneſſe of our ſinnes: for if Saint Paule were a mediator, the other Apoſtles ſhould be alſo, and ſo there woulde be manye mediators, the which will not agree with that which is ſayde in an other place, that there is one God, and one mediator betweene God and man. &c.

Ambroſe in his boke of Iſaac, and of bleſſed lyfe.

Ieſus Chriſt is our mouth by whome we doe ſpeake vnto the father, or eye by whome we doe ſee the father, or right hand, by whom we do offer vnto the father, with out which mediator there is no nereneſſe toward God, neyther to vs, nor to all the Saintes.

Auguſtine in his Quinquageſima vpon the.94. pſalme.

If thou doe ſeeke thy mediator for to bring thee vnto God, he is in heauen, and prayeth there for thee, as he dyed for thee in earth. It is moſt true that we doe not imagine that he kneeling vpon his knees maketh humble ſupplication: But we doe vnderſtand it with the Apoſtle, that he appeareth ſo before the face of God, that the vertue of his death is auaylable to perpetuall intercession. And he being entred into the sanctuary of heauen, representeth only the prayers of the people, who haue not neare accesse vnto God. Rom. 8.

Augustine vpon the Epistle of S. Iohn. 2. Treatise.

But in whose name be our sinnes pardoned? Is it by the name of Augustine? Then it is not also through the name of Donatus. Doest thou see that it is of Augustine, or of Donatus? neyther is it by the name of Paull nor of Peter. In loue the mother bringing forth the little children, openeth hir bowells in the Apostle, vnto those which deuyded the church, and which desired to make many partes of the vnity. And by words doth somwhat breake his wordes, and bewayleth those whom he seeth to be carryed out, and calleth againe vnto one name, those which woulde make them many names, and repealeth them backe from his loue, that Christ be onelye loued: and saith, was Paule crucified for you? eyther were ye baptised in the name of Paule? what saith he? I wyll not that ye be to me, but with me, be with me, wee

Our sinnes are not pardoned vs in the name of S. Paule, nor of S. Peter.

1. Cor. 1.

are all to him which is deade for vs, who is crucified for vs.

Augustine in his Quinquagesima, vpon the 108. Psalme.

The prayer which is not made through Jesus Christ, not onely doth not put away sinnes, but it is sinne it selfe.

Chrysostome in the. 16. homilie, of the profite of the Gospell.

Mat. 15. The Cananite prayed not the Apostles, but only Christ Iesus.

Speaking of the woman that was a Cananite. But tell me O thou woman, howe hast thou bene so bolde to come vnto him, in as muche as thou art a poore sinner? I know very well, sayde she, what I doe. Beholde the wisedome of the woman, she neyther prayed to James nor John, she did not go vnto Peter, and regarded not all the assembly of the Apostles, shee sought not a mediator, but in steade of all those, she tooke repentaunce for hir companion, who holdeth the place of an aduocate. &c.

In the same.

Wilt thou knowe that when we do pray for our selues, we doe more towards God, than when other doe praye for vs: This

Mat. 15. woman did crie out, and the disciples ap-

prochedt

proched vnto him, and sayde: sende hir awaye, for she cryeth after vs. And he sayd vnto them: I am not sent, but vnto the lost sheepe of the house of Israel. Then shee came and worshipped him, saying: Lorde helpe me. But he answered and sayde: It is not good to take the childrens breade, and to cast it to whelpes. And she sayde: truth Lorde, for in deede the whelpes eate of the crummes which fall from their maisters table. Then Jesus answered and said vnto hir: O woman great is thy fayth, be it vnto thee, euen as thou desirest. Doest thou see howe he refused, when the other desired him? But when she hirself cried in praying for the gift, he accorded vnto hir. For he sayde vnto them (when they intreated him) I am not sent but to the lost sheepe of the house of Israel. But he sayde vnto that woman: great is thy fayth, be it vnto thee euen as thou desirest.

God vvill giue vnto vs rather or sooner that vvhich vve desire, vvhen vve pray, thā vvhen other praye for vs.

In the same.

It is not needefull to haue patrons with God, nor to runne much here and there for to entreate others, but althoughe that thou art alone, and that thou art without a patron, and that by thy selfe thou doest

It is not nedefull to haue patrōs vvith God.

pray vnto God, thou shalt haue altogither that thou desirest. For God will not so easily giue it when other men doe praye for vs, as when wee doe praye our selues: yea although that we are full of many euils.

Chrysostome vpon Genesis. 43. Chapter.

We are constrayned to set forth all this hystorie, to the ende to learne, that we doe not so muche by others as by our selues. So that we doe approche or come with a pure and vigilant thought. Also the same woman hauing the disciples praying for hir, profited nothing at all, vntill suche time as she presented hir selfe, for to draw vnto hir the mercie of the Lorde.

Chrysostome in the first Tome. 5. homilie of the first chapter of S. Mathewe.

We may a great deale sooner bee assured by our prayer and supplication, than by the prayer of another. For God will will not giue so soone our health vnto others which doe praye for vs, as vnto our selues, to the ende that by the same that we desire, his ire and wrath maye be ap-

peased

peased in vs: We may come to do better, and that wee maye gather the trust of a good conscience.

Euen so truely had he pitie of that Cananite. And in like manner he did giue saluation vnto the harlote. Euen so did hee transporte and carye the theefe that did hang vpon the crosse into Paradise, not entreated of any patrons, neyther through the puritie of any. Mat.15. Luc.7. Luc.23.

There is one God and one mediator betweene God and man, which is the man Christe Jesus. 1.Tim.2.

Jesus Christ is rysen againe: who is also at the right hand of God, and maketh intercession for vs. Rom.8.

He is able also perfectly to saue them that come vnto God by him, seeing hee euer liueth to make intercession for them. Heb.7.

Jesus Christe saith. I am the waye, and the truth and the life, no man commethe vnto the father but by me. Iohn.14.

I am the dore, he that entereth not in by the dore into the sheepefolde, but clymeth vp some other way, the same is a theefe and a robber. Iohn.10.

Thou O Lorde onely doest knowe the 3.Reg.8.

heartes of all men.

Psal.44. God knoweth the very secretes of the hearte.

Luk.16. Jesus Christe saith. God knoweth your heartes.

Mat.11. Also: Come unto me al ye that are wearye and laden, and I will ease you.

Galat.6. While we haue time let vs doe good vnto all men.

S. Ambrose vpon the fyrst Epistle to the Romans fyrst Chapter.

Men haue of custome vsed a miserable excuse, saying, that by them men may goe vnto God, euen as men come vnto kinges by the earles and lordes. Is there anye man so mad, and so obliuyous of his safety which doth attrybute and giue the honor of a king vnto an earle or lorde, for if any such be found which dare saye the same, they are worthely condemned as culpable of his maiestie. And yet those doe not hold those men gyltye or culpable which doe attrybute the honor of the name of God vnto the creatures. And in forsaking the Lord, they doe worship those whiche are seruantes with them. As though the seruing of God were worldly gaines. For the

Men forsake God, and do vvorship the seruants.

the same cause men doe finde to haue accesse and comming vnto the king by the meanes of the earles and lordes: bicause that the king is a man, and doth not well knowe whom he ought to truste of his common wealth. But for to winne and obtayne the fauor of God, vnto whome nothing is hydde (for he knoweth the hearts of all men) we haue no neede that any doe entreat for to present our supplication, but with an humble and lowlye heart.

Of images.

Whether it be lawefull to haue them in the temples of the christians.

Moyses saide: Take heede vnto your selues therefore, that ye forget not the appoyntment of the Lord your God, whiche hee made with you: and that ye make you no grauen image, of what soeuer it be that the Lorde thy God hath forbidden thee. For the Lorde thy God is a consuming fire, and a ielous God. If after thou

> *Deut. 4.*

> VVe ought to make no Images.

thou haste gotten children and childrens children, and hast dwelt long in the land, ye shall marrye your selues and make grauen images after the likenesse of what soeuer it be, and shall worke wickednesse in the sight of the Lord thy God to prouoke him. I call heauen and earth to record vnto you this daye, that ye shall shortlye perishe from the lande, &c.

Deut.4.

Againe: The Lord spake vnto you out of the fire, and ye heard the voyce of the wordes, but sawe no image, but hearde a voyce onely. And he declared vnto you his couenante, which he commaunded you to doe, euen tenne verses and wrote them in two tables of stone. And the Lorde commaunded me the same season, to teach you ordinances and lawes, for to doe them in the lande whyther ye goe to possesse it. Take heede vnto your selues, diligentlye as pertayning vnto your soules, for yee sawe no manner of image the daye when the Lorde spake vnto you in Horeb out of the fire: least ye marre your selues, and make you grauen images, after what soeuer likenesse it be: whither after the likenesse of man or woman.

Those are greatly deceyued vvho vvoulde figure God being inuisible by visible things.

I my selfe whose name is the Lorde, which giue my power to none other, neyther mine honor to the Gods. *Esay. 42.*

Thou shalt worshippe no strange God, for the Lorde is called ielous, bicause he is a ielous God: &c. Thou shalt make thee no Gods of mettall. *Exod. 34.*

To whom then will ye liken God? or what similytude will ye set vp vnto him? shal the caruer make him a carued image? and shall the goldsmith couer him with golde? or cast him into a forme of siluer plates. &c. Knowe ye not this? hearde ye neuer of it? hath it not bene preached vnto you sence the beginning. &c. To whom nowe will ye liken me, and to whom shall I be like saith the holy one? lift vp your eyes on hie, and consider, who hath made those thinges. *Esay. 40.* Vnto whō shall we liken God, he is a spirite incomprehensible.

Whome will ye make me like in fashion or image, that I may be like him? ye will take out siluer and golde out of your purses, and waye it, and hyre a goldsmith to make a God of it, that men may kneele downe and worshippe it: yet must hee bee taken on mens shoulders and borne, and set in his place, that he may stand and not moue. *Esay. 46.*

moue. Alas that men should crye vnto him which giueth no aunswere: and deliuereth not the man that calleth vpon him, from his trouble. Consider this well, and be ashamed. Goe into your owne selues (O ye runnagates) Remember the things which are paste, sence the beginning of the worlde, that I am God, and that there is els no God, yea and that there is nothing like vnto me.

Sapien. 15. No man can make a God like vnto him: for seeing he is but mortall him selfe, it is but mortall that he maketh with vnrighteous handes. He him selfe is better then they whom he worshippeth, for he liued though he was mortall, but so did neuer they.

Leuit. 26. The Lord hath saide, ye shall make you no Idolles nor grauen image, neyther reare you vp any pillers, neyther ye shall set vp any images of stone in your lande to bowe your selues thereto, for I am the Lorde your God.

Deut. 11. Beware that your heartes deceiue you not, that ye turne aside, and serue strange Gods, and worshippe them.

Deut. 27. Cursed be the man that maketh any

carued

carued image, or image of mettall (an abhomination vnto the Lorde the worke of the handes of the craftesman) and putteth it in a secret place: and all the people shal aunswere and say Amen. The caruers of Images are accursed.

The Images of the people are but siluer and golde, euen the worke of mens handes. *Psal.115.* *Psal.135.*

The Lorde God sayde: ye shall ouerthrowe their aultars, breake downe their pyllers, cut downe their groues, and burn their grauen images with fire. For thou art an holye Nation vnto the Lorde thy God. *Deut.7.* *Exod.34.*

They hewe downe a tree in the woode, with the handes of the workeman, and fashion it with the axe: they couer it ouer with golde or siluer, they fasten it with nayles and hammers that it moue not. &c. All these things are the works of ye craftie workeman. But the Lorde is a true God, a liuing God, and an euerlasting king. *Iere.10.*

Jeroboam sayde: Beholde your Gods, O Israel, which brought you out of the lande of Egypt. And he put the one in Bethel, and the other in Dan. And that doing was a cause of sinne. 3.*Reg.*12

Nowe

Iosua.24. Nowe then feare the Lorde, and serue him in purenesse and truth: and put away the Gods which your fathers serued on the other side of the floude, and in Egypt, and serue the Lorde. But if it seeme euill vnto you to serue the Lorde, then choose you this daye whome you will serue.&c. And the people aunswered and sayd: God forbyd that we shoulde forsake the Lorde, and serue straunge Gods.

Sapien.14 The honoring of abhominable Images is the cause, the beginning and ende of all euill.

Act.17. We ought not to thinke that the Godheade is lyke vnto golde, siluer, or stone, grauen by craft and imagination of man.

Rom.1. The foolish men vvould resemble God to a man. When they counted themselues wyse, they became fooles: for they turned the glorie of the incorruptible God, to the similitude of the image of mortall man, and of birdes, and of foure footed beastes, and of creeping beastes: wherefore God gaue them euen vp vnto their heartes lust, vnto vncleannesse, to defile their owne bodies betweene themselues, which turned the truth of God vnto a lie, and worshipped and serued the creatures, neglecting the

the Creator, whiche is blessed for euer. Amen. For this cause also God gaue them vp vnto shamefull lustes. &c.

Be yee no worshippers of Images as were some of them, according as it is written: the people sat downe to eate and drinke, and rose vp agayne to playe. *1. Cor. 10*

Flie from idolatrie. *1. Cor. 10.*

Babes keepe your selues from Idols. *1. Iohn. 5.*

We knowe that an Idoll is nothing in the worlde, and that there is none other God but one. And though there be that are called Gods, whether in heauen or in earth (as there be many Gods and manye Lordes) yet vnto vs there is but one God, which is ye father, of whom are all things, and wee in him: and one Lorde Iesus Christ, by whome are all things, and wee by him. *1. Cor. 8.*

Athanasius agaynst the Gentiles.

The Gentiles and Paynims saye vnto me: how is God knowne by the Images, is it by the thing or cause whiche is outwardly, or by the forme and figure which is grauen and put within the thing? If it be through the thing it selfe, what nede is there to make the forme or figure? For as

much

much then, as before that suche portraytures were made, God was manifested and shewed forth, by the meanes of all things: Inasmuch also as all things doe giue witnesse of the glorie of God. If the pourtracture be the cause of the heauenlye knowledge, what needeth it painting or any other matter or thing? And wherfore doe not men come unto the knowledge of God by the true creatures rather then by figures and remembrances? for truly the glorye of God should be more clearly knowen if it were manifested by the resonable and unreasonable creatures then by those which are without soules and immouable. Then when you doe engraue and make the images and pourtractures for to make us to knowe God, truely you doe a wicked thing.

Those which doe graue Images for to represent God, doe wicked things.

Lactantius Firmianus of his godly institutions, against the Gentils and idolaters. 2. booke.

God is aboue man, and is not set here by lowe, but we must seeke him in the hie region, and therefore it is most certayne ŷ religion is not in the places where there are images. For if religion cōsisteth in diuine

uine thinges, and that it is so that there is nothing diuine but in heauenly and celestiall thinges, we must then conclude that there is no religion in images.

Religion is not vvhere there are Images.

He saith further in his second booke and second chapter. That God whose spirite and puissance is spreade abroade euerye where, cannot be absent. The image then is alwayes superfluous.

Reade the 3.4.and 5. Chapters.

Lactantius Firmianus in the.2 booke and.4.Chapter.

Seneca did deryde and mocke the folly of the auncientes, saying: Wee are not twyse children (as the prouerbe is) there is notwithstanding great difference by the same that we being old, and of age to iudge and discerne the good, shoulde occupye our minde to such follyes, that to these great puppets, beutified and decked vp, men should offer oyntmentes, incens, and good smells, to those that haue mouthes without teeth.

Clement in his.5.booke vnto Iames the brother of the Lorde.

Men doe adore images in the honor of God, vvhich is against God

We doe adore and worshippe the visible images in the honor of the inuisible God, the which truely is false. For if ye wyll truely worship the image of God in doing good unto man, you shall worship the true image of God in him. For the image of God is in all men, and the similitude is not in all. But only there where the soule is gentle, and the thought pure. If thē you will truly honor the Image of God, wee shall declare unto you that which is veritable and true, that you doe good unto man which is made after the Image of God, that you doe honour and reverence him, that you administer meate unto him which is an hungred, and drinke unto him that is a thirst, clothing unto him whiche is naked, visite those that bee sicke, and lodge and harbour the stranger, and helpe the necessities of him that is put in prison. The same is the thing which shall be reputed truly to bee done unto God. And therefore those things doe come unto the honor of the Image of God, insomuche that he which hath not done them, shall be esteemed to haue done iniurie unto the Image of God. What is that then to honor God, to runne here and there after Images of stone and woode: and to honor the vayne figures & without soules, as diuine

The honor of the image of God.

Mat. 25.

things,

things, and to despyse man, in whom truly is the Image of God? And which is more, be ye certayne that he which doth commit homicide or adultrie, and all that which is payne or iniurie to men, the Image of God is violated and defiled in all such things. For it is great infidelitie agaynst God, to hurt man. Then when thou doest unto another, that whiche thou wouldest not suffer, thou doest defile and marre the Image of God most wickedly. Understande then that such subiection is of the serpent which is hydde within you, the which doth make you beleeue that you may be faythfull when you doe honor the insensible things, and that you are not unfaythfull, when ye hurt those that be sensible, and haue reason.

In the same booke.

It is great infidelitie to receyue the goodnesse of God, and to render thākes vnto the Images of wood or stone.

Who is so wicked, or so unthankfull, which to obtayne and receyue the benefite of God, doth render thankes unto woode or stones. Therefore awake ye, and gyue good eare unto your health. Trulye God hath no neede of any man, and requireth nothing, and is nothing at all hurt. But it is onely we whiche are ayded or hurt, in that that wee are eyther thankefull or vnthankefull.

Agayne in the same booke.

They are esteemed verilye to be righteous and iust, whiche haue in veneration, not the things which are done for the administration of the worlde, but the creator of them and of the worlde: also those thinges doe reioyce themselues when he is honoured and worshipped: and cannot abide to see that the honor of the creator shoulde be giuen to the creature. For adoration is a thing belonging vnto God alone, who onely was not created: And all things are his workes. As then it is the propertie of him whiche onely was not created to bee God: in lyke maner, all that which hath bene made, is not truly God. We ought then before all things to vnderstande the deception of the olde serpent, and his cautelous suggestions, who as through wisedome hath deceiued you: As by a certaine reason doth creepe into your senses. And begynning at the head, doth slyde vnto the interior partes, esteeming your deception to be great gayne.

Adoration apertaineth only vnto the true God.

Lactan-

Lactantius Firmianus. 6. booke. 2. Chapter.

Woulde not a man iudge him to be out of his wit, which doth offer candles of wax for an oblation and gift vnto God, whiche is the author and giuer of light?

S. Ambrose in his. 4. Tome vpon the 118. Psalme. 10. Sermon.

The Gentyles doe adore and worshippe the woode, bicause they thinke that the same was the image of God: but ẏ image of the inuisible God is not in that whiche is seene, but is altogither in that which is not seene. Thou doest then see that we doe walke among manye of the images of Christ. Let vs take heede that wee be not found to take the crowne from the image, which crowne Christ hath put vpon euery one. Let vs take heede to take nothing from them, vnto whome we ought to adde and giue. &c.

Ambrose of the death of Theodosius. Tome. 3.

Helena then did finde the title, she worshipped the king, and not the wood: For the same is the error of the Gentils, and the vanitie of the infidels: But shee worshipped him which did hang on the wood, written in the tytle. &c.

Lucyan Byshoppe of Antioche confessed his fayth before the Judges, as recyteth Eusebius in his ecclesiasticall history the. 9. booke and. 3. chapter. Saying thus among other thinges. The omnipotente God who was not made by our handes, but by whom we are created and composed hauing pitie of our error, hath sent his wysedome in this world, taking vpon him our fleshe, for to shewe and teach vs, that we ought to seke the same God (who hath made heauen and earth) not in images made with mans handes, but in eternall thinges.

VVe ought not to secke God by the Images.

The counsell of Illyberis or Granado, the. 36. decretall.

It hath benne concluded ye there shoulde be no painting in the temples: to the ende that the same which ought to be worshipped and serued be not painted on the wals.

Augustine of the citie of God. 4. booke. 9. and. 31. Chapters.

Those which haue put forth first of all the images, haue taken from the world the feare of God: And haue augmented error.

Augu-

Augustine vpon the. 113. psalme.

No man can pray or worshippe, beholding and looking so towards the images, but that he is touched as if he were heard from thence, or els he looketh and hopeth to haue that he doth demaunde.

Furthermore he saith, men cannot place and set the images in hie and honorable places, for to be looked on of those that praye and worshippe, but that they doe drawe the senses of the weake, as if they had senses and soules.

Images doe drawe the senses of the weake vnto vayn things.

S. Augustine in his Cataloge of heresyes.

There was a woman named Marcelin, one of the secte of the Carpocratines, which did worshippe the image of Iesus Christe, and of Saint Paule, of Homer and of Pythagoras: prostrating hirselfe before them, and offering vnto them incence.

Shee is put in the rolle of the heresyes by Saint Augustine.

The counsel of Constantinople celebrated by Constantine the fift, and by. 38. Bishoppes of Asya and of Grece (people excellently lerned, amonge whome the chee-

Eutropius of the dedes of the Romanes.

feste were the Byshoppe of Ephesus, the Byshoppe of Perga, and the Byshoppe of Constantinople, and was begonne the. 15. day of Februarye, continuing untill the 15. day of August, decreed that it was not lawfull for those that beleeue in God through Iesus Christe, to haue any images of the creator nor of creatures in the temples for to worshippe them: But that all such thinges ought to be taken awaye out of the temples, according to Gods lawe. and for to auoyde offence.

Images forbidden in Temples.

Asmuch hath the second counsell of Toledo decreed condemning images.

The counsell of Illyberis or Granado. in the. 48. Canon.

We haue often times admonished the faithfull, that they doe let and hinder asmuch as they can that there be no images in their houses, which if they feare the force and strength of their seruants, yet at the leaste they them selues auoyde from them: And if they doe it not, that they bee reputed as strangers from the Churche.

Those are reiected frõ the Church, vvhich vvill not abstaine frõ Images.

Origen against Celsus. 8. booke.

Celsus sayth: That we doe auoyde the Tem-

Temples, Aultars, and Images, to the end that they be not builded nor edified by vs, forasmuch as hee esteemeth that the fayth of this our inuincible communion & charitie, and the which cannot be expressed that it is a faction or sect. In the meane season notwithstanding hee doth not see, that there is in vs a spirite of righteousnesse, in stead of the Aultar and of the temple, out of whom without doubte doe goe most sweete sauors and encense, that is to saye prayers and requestes proceeding from a pure conscience. And to that effecte Saint John saith thus in his Apocalips, that the incense and odours are the prayers of the Saintes. And Dauid prayed saying: Let my prayer be set forth in thy sight as the incense Lorde. Furthermore these are images and oblations agreable vnto God, which are not made by vncleane workes, but formed and fashioned in vs by the worde of God: Euen so then all men haue such images in them, I doe meane those which haue acquired and gotten by heauenly doctrine, continency, righteousnesse, strength wisedome, and a true feare of God: And the buyldinges of all

Apoc. 8.

Psal. 141.

other

other vertues, the which I doe beleeue to be reasonable to beare honor vnto that which is the true patron of all images, to wete the image of the inuisible God, which is the only God, or rather those which doe kill the olde man with his workes, putting on the newe man, the which is renued in the knowledge of God, after the image of him which hath created him. And then they shall make such images, as that great and soueraigne workeman desireth. And incontinently afterwardes he saith, to the ende that I may speake in fewe wordes, all christians doe endeuer them selues greatly to buyld such Aulters as we haue spoken of, and such images as we haue declared, not of thinges insensible and without life, neyther of Gods and Idolles of wicked spirites, neyther of dwellinges where the diuells doe make their abiding: But of places capable of the spirit of God which dwelleth where vertue is: and also of that great God which hath created vs to his owne image, and which doth approche nigh vnto vs, as comming to his domesticall and familiar freendes: And in such sorte that the spirite of Christ be resi-

A recital for to make suche Images vvhiche are pleasing vnto God.

Rom.6.

The diuels dvvell in the temples of Idolaters.

dent

dent in vs, which are so figured and fashioned. And the heauenly worde willing to set the same foorth, hath described God making promise to the righteous, and speaking vnto them after this manner: I will walke among you, and will be youre God, and ye shall be my people. And the heauenly word hath also described the sauiour saying thus: He that hath my commandementes and keepeth them, the same is he that loueth me, and he that loueth me shall be loued of my father, and I wil loue him, and will shewe mine owne selfe vnto him manifestlye. Whosoeuer then woulde haue suche aultars, as I haue lately declared, that he doe seeke diligentlye, and if he thinke it good, that he doe conferre with such aultars. Immediatlye afterwardes he sayth, speaking of Images: Truly one ought to knowe that they are insensible, and without mouing: and in processe of time they will become rotten and corrupt: and that ours shall dwell and abyde in the immortall soule, as long as it shall haue any reasonable soule dwelling in it.

Leuit.26
2.Cor.6.
Iohn.14.

S.Cy-

S. Cyprian wryting agaynst Demetrius. first Treatise.

What beastlynesse of mynde is it, or rather what blynde foolishe rage of madde men is it, not to go from darkenesse, for to come vnto the light. And when those which are tyed and bounde with the bonds of eternall death, will not receiue ẏ hope of immortalitie, and not to feare God, threatening and saying that hee that doth sacrifice vnto anye Gods, saue vnto the Lorde onely, let him die without redemption. Also: They haue worshipped those which their hands haue made and fashioned, and man did prostrate and humble himselfe before it, and I will not pardon them. Wherefore doest thou humble and bowe thy selfe before the false Goddes? Wherefore doste thou bowe thy wretched body before Images that are filthye, and that haue no vnderstanding, and before the workes of the earth? God hath made thee right and straight, in comparison of other crooked creatures, making them to looke downe on the earth. Thou hast a hie looke, and a face to beholde thy God: beholde him, fixe thine eyes on him, seeke God on hie,

Exo. 22.
Esay. 2.

hie, that thou mayst be exempted from the lowe hell: lyft vp thine heart vnto celestiall and heauenly things. Wherefore doste thou cast thy selfe agayne to the grounde, in the fall of death with the serpent whom thou honourest? why doste thou fall headlong in the ruine of the diuell throughe him? Keepe the highnesse in the whiche thou art borne, perseuere and continue to be such a one as thou wast made of God: lyft vp thy hearte with the stature of thy bodye, and the shape of thy visage, that thou mayest knowe God, knowe thy selfe first: leaue and forsake Idols which mans error hath founde out. Turne vnto God, who will assist and helpe thee after when thou shalt call vpon him. Beleeue in Iesus Christ whome the father hath sent for to quicken and amende vs. &c.

Those vvhiche doe honor images, doe honor the deuill.

Confounded be all they that worship Images, and delite in their Idols.

Psal. 97.

Those are cursed that vvorship Images.

Howe agreeth the temple of God with Images.

2. Cor. 6.

God did expressely forbid in the old lawe Images, saying thus: Thou shalt haue none other Gods in my sight. Thou shalt make thee no grauen Image, neyther any simili-

Exod. 20.
Deut. 5.
Psal. 81.

similitude that is in heauen aboue, eyther in the earth beneath, or in the waters that are beneath the earth. See that thou neyther bowe thy selfe unto them, neyther serue them: for I the Lorde thy God, am a iealous God.

4.Reg.18. Ezechias king of Iuda, ordeyned that the Image of Christ shoulde bee burned (that is to saye, the brasen Serpent that God commaunded to be made in the wildernesse) bicause that when it was borne about by the people, they did burne sacrifice unto it, and honoured it, yet the sayde Serpent was the image of Christ, prefiguring him as he himselfe hath said in the Gospell. Notwithstanding Ezechias brake it in peeces, bicause that they abused it: And he was greatly praysed for it of the Lorde.

Ezechias did burne the Image of Iesus Christ, bicause it vvas abused.

Obiection.

The Canon lawe in the Chapter which beginneth Prælatum of consecration, distinct. 3.

That which the Scripture doth unto the readers, the very same doth the payntor unto the gasing fooles or Idiotes. For in the same the ignorant people doe see that

The Canon lavve permitteth those vvhich can reade, to haue the scriptures.

that which they ought to followe, in the same those doe reade which doe not know any letters.

Aunswere.

The Prophet Abacuc in his.2.chap. aunswereth to the same Canon.

What helpeth then the grauen images for the workeman hath left it, it is molted and an image & a thing shewing dreames and lyes. *Abac.2*

Gregory writing vnto the Byshoppe Marsill, in his.4. Epistle.

We had praysed thy doing, if thou haddest forbidden to worship images: which haue bene set in the Temple not for to worship, but onely for to instruct the spirites of the ignorant.&c.

The Prophet Ieremye in his.10.Chap. aunswereth vnto Gregory.

In that onely poynt they are altogither brutish and doe folishly, for the wood is an instruction of vanitie. *Iere.10.*

Jesus Christe saith: In vaine they worship me, teaching for doctrines the commaundementes of men. For ye laye the commaundement of God aparte, and obserue *Marc.7.*

serue the tradition of men.

S. Ierome vpon the Prophet Esay. 57. Chapter.

Esa.57. There was not a place that was left vndefiled with the filthinesse of Idolatrye, in such sort that behind the doores and postes of their houses they haue set vp images, whom they doe call their priuye and familiar Gods. And by and by after he saithe: The Cities of many countreys and prouinces are in that error, and doe keepe that wicked custome of the elders. Yea and Rome the mistres of the worlde, doth the like honouring the image of Ceres, as their sauegarde, through out euery house, with torches and candels, to the ende that they haue memorialls, which should admonish them of their inuented error, aswel in the comming in as at the going out of the house. &c.

Gala.3. O foolish Galatians, who hath bewitched you that ye should not obey the truth? to whom Jesus Christ before was descrybed in your sight, and among you crucified.

VVe haue a true Image of the crucifixe in the Gospell.

Ephipha-

Epiphanius the good Doctor in the Epistle written vnto Iohn Byshoppe of Ierusalem, and afterwarde translated by S. Ierome out of Greeke into Latine.

Beside that that I haue heard (saith he) that some did murmure against me, for asmuche as when we did goe vnto a holye place which is called Bethel, to the ende that I might make there with thee some prayer, according to the ecclesiasticall custome: and after that we were arryued to the village, which is called Anablatha, I sawe in passing by a Lampe burning, and after I demaunding what place that was, one aunswered to me, it was a Temple. And when I was entred in for to praye, I found therein a vayle hanging at the gate painted, hauing the image of Iesus Christ or of some kind of Saint: For I doe not well remember whose image that was: Then as I sawe in the churche of Iesus Christe an image of a man hanging, against the authorytie of the holy Scriptures, I did teare and rent it in peeces, and gaue counsell vnto the keepers of the sayd place, rather to wrappe some poore deade body in it, and to carry it awaye. They did mur-

Epiphanius entring into a temple of the christians, founde there the Image of Iesus Christ, the vvhich he did teare in peeces.

murmure against me saying: if he woulde haue cut it of, were it not reasonable that he should giue an other vayle in change? I hearing the same promised to giue one, and to send it incontinent. But there was a little time betweene them, whilest that I searched for a certayne vayle of price for to sende in steade of the other. For I dyd thinke that I must sende one of Cypres, but nowe I haue sent one such as I could finde, and I desire thee that thou doeste commaund the priestes of the saide place to receiue this vayle of this bringer which is sent from vs. And to commaunde from-henceforth in the Churche of Christe that they doe hang no more any such vayles, which are against our religion: For it becommeth thy honestye and it is also reasonable that rather thou haue a care to take from the Church of Iesus Christ all scrupulous thinges, which are not meete for the people giuen thee in charge.

S. Ierome doth giue witnesse of Epiphanius writing to Pammachius against the errors of Iohn Byshoppe of Ierusalem.

Thou hast Epiphanius the Byshoppe, who

who by the letters that he hath sent unto thee, hath called thee openly Heriticke: Truely thou art no greater then he, neyther of age nor of knowledge, neyther in holynesse of life, neyther according to the testimonye of all the worlde, during the time that the heresye of the Aryans and Eunomians did raigne in all the Easte countreys, except Pope Athanasius and Paulin: when thou wouldest not communicate, or haue felowship with those of the West partes, neyther with those that did confesse the name of God in exile. Eyther he was not heard of Euticius during the time that he was but priest of the Monastery, nor after that he was Byshop of Cypres, he was not touched of Valens, for he was alwayes so honored and esteemed that the Heritickes them selues being in their kingdome, would haue thought that the same should haue turned to their ignomynie and sclander if they should haue persecuted so excellent a man.

The heretikes had thought that it had turned to their dishonestie, if they had persecuted Epiphanius for his holy life.

Also the history Tripartite. 9. booke. Chapter. 48. affirmeth.

That he did many myracles.

The saide Epiphanius hath written a

booke called the booke of heresyes, out of which Saint Augustine allegeth witnesses. He liued in the time of Theodosius about the yeere of our Lorde, 390.

Of fastings and of meates.

1. *Tim*. 4.
Those vvho doe forbid mariage, and to eate of certayne meates, doe teache the doctrine of diuels.

The spirit speaketh euidently that in the latter times some shal depart frō ÿ faith, and shal giue hede unto spirites of error and doctrines of diuelles, which speake false lyes through hipocrysie, & haue their consciences burned with an hotte yron, forbidding to marrye, and commaunding to abstayne from meates, which God hath created to be receiued with giuing thanks of them which beleeue and knowe the truth. For all creatures of God are good, and nothing ought to be refused, if it be receiued with thanks giuing. For it is sanctyfied by the worde of God, and prayer.

S. Athanasius in his expositions vpon the Epistle to the Hebreus 13. Chapter.

These are truly strange doctrines. And he

he rebuked those which had brought in the Jewishe abstinences and obseruations of meates. For (he sayth) you ought to be fortified with grace, that is to saye, with fayth, and ye ought to be moste sure, that nothing is defiled, and that all thinges are pure and cleane vnto him that beleeueth, and so that faith is necessary: and not the obseruation of meates. For those whiche doe abstayne from meates, that is to saye, those which haue their affection alwayes to obserue in such manner meates, it is most manifest, that such haue nothing profited, no more then those which doe seperate them selues from the bonds and lymytes of the true faith, and serue wholy a lawe altogither vnprofitable.

Faith is necessarie, and not the obseruation of meates.

What soeuer is solde in the fleshe market, that eate ye, and aske no question for conscience sake.

I. Cor. 10.

S. Ierome vpon the first Chapter, of Malachye.

Turne neyther to the right hand neyther to the left: to decline and turne to the right hand is to abstaine from meates whiche God hathe created to bee vsed. Also to condemne and forbyd marriage, is to fall into that whiche is written in another place: be not righteous in thy selfe beyonde measure.

Jesus Christ sayth: that whiche goeth into the mouth defileth not a man: but that which commeth out of the mouth defileth the man.

The Councell of Bracara or Braga. 2. 30. distinct. Chapter which beginneth, Si quis. Helde in the yeare. 619.

Hath excommunicated those which did abstayne themselues from eating of fleshe through superstition.

Eusebius in the ecclesiasticall historie, the. 5. booke. Chapter. 3.

Rehearseth, that among those whiche were prisoners for the fayth at Lyons, there was one named Alcibiades, who led a very strayte life: for he woulde eate nothing but breade, and drinke water wyth salt, the which lyfe he was willing to continue being in prison. He was notified unto Attalus (the true martyr of Jesus Christ) after his first confession that hee made in the theater) that the same Alcibiades did euill, in not eating those creatures

tures

tures which God hath made, and that the same was an offence vnto others: the which thing being come to the knowledge of Alcibiades, he did eate (by the admonishing of Attalus) all things as others did, rendring thankes vnto God, for that the holy ghost reuealed vnto the same Attalus that which he did teach.

S. Augustine of ecclesiasticall maners, 33. vpon the letter K.

Speaking of the Monkes of Millaine, whose straytnesse he sawe: None is constreyned to beare a heauyer burthen than he can, else let him refuse to beare it, and he which is weaker than the other, is not therefore condemned of them. They all do knowe howe greatlye loue and charitie is commended. They doe knowe very well that all meates are cleane to those that are cleane: therefore all their industrie is not to reiect any meates as vncleane, but only to tame their concupiscence and lust, and to holde and keepe themselues in brotherly loue. They do remember this sentence, Meates are ordeyned for the belly, and the bellye for meates: neuerthelesse, manye which are strong shall abstayne bicause of

Behold the order of the Monkes in times past.

1. Cor. 6.

the weake. Many haue another reason, to wete, bicause that they had rather to bee fedde with grosse meates, and not with sumptuous and delicate, therefore those which in health doe abstayne from one kynde of meate, make no doubt being sick to eate of it. Many doe not drinke wyne, yet neuerthelesse they doe not thinke to be defiled therewith: for they themselues doe ordeyne, that one shoulde giue vnto those that are of a weake complexion, and can none otherwise keepe their health: if there be any that refuseth to drinke, they admonishe them brotherly, not to make themselues through vayne superstitions more weake than holpe. Euen so they doe diligently exercise themselues in the feare of God. And as touching the exercise of the bodye, they doe knowe verye well, that it profiteth onely for a little time. Loue is chieflye kept, and therevnto is applyed meates, wordes, apparayle, and the countenances: euery one doth consent vnto a mutuall loue and charitie, and doe abhorre to violate it, as much as God doth, if any one do resist the same, he is cast out: & if any one doe disagree from the same, they will

VVe ought to giue meates according to charitie.

will not suffer him one day. *Titus.1*

Rebuke them sharply, that they maye be sounde in fayth, and not taking heede to Jewishe fables, and commaundements of men, that turne from the truth. Unto the pure al things are pure: but unto them that are defiled and unbeleeuing, is nothing pure: but euen the very mindes and consciences of them are defiled.

The Councell of Toledo.13. hath excõmunicated those whiche forbydde to eate fleshe.

The Councell of Pope Martin hath ordayned as much.

Pope Elutherius hath ordayned, that none sholde keepe himselfe through superstition from eating of any meates, whiche are agreable to mans nature.

Let no man therefore condemne you about meate and drinke, or for a peece of an holy day, or of the newe Moone, or of the Saboth dayes, which are nothing but shadowes of things to come, but the bodie is in Christ. Let no man wilfully beare rule ouer you by humblenesse, and worshipping of Aungels, aduauncing himselfe in those things which he neuer sawe, rashlye *Collos.2.*

puft

puft vp with his fleshly minde. &c. Wherefore if ye be dead with Christ, and are free from the ordinances of the worlde. Why, as though ye yet liued in the worlde, are ye yet burdened with traditions of them that say: touch not, taste not, handle not, which all perysshe with the vsing of them, and are after the commaundementes and doctrines of men: Which things haue in deede a shewe of wisedome, in voluntarie worshipping and humblenesse, and in not sparing the bodie, yet are of no value, but appertayne to those thinges wherewith the flesh is crammed.

The bodily exercise profiteth little: but godlynesse is profitable vnto all things.

In the first booke of the historie tripartite. Chap. 10.

The holy Bishop of Cypres, Spiridion sayth, that freely he dare eate fleshe in Lent, when others doe abstayne from it, bicause he was a Christian (sayth he.)

Let vs not therefore iudge one another any more: but vse your iudgement rather in this, that no man put a stumbling blocke, or an occasion to fall, in his brothers waye. I knowe and am fully certified

fied through the Lorde Iesus, that there is nothing uncleane of it selfe: but unto him that iudgeth it to be uncleane, to him it is unclean. But if thy brother be grieued with thy meate, nowe walkest thou not charytably. Destroy not him with thy meate, for whom Christ dyed. Cause not your commoditie to be euill spoken of. For the kingdome of God is not meate and drinke, but righteousnesse, peace, and ioye in the holy ghoste. &c. But why doest thou iudge thy brother? or why doest thou despise thy brother? for we shalbe all brought before the iudgement seate of Christ. *1. Cor. 8.* *Rom. 14.*

He that eateth, eateth to the Lorde: for he giueth God thankes: And he that eateth not, eateth not to the Lorde, and giueth God thankes. *Rom. 14.*

Meate maketh us not acceptable to God for neyther if we eate, are we the richer: neyther if we eate not, are we the poorer. But take heede least by any meanes this liberty of yours be an occasion of falling to them that are weake. &c. Wherefore if meate offend my brother, I will eate no fleshe while the world standeth, bicause I will not offend my brother. *1. Cor. 8.* *1. Cor. 8.*

The

Esa.58. The Lord sayd vnto the Prophet Esay, crye nowe as loude as thou canst. Leaue not of, lift vp thy voyce like a Trompet, and shewe my people their offences, and the house of Jacob their sinnes. For they seeke me dayly and wil knowe my wayes, euen as it were a people that did right, and had not forsaken the statutes of their God. They argue with me concerning right iudgemente, and will pleade at the lawe with their God. Wherefore faste we (saye they) and thou seest it not? We put our liues to straitnesse, and thou regardest it not? Beholde when ye fast, your luste remayneth stil: for ye doe no lesse violence to your detters: Loe, ye faste to strife and debate, and to smyte him with your fyste that speaketh vnto you. Ye faste not (as sometime) that your voyce might be heard aboue. Thinke ye this faste pleaseth me, that a man shoulde chasten himselfe for a daye, and to writhe his heade about like a hoke in an heary clothe, and to lye vpon the earthe? Should that be called fasting, or a daye that pleaseth the Lorde? But this fasting pleaseth not me, tyll the time be, thou loose him out of bondage, that is

The true fast vvhich pleaseth god is to abstayn from all euils.

in thy danger: that thou breake the othe of the wicked bargaynes, that thou let the oppressed goe free, and take from them all manner of burthens. It pleaseth not me, till thou deale thy breade to the hungrye, and bring the poore fatherlesse home into thy house, when thou seest the naked that thou couer him, and hyde not thy face from thine owne fleshe.

Origen vpon Leuiticus. 10. homely 16. Chapter.

If thou wilt faste as Christ commaundeth thee, and humble thy soule, it is conuenient that thou doe it all the time of the yeere, yea, doe the same all the dayes of thy life for to humble thy soule, neuerthelesse if thou haste learned of the Lorde our Sauiour, that he is gentle and lowly of hearte, then if thou wilt faste, after the commaundementes of the Gospell: and keepe in thy fastinges the euangelicall lawes, the which the Sauiour hath commaunded to faste in such manner. But if thou do fast, annoynt thine head, and wash thy face. &c. *Math. 6.* Wilt thou that I doe shewe vnto thee what fasting thou must faste? fast from all thy sinnes, take no meate of malyce, take

no meate of pleasure, be not to hotte with the wine of luxurye, fast from doing euill, abstaine from euill wordes, keepe thy selfe from euill thoughtes, touch not the breade
Col.2. of thefte, of wicked doctrines, couete not the meates of false Philosophy, which doe seduce thee from the truth. Such fasting
1.Tim 4. pleaseth God, but to abstaine from meates which God hath created for the faithfull to take with giuing of thankes, and to doe the same with them which haue crucified Jesus Christ, it cannot please God. The Pharyses were offended with Christe bicause that his disciples did not faste, vnto
Math.9. *Mar.2.* *Luc.5.* whom he aunswered, that the wedding children cãnot mourne as long as ẏ bridegrome is with them. Those then doe faste which haue lost the brydegrome, we which haue with vs the bridegrome cannot faste, but therefore we saye not this, that we woulde let slacke the brydle of christian abstynence. This is verily the Christian libertye to faste alwayes, not through superstition of obseruance: but by vertue of continencye. For howe can they keepe them selues chaste and not defiled and marred, if they bee not holpen and sustayned

Christian libertie is to fast alvvayes, and not by obseruing of dayes.

stayned through the ayde of continencye? Howe shall they understand the Scriptures? Howe shall they studye in knowledge and wisedome? Shall not that bee through the continencie of the bellye, and of the mouth: howe shall euery one make himselfe chaste for the kingdome of heauen, if he doe not cut awaye the affluence of these meates? The Christians then haue that reason to fast.

Augustine in the. 86. Epistle written to Lasulanus.

In the diuine and Apostolicall scriptures, and also throughout the newe testament, in feruentnesse of courage beholding it, I doe see fasting to bee commaunded, but I do not finde it to be defined by Gods commaundement, or of the Apostles, in what time or day we must fast or not fast: wherefore by this I doe understande that the commaundement to fast, is not for to obtaine righteousnesse, the which inwardly is the beautie of the kings daughter.

VVe finde not in the Scripture in vvhat time vvee must fast.

Chrysostome in the 4. tome, of fasting in Lent. Homilie. 73.

If we doe dayly here agree, and that we doe fast all the Lent, and doe not amende our lyues, greater occasion of damnation shall be done vnto vs.

Gregorie the 7. hath commaunded to fast the Lent, vpon payne of deadly sinne. Reade *Platyna*, Pag.171. in his life.

Apollonius the martyr of Iesus Christ in the ecclesiasticall hystorie. 5. booke. Chapt. 11.

Rebuked the heretike Montanus, bicause he was the first which made the law of fastings.

Saint Ierome to Nepotian, first tome.

Laye vpon thee such maner of fasting, as thou canst beare. That thou haue pure, chaste, simple, and moderate fastings, not superstitious. What profiteth it, not to eate of the oyle, and to seeke certayne dainties, and difficult kyndes of meates, as figges, peares, nuttes, fruites of palmes, or dates, the flower of wheate, of honie, and such maner of meates? There is no kynde of garden fruite wherewith we do not torment our selues, to the ende we eate not of breade, and whylest we doe folowe our pleasures, we are drawen from the kingdome of heauen. Further-

Superstitious fastings.

more,

more, I haue hearde of some, who against the rule of the nature of men drinke not water, and eate no breade, but doe eate of delicate suppings, and of punned Leekes, and drinke not the pottage in a cuppe, but in a dishe. What shame is this, howe are we not ashamed of such maner of follies? how are we not weried with such superstitions? Furthermore also, we seeke in delicates the renowme of abstinence. The strongest fasting is breade and water, but bicause that there is no glorie therein, and bicause all liue of breade and water, as of a common thing, we doe not esteeme it to be fasting.

The most strong fasting.

In the olde time they fasted vntill night. *Iudg.20.*

The fasting without workes of mercie displeaseth God. *Zacha.7.*

Cassiodorus reciteth in the 9.boke of his historie,

That the Romaynes had but three weekes for the Lent, fasting euery day except the Sundaye and Saterdaye: The Illerickes and the Grecians had sixe, and the other seauen: but they fasted by space betweene.

Reade of fasting, Actes.13. 1.Cor.16.

Math.4.Luc.2.Tobi.2. 1.Reg.6. 2.Cro 20. 1.Esdras.8.Ioel.2.Ionas.3.Hester. 4.and.14. Psalme.35. and.69. and .109. Deut.9. 3.Reg.19.

2.Reg.1. David and his people fasted vntill euening, hearing that Saule and Ionathas were dead.

2.Reg.12 David fasted and prayed for the people which were stroken of God.

3.Reg.21. Achab fasted and slept hauing on sackecloth, walking comfortlesse, and the Lord had compassion and pitie on him.

Iudith.8. Iudith fasted all the dayes of hir life.

Hest.4. Hester purposing to enter vnto the king for to speake vnto him, fasted three dayes and three nightes.

Iere.36. Iosias declareth the fasting to all the people, and caused the wordes of the booke of Ieremye to be reade openly.

Math.4. Iesus Christ humbled his soule with fasting psalm.35.and .69.and.109.

Esay.58. Unto whome is he like that fasteth, and neuerthelesse ceaseth not to sinne?

Ierem.14. Fasting profiteth nothing at all to the wicked and obstinate people.

Luc.21. Iesus Christ saith: Take heede to your
Rom.13. selues, least at any time your heartes bee

ouercome with surfeting and drunkennesse and cares of this worlde.

Ye haue bene called vnto liberty, onely let not your libertye be an occasion vnto the fleshe, but in loue serue one an other. Gal.5.

Of maryage and of vowes.

The spirite speaketh euidently, that in the latter time some shal depart from the faith, and shal giue heede vnto spirites of error, and doctrins of deuills, which speake false lies through hipocrysie, and haue their consciences marked with an hotte iron: forbidding to mary. 1.Tim.4.

Jesus Christe saithe, haue ye not reade, howe that he whiche made man at the beginning, made them man and woman, and sayde, for this cause, shall a man leaue father and mother, and cleaue vnto his wyfe, and they twayne shall be made one fleshe, wherfore they are no more twayne, but one fleshe. Let not man therefore put asunder that which God hath coupled togither. Mat.19. Genes.1. Genes.2. Ephes.5. 1.Cor.6.

Origene vpon Saint Mathew.
23. Homilye.

The Scribes and Pharyses are set in Moyses chayre. &c. He doth rebuke then such manner of preachers, who doe not only that they saye, but allso doe cruelly and without mercy, great thinges, whiche one cannot doe, not esteeming, or iudgeing what is the vertue of euery one of the hearers, as those which forbid to mary: And doe constraine the people to a moste vyle vyllanye, for that they doe forbydde that which is expedient. Those allso which doe teach to abstayne from meates, and other such manner of thinges, to the which the faithfull ought in no wyse to be constrayned. They do laye great burthens through the worde of their expositions, against the will of Christ saying, my yoke is easie, and my burthen is light: And often times we doe see that those that doe teache suche thinges, doe liue altogither contrarye to their sayings, doing all thinges for the regarde of men, and for vaine glorye, as the word following doth shewe it, saying. All their workes they doe for to be seene of men.

No constraint from mariage.

Mat. 23.

Salomon

Salomon in the.18.Chapter of the pro-uerbes doth describe the blessing of maryage. *Pro.18.*

The Prophet Dauid in the.128 psalme dothe describe the blessing of God vppon those that are maryed. *Psal.128*

The angell Raphael did teache Tobie howe hee ought to marie as God commaundeth. *Tob.6.*

The confirmation of mariage is in the 9.Chapter of Genesis vnder the letter *A.* *Genes.9.*

Eusebius in the Ecclesiasticall hystorie, 3.booke.27.Chap.

Saint Clement, as Eusebius of Cesaria doth recite, hath written agaynst those who doe despyse mariage. Among other things that he hath written, sayth as followeth: Will they also reproue the Apostles? Saint Peter and Saint Philip had wyues, and maried their daughters, and Saint Paule in one of his Epistles, was not ashamed to make recommendations and salutations vnto his wife, whom he sayth he woulde not leade with him about the countrie, to the ende he might be the more free to preache the gospell. And by and by after hee sayth, that

The Apostles vvere maried.

Clement sayth that Saint Paule vvas maried.

Clement in his 7. booke of his work, sayth as followeth: It is sayde that S. Peter when he did see his wyfe to be martyred, reioyced, seeing that by that meanes shee was of the number of the elect, and that she returned unto hir owne house of Paradise, and that he cryed after hir when they brought hir to hir death, calling hir by hir name, saying unto hir: O deare wyfe remember God. Such were the mariages of the Saintes, and their affections perfect.

In the 4. of the sentences, distinction. 17. Chapter. 4. and in the 27. decret. question. 2. Chapter which beginneth, Cum societas. &c.

The Pope in his Decretals calleth mariage, uncleannesse, pollution, and carnall filthynesse.

Heb. 13. Saint Paule answereth the Pope, saying: Wedlocke is to be had in honor among all men, and the bed undefiled, for whore keepers and adulterers God wyll iudge.

Iohn. 2. Iesus Christ allowed mariage, for hee and his mother were at the mariage in Cana

Cana of Galile.

Augustine in his treatise of the goodnesse of mariage.21.chap.

I dare not preferre the virginitie of Saint Iohn, before the mariage of Abraham.

The historie tripartite, 2.booke, Chapt.14. rehearseth or doth make declaration of the Councell of Nice, how it hath decreed that Priests ought not to marry.

But the holy man of God named Pahnutius bishop of Egipt, who had his right eye pluckt out, and the right leg cut of in the hamme, and condemned by the Emperour Maximine to be boyled in melten leade. All these great euils did he suffer for the Gospell of Iesus Christ. The same holy man, seeing that the Councell had ordayned that decree, resisted it boldly, saying that mariage is honourable, and that the companie of his owne wyfe was chastitie, persuading the Councell neuer to establishe such a lawe, saying: that if they doe make such a lawe, it will be vnto them a great occasion of fornication. Then the Synode praysed the sentence and aduice

Note what chastitie is.

The Councell of Nice vvould not make a lavve that the Priestes shoulde not marie.

of that holye man, and woulde constitute nothing touching that matter, but left it to vse at euery mans libertie, not making lawe or necessitie, yet notwithstanding the sayde Pahnutius was not maryed. This Councell was celebrated in the yeare of our Lorde. 328.

Platyna in the lyfe of Siluester the first.

The Councell of Gangres in Galatia celebrated in the yeare of our Lorde 333. hath permitted mariage vnto Priests, and hath excommunicated those whiche shall forsake their father and mother and wyfe, vnder coulor of religion.

Distinction. 31. Chapter. which beginneth, Quoniam.

The counsell of Constantinople the first, hath in like manner ordayned not to make any vowes not to mary, & that the priestes which doe seperate them selues from their wyues, bicause of their holy orders, should be excluded from the communion.

Distinction. 27. Chapter, Quidam, and in the Canon of the Apostles. Chapter. 6.

The counsell of Anticyra whiche was celebrated the yeere of our Lord, 304. like wyse

wyse did permit the Deacons to be maryed, after that they haue taken their orders.

Iohn le Maire of the differences of schismes and of the counsells of the Church.

I founde in the library of the Abbey of Desnay at Lyons in an olde booke: that in Fraunce in the time of Pope Formosus, and King Lewes the second of that name, who was surnamyd the stammerer or stutter, the priestes were maryed. Priestes maried in France.

The Canon of the Apostles saith, if there be any which saith or teacheth vnder the title and cloke of religion, that priestes ought to forsake their wyues, let them bee cursed.

Long time after the counsell of Nice, in the church of the Latines, many Byshoppes were maryed: among other S. Hilary Byshoppe of Poictiers, as wee may see by his Epistle which he wrote being in exile vnto his daughter being a virgin, in which Epistle he made also mention of his wyfe the mother of hir. S.Hilarie bishop of Poictiers vvas maried.

A Byshoppe therefore must be fautlesse the husband of one wyfe, watching, sober, modest, herberous, apt to teach not giuen to *1.Tim.3.* S.Paule teacheth that the byshops may be maried.

to wine, no fighter, not giuen to filthy lucre but gentill, abhorring fighting, abhorring couetousnesse, one that can rule his owne house honestly, hauing children vnder obedience with all honesty. For if a man cannot rule his owne house, how shall he care for the church of God. &c. Likewyse muste Deacons be honest, not double tõgued, not giuen vnto much wyne, neyther to filthie lucre: but hauing the mysterie of the faith in pure conscience: and let them first bee proued, & then let them minister if they be founde faultlesse. Euen so must their wyues be honest, not euill speakers, but sober, and faythfull in all things. Let the Deacons bee the husbande of one wyfe, and such as can rule their children well, and their owne housholdes. After these wordes in the beginning of the fourth chapter, he sayth: the spirite speaketh euidently, that in the latter times some shal depart from the fayth, and shall giue hede vnto spirites of error, and doctrines of deuils, which speake false lyes through hypocrisie, and haue their consciences marked with an hote yron: Forbidding to marie.

The Deacons vvere maried in the primatiue church.

1. Tim. 4.

Againe:

Agayne: For this cause haue I left thee in Creta, that thou shouldest continue to redresse that which resteth, and shouldest ordayne Elders in euerye citie, as I appoynted thee. If any be faultlesse, the husbande of one wyfe, hauing faythfull children, which are not slaundered of ryote, neyther that are disobedient, that hee bee chosen. *Titus.1.*

Obiection.

Pope Gregorie the 7. Monke of Cluny otherwise called Hildebrande, who was Pope in the time of the Emperor Henrie the 4. hath commaunded by letters, vnto Otto bishop of Constance, that he should forbyd in his Dioces, the Priestes to marie, and that he doe vnlose or make frustrate the mariages of those which were already maried. Naucler. Albertus. Crantzius. Lambert. Hirsued.

Aunswere.

The Lorde aunswered vnto the same, saying: It is not good that man should be alone. *Genes.2.*

Extra de Cle.conf.lib.6.Cap.1.

Pope Boniface the 8. hath permitted all libertie vnto ẏ religious people, although they were maried.

Saint

Saint Ambrose in his first booke of Virgins.

1.Cor.7. As concerning Virgins, I haue no commaundement of the Lorde: but I giue vnto you myne aduice. If the Doctor of the Gentiles had no commaundement, what is he that can haue it? And in very deede he had no commaundement, but he hath had an example. For virginite cannot be commaunded, but be desired. For the things whiche are not in our power, are more to be desired, than to bee commaunded. &c.

Virginitie not commanded, but desired.

After that Paule hath counsayled that it were good, if we coulde liue vnmaried, bicause that we are more free to thinke on God, he sayth: And this I speake to declare what is profitable for you, not to tangle you in a snare: but that ye followe that which is honest and comely, and that yee maye quietly cleaue vnto the Lorde without separation.

1.Cor.7.

1.Cor.7. To auoyde fornication, let euerye man haue his wife, and let euery woman haue hir owne husbande. I woulde wish that all men were as I am: but euerye man hath his proper gyft of God, one after this maner,

ner, another after that.&c. If they cannot abstayne, let them marie: for it is better to marie, than to burne.&c.

S. Vldaric bishop of Augsparge, in the Epistle that he sent to Nicholas the first, concerning the forbidding of mariage vnto Priestes.

The forbidding of mariage was altogither contrarie both to the worde of God, the decrees of the Councell of Nice, and to the auncient Church. After he declareth vnto him the great euilles and daungers which therein were. And among other things he declared that which chaunced in the time of Gregorie the first, through the occasion of such forbidding, whiche constrayned him to chaunge his mynde in that case. At a certayne day the said Gregorie sent to his fishe ponde or stewe, for to drawe fishe, and there were brought vnto him more than sixe thousande heades of little children, whiche had bene cast in there, for to couer and hide the whoredome of the Priestes and other Ecclesiasticall ersons. Wherefore Gregorie seeing the same, was constrayned to saye, condeming the decree that he had made against

Note the fruite vvhich came of the forbidding of mariage vnto Priests.

the maryage of the ecclesiasticall persons. The Apostle saithe, it is better to marye then to burne: And I say also for my part, that it is better to mary, then to giue occasion of death. This Epistle was founde in a librarye of the towne of Hollande, called Aldwater.

Of vowes.

S. Ambrose vpon the fyrst to the Corinthians. 7. Chap.

No man ought to be constrayned, least hauing forbid things that are lawfull he doe fall into thinges vnlawfull.

VVe maye breake the vovves made agaynst the fayth.

The counsell of Toledo. 8. did permitte to breake the vowes and othes made against the faith.

1. Sam. 25 The vovve of Dauid.

Dauid sinned in swearing that he would put to death Nabal and all his men, hee did very well to breake that vowe, whiche was against God: And therefore he praysed greatly God for that he letted him to shead bloud, by Abigail.

Mat. 14.

Herode made a vowe to giue vnto the daugh-

daughter of Herodias that daunced before him, what soeuer shee would aske. And she being before instructed of hir mother, said, giue me here John Baptist his heade in a platter. And ye king sorowed: neuerthelesse for his othes sake, & for their sakes which sat also at the table, he commaunded it to be giuen hir. He did euill in fulfilling that vowe against God.

The vowe of Herode.

Saule did euill to vowe to put to deathe his sonne Jonathas, who was hindred to accomplishe his vowe by the people.

1. *Sam.* 14
The vowe of Saule.

God hath sayde and commaunded, thou shalt not kill.

Exod. 20.

Jephtha vowed a vowe vnto the Lorde and sayde, if thou shalt deliuer the children of Ammon into my handes, then that thing that commeth out of the dores of my house against me, when I com home in peace, from the children of Ammon, shall be the Lordes, and I will offer it vp a burnt offring. After the wars were ended he came home, and see his daughter came out against him with Timbreles and daunces. And when he sawe hir, he rente his clothes, and sayde: Alas my daughter, thou hast made me stoupe and art one of

Iudg. 11.
The vowe of Iephtha.

them

them that trouble me. For I haue opened my mouth vnto the Lorde, and cannot goe backe. &c. And he killed his daughter against the commandement of God, which forbyddeth to kill.

Saint Cyprian the Martyr of Iesus Christ. 11. Epistle fyrst booke.

If the virgins haue giuen them selues with a good wil vnto Christ, let them perseuere in chastitie not dissembling, being so strong and constant that they attend the rewarde of their virginnitie: if they will not or cannot perseuere, it is better for them to mary, then to be throwne hedlong into the fire through their pleasures.

If the virgins vvil not or cannot perseuere in their virginitie, let them marie.

The counsel of Arausique or Orenge the 11. chapter hath decreed, that we can vowe nothing rightly vnto God, but that which we haue receiued at his hand: In asmuch as all thinges which we can offer vnto him, are gyftes proceeding from him.

The counsell of Gangres in Galatia, in a Canon and rule saith, if any of those which keepe virginitie for the loue of Iesus Christe, doe eleuate them selues against those that are maryed, let them bee excommu-

excommunicated, or giuen to the diuell. In an other Canon it is saide, when a man bicause of dissembling countenance, vseth strange apparell, beleeuing that thereby he hath righteousnesse in him selfe, and despiseth others, which with honesty and reuerence doe weare caps and other comely apparell, that he be excommunicated.

If the Monkes do think themselues more holy than the maried folk, they ought to be excommunicated, or giuen vnto the deuill.

Iohn le Maire of the difference of schismes and of the counsels of the Churche.

Pope Gregory the seuenth, was the first which made a lawe that priestes shoulde not mary.

Platyna in the life of Pope Pius. 2. or Æneas Syluius.

The Pope Pius borne at Senee, afore named Aeneas Syluius, among other prouerbes, which he was wont to speake, was accustomed also to saye, by good right and by good cause, they haue taken awaye maryage from priestes, but for better cause they ought to restore it vnto them againe.

The prouerbe of the Pope.

Jesus Christ sayth in vayne they worshippe me, teaching for doctrines, whiche are but mens preceptes.

Mat. 15.

*Math.*15. All plantes whiche my heauenly father hath not planted, shall be plucked vp by the rootes.

1.*Cor.*7. It is better to mary then to burne.

Of the church, and howe it may be knowen and of hir authorytie.

Chrysostome vpon S. Mathewe.48. homily.24.Chapter.

The wicked haue Churches, Preachers, Orders, and Clarkes.

There be some who doe greatly seduce, althoughe that it be through liyng, yet neuerthelesse they doe preache Christe, they declare the faith: For they also haue orders, and priestes aswell as the faithfull. They doe also reade the holy Scriptures. Also they doe thinke that they do giue the same Baptisme, and the same Sacramentes of the body and of the bloud of Christe: likewyse they doe honor the Apostles, & Martyrs, and thereby doe cause the thoughtes of men greatly to erre, not onely of the meane and simple people, but also of the

prudent

prudent and wyse. Who shall he be whom Antechrist will not moue? partly doing the workes of Christe, and fulfilling al the offyces of the Christans, before the Christians: excepte it bee paraduenture hee which considereth that which the Apostle hath sayde: Forasmuch then as Sathan himselfe is changed into the fashion of an angell of light. Therefore it is no great matter, though his ministers fashion them selues as though they were the ministers of righteousnesse, whose ende shall be according to their deedes, and not after the fayning and forme of their christianitie. 2. Cor. 11.

Chrysostome vpon S. Mathew, 9. Homilie. Chapt. 24.

All the Christians in this present time, ought to conferre themselues in the holye Scriptures. For sithence the time that heresie hath obtayned and gotten hir churches, men can haue no certayne proofe or triall of true christianitie: And there can be no other refuge for the Christians, who are willing to know the truth of the faith, but the holy Scriptures. Afterwardes he sayth: Whosoeuer then will knowe what the true church of Jesus Christ is, howe

The true Church knovvne by the holye Scriptures.

shall he knowe it but onely by the Scriptures?

Saint Augustine, 2.Tome, 166.Epistle.

In the holy Scriptures we haue learned Jesus Christ: and in the Church we haue commonly those holye Scriptures. Wherefore then is it, that in them we kepe and holde not altogither, in common both Jesus Christ and his Church?

S.Augustine. 7.Tome, in the Epistle against Petilian a Donatist. Chapter.2.3.4.

The Church is in the vvordes of Iesus Christ.

Amongst vs and the Donatistes is a question where the Church is. What is it then that we shall doe? Ought we to seke it in our wordes, or in those of our heade Jesus Christ? Truly we ought to seeke it in the wordes of him whiche is the truth, and which also knoweth his bodie.

Chrysostome vpon Saint Mathewe, 49.Homilie. Chap.24.

Heresie the troupe of the souldiers of Antichrist.

Heresies are the bandes and troupe of the souldiers of Antichrist, chiefly those whiche haue obtayned the place of the church. And it is holden in the holy place, insomuche that it seemeth that they are

there

there holden, as the worde of truth: but it is the abhomination of desolation, that is to saye, of the hoste and bande of Antichrist, the which hath made the soules of many men desolate, forsaken, and destitute of God. And peraduenture that is that which the Apostle speaketh of, which is an aduersarie, and is exalted aboue all that is called God, or that is worshipped: so that he shall sit as God in the temple of God, and beare in hande that he is God. And so all his euils of diuerse heresies, the which were before but only hearde of, are afterwarde holden in the holye place, in ouerthrowing the Churche of Jesus Christ. &c.

2. Thess. 2

Chrysostome vpon Saint Mathewe, Chapt. 24. Homilie. 49.

He then which woulde knowe what is the true Church of Jesus Christ, howe shall he knowe it in so great confusion of such likelyhoode, but by the scriptures?

In the same.

The Lorde then knowing so great confusion to be come in the latter dayes, therfore willed that the Christians which are in Christianitie, which will take the surenesse

For to haue the surenesse of the true fayth, wee must haue regard vnto the holy Scripture.

nesse of the true fayth, should haue refuge vnto nothing but vnto the Scriptures: Otherwyse if they regarded other things, they shall be euill spoken of, and shall perishe, not vnderstanding what the true Church is, and thereby shall fall headlong
Mat. 24. into the Abhomination of Desolation which standeth in the holye place of the Church, &c.

In the same.

Mat. 24. If any mā shal say vnto you, beholde here is Christ in the houses, beleeue it not. For nowe you doe iniurie and wrong to the Godheade, if you seeke it in houses, that which filleth both heauen and earth: or if ye think that he which is come for to resist the proude, and for to exalt the humble and meeke, is hydde there: shewing by suche things, howe of his true Churche oftentimes doe ryse vp seducers. Therefore we must in no wyse beleeue them, if they saye not or doe not that whiche is agreeable to the Scriptures, beleeue them not: for as the smoke goeth before ỹ fire, and the battaile before the victorie: euen so the temptation of Antichrist, preceedeth and goeth before the glorie of Christ, &c.

VVe must beleeue no men if they do not teach the scriptures.

Saint

Saint Barnard vpon the Canticles 33. Sermon.

From whom shall the church hide hirselfe? all are freendes, and all are enemies: all are kinsefolkes, and al are aduersaries: all are housholo seruantes, and there is none at peace: all are neighbours, and all seeke but their owne profite: They are the ministers of Christ, and serue Antechrist: they do walke in the honor of the gooneds of the Lorde, unto whom they doe no honor: thereby commeth that beauty of the harlotte, whiche thou seest dayly in their apparell, as the players of Comedyes, as in the apparell of a King: thereby thou seest the golde in the brydels, saddels and spurres: Thereby are the tables beautified with meates and vessells. Thereby commeth drunkennesse, and gloutonye, thereby proceedeth the harpe and the viol, thereby are the priestes ouerrunning, and the garners full, aunswering the one the other: Thereby are the boxes full of oyntementes and sweete sauor, thereby are the purses filled, therefore would they be, and are the princes of the Churches, the Prouostes, Deanes, Archedeacons, Bishops,

Iudges of the Church in our time.

The Priestes are apparailed pompously like harlots, and those that play in comedies or tragedies when they doe their diuine office.

Archebyshoppes, and such thinges come not lawfully, but bicause they doe walke in the businesse of darkenesse. By that before it hath bene forespoken, and nowe is come the time of the fulfilling of the same, Behold nowe in peace my bitternesse is most bitter, it hath bene before bitter, in the death of Martyrs, afterwardes more bitter in the controuersye of Heretickes, now it is most bitter in the manners of those of our owne house: we can neyther chase them nor driue them away, they are so mighty and multiplyed without number. The sores and plagues of the Church are entred into the inwarde partes, and are incurable, and therefore is hir bitternesse most bitter. &c.

Esay. 38.

S. Hilary writing against Auxentius.

I doe admonishe you to take heede of Antechriste, ye staye your selues to muche on the walles, seeking the church of God, in the fairenesse of buyldings, thinking that the unitie of the faithfull is there contayned: doe wee doubte that Antechriste ought there to haue his seate? The mountaines and the woodes, lakes, prisons, and desertes are more sure unto me and of bet-

VVe ought to take hede of Antichrist, for if vvee doe marke vvell the scriptures, vve shall finde him in the Church.

ter truste, for the Prophets being therein hid haue prophecied.

Saint Barnard vpon the. 90. psalm, Qui habitabit. verse. 6.

O Lorde Jesus thou hast multiplied the people, and thou hast not increased theyr ioye: for many be called, but fewe bee chosen: Al the Christians, almost al doe seeke their owne profite, & not of Jesus Christe. And haue remoued the offyces from the ecclesiasticall dignitie into shameful gaine, and into workes of darkenesse, and the health of soules is not searched for in suche thinges: but the pleasure of riches. Therefore are they shoren, therefore doe they frequent the Churches, and doe celebrate masses, and sing psalmes. They stryue and contende most impudently dayly by proces for Byshopryks, Archebyshopprykes, in somuch that the reuenewes of the Churches are bestowed and wasted in superfluyties, and to vayne vses. There remayneth nothing but that the man of sinne be reueled, the sonne of perdition. &c.

Esa. 9. Mat. 20. Philip. 2.

The Priests are shoren and shauen, and doe all their ceremonies for couetousnes

S. Barnard in his Sermon of the conuersion of S. Paule.

Alas O Lord God, for these are the first *Esay. 1.*

which

The heades of the Church doe persecute the Church.

which doe persecute thee, whome we doe see to loue the hyest places in thy Church, and to holde the principalitie. They haue taken the Arches from Sion, they haue occupied the Castle, and afterwards haue freely & by power and strength, set all the citie on fire: their cōuersation is miserable, the subuertion of thy people is pitifull.

S. Ierome vpon the. 9. Chapter of the Prophete Oseas.

I doe not finde in the olde hystories any other to haue seperated and diuided the Churche, and seduced the people from the house of God, than the Priests and Prelates which are placed of God, for to bee the spyes and watchmen for the Christian people, agaynst the enimies of the church.

S. Barnarde in his first booke, De considera. to Eugenius.

Speaking vnto Pope Eugenius: what are those thy flatterers whiche saye vnto thee: nowe vp boldly: thou doste by them of the spoyle of the Churches? The lyfe of the poore is sowen in the places of the riche. Siluer shyneth in the myre, they runne thither out of all partes, the poorest sort doe not carie it awaye, but the most

strong,

strong, or hee that runneth swyftest: this custome, or rather this mortall corruption, hath not begon in thy time, but I beseeche God that it may ende in thine. In the meane time thou art apparayled and decked vp very gorgeously and sumptuously. If I durst speake it, thy seate is rather a Parke of diuels, than of sheepe? Did S. Peter so? Did S. Paule mocke after that sort? Thy Court ought rather of custome to receyue the good, than to make them such. For the wicked do profite nothing, but the good doe very muche empayre. Afterwardes hee concludeth: Beholde the murmuring and common complaynt of all Churches, they doe crie out that they are cut in peeces and dismembred. There are very fewe, or almost none, whiche doe not feare the stroke or wounde: Doest thou demaunde what? The Abbots are drawen away from their Bishops, the Bishops from their Archbishops. It is great maruayle if one can excuse the same. In doing so, you doe shewe very wel, that you haue fulnesse of power, but not of Justice. You doe the same, bicause that you can doe it: but the question

is,

is, whether you ought to doe it. You are there constituted and placed for to keepe and preserue vnto euery one his honour, and his degree, and not for to beare him enuie and malice.

In the 34. distinction, Chapter, Lector. Glose and distinct. 82. Chap. Presbyter, & Glose. And in the Canon of the Apostles. 17. quest. 4. Chapt. And distinct. 40. Chapt. Si Papa. And distinction. 96. Chapt. Satis. And Chapter, Simplici. And Incipitis.

The Pope sayth that he hath povver to make lavves against nature, and agaynst the Gospell.

It is written in those Canons, that the Popes haue such power and authoritie, that they may dispence agaynst the Apostolicall doctrine, and agaynst the right of nature, and consequently agaynst the Gospell and the worde of God. For the Pope hath all the rightes as well diuine as humane, in the inwarde partes of his brest, wherefore he ought to iudge euerye man, and ought to be iudged of none: Insomuch that though he should lead a great number of people into hell, yet no mortall man ought to presume to rebuke his faultes: For he is God which cannot be iudged of men.

Saint

Saint Paule aunswereth vnto the same saying. Let no man deceiue you by anye meanes, for the Lorde commeth not, except there come a departing first, and that that sinnefull man be opened, the sonne of perdition which is an aduersary, & is exalted aboue all that is called God, or that is worshipped: so that he shall sitte as God in the Temple of God, and shewe himselfe as God. *2. Thes. 2.* Iudge yee novve vvho is Antichrist according to the Canon, and according to the vvord of God.

Saint Hilary in his booke against Auxentius.

Whosoeuer denieth Christe to be suche as he hath bene preached by the Apostles, he is Antechrist. The property of the name of Antechriste, is to bee contrary vnto Christe.

The Priestes doe saye that the Pope cannot erre, neyther the counsels.

Iesus Christ hath sayde vnto S. Peter, I haue prayed for thee, that thy faith faile not. *Luc. 22.*

Vnto the same their owne Canons doe aunswere in the. 40. distinction Chap. which beginneth, Si Papa.

If the Pope doe fall into an error in the faith,

in the faith, and that he be an Hereticke one may very well rebuke and checke him in his faultes.

Alexander.6 Pope.227. in the yeare of our Lorde 1492. Reade Guliel.Bud.

Pope Alexander the.6. speaking once vnto an Embassadour of ye king of Fraunce, vnto whome he had these wordes, this fable of Jesus Christe hath gotten vnto vs great riches.

Sanazarius an Italian Poet in his Epigrammes in the.2.booke.

Beholde the enormitie of the Popes, and their life more than diabolicall.

Speaking of that Pope Alexander, noting the inceste of him, with his owne daughter Lucrecia, and asking hir, Lucrecia wil Alexander desire thee alwayes? afterwardes aunswered, O wicked case: it is thy father. Behold the witnesse whiche the writers of his time haue, declared of that head of the churche.

Abbas Vrspurgensis reciteth of Gregory the.7. otherwise called Hildebrand.

The Popes may verye vvell erre.

That the common wealth of Rome, and all the Churche hath bene vnder him in great danger, through the error of newe schismes, and not heard of, and that he hath vsurped the Papall seate through tyrannye, and not by lawfull election.

The

The counsell holden at Wormes in the yeere. 1080.

Affirmed of Gregory the seuenth, that it is most true that he was not chosen of god, but that hee exalted him selfe, without all shame through disceit, and money, and that he hath turned vpside downe the ecclesiasticall order, and that he hath troubled the kingdome of the Christian Empyre: and that he hath attempted the deathe both of the bodye and soule of that Catholicke and quiet king, and that he hath defended and holden vp the wicked and periured king, and that he hath sowen discorde, among those that agreed togither, and strifes amongest the peace makers, and offences amongest brethren, and diuorcement betweene maryed folke, and that he hath remoued and troubled all that was at reste, quiet and in peace betweene the good lyuers. We being assembled togither of God agaynst the sayde Hyldebrand, preaching sacrileges, and fires, mayntayning periured persons and homycides or men slears, putting in question or doubt the catholicke and Apostolicke faith of the body and bloud of the Lorde, being an obseruer

Gregorie was not chosen of God.

Gregorie hath put in question the catholike fayth, and hath bene a coniurer & necromancer.

and

and keeper of diuinacion and coniuring, and of dreames, and a most manifest Necromancyer, hauing familiar spirites, and for that cause swaruing from the true faith, we doe iudge that he ought to be canonically deposed driuen away, banished, and condemned perpetually, if he doe not leaue of his seate, after that he hath heard these thinges.

Benno Cardinall in the life of the sayde Gregorye.

Amongest many wickednesses that he alledged of him, sayde, that he alwayes vsed to beare about with him a booke of Necromancye, the which was vnto him very familiar, and that he did cast through his enchauntments, the consecrated hoste into a fire, that by that meanes he might faine to haue had a heauenly reuelation, against the Emperor Henry: Benno alledgeth for witnesse, Iohn Byshop of Porta, Secretary of the said Hildebrand.

Note the lyfe of Gregorie.

Platyna in the lyfe of Iohn the 8. And Sabellicus, lib. 1. of the 9. Ennead.

The woman called Iohn the eyght, was borne in Englande, and hir parents were of

The Papesse Iohn. 8. Pope. 107. Yeare. 855.

of Mentz. She followed in hir yong age, a yong scholler in the studies of learning, and profited so well at studie, that she was esteemed at Rome amongst the wysest: for which cause she was chosen to be Pope, thinking that shee had bene a man, and was chosen with as great consent as euer was Pope, following still the studie that she had learned with hir studie felow. *Apoc. 17.* At the time that she was chosen Pope, she was founde with childe with one of hir *Esay. 3.* owne seruants, who perceiuing hirself big, knewe so well to prouide for hir great belly, that none coulde perceiue it, untill such time as she trauayled of childe in the open streete, and in the open procession, uppon the shoulders of those that did beare hir, & dyed in the same trauayle, the second yere after hir Papacie.

Beholde the goodly stuffe that hath bene holden by the popes.

One maye nowe well see whether the Pope cannot erre.

Platyna in the life of Syluester. And Sabellicus. Lib. 2. of the 9. Ennead.

Syluester. 2. Pope. 147. Yeare. 999.

Syluester the 2. was a Monke in his youth, afterwards did giue himselfe unto the diuell, as a right sorcerer, upon condicion that his bodie and soule, should be his

The Pope giueth himselfe to the deuill.

after his death. Prouided that the diuell doe helpe to obtayne that that he desireth, by which meanes he came afterwardes to be Pope.

Platyna in the life of Bennet.8. And Sabellicus lib. 2. of the 9. Ennead.

Benet.8. Pope.152. Yeare.1012. The Pope did shevve himselfe a diuell being aliue, and the diuell appeared Pope after his death.

Bennet the.8. appeared damned after his death in a monstruous and horrible likenesse hauing an heade and tayle like vnto an Asse, and the residewe of the body like vnto a Beare, saying that he did shew himselfe after such sorte, bicause that being Pope he hath liued beastly.

The Pope vvas founde in a lie, and proued a lier

The yeere.457. The counsell of Carthage was holden in which S. Augustine ruled. In the same a lawe was made, vpon the appellations in Ecclesiasticall iudgement. The Pope required that it might be lawfull to euery one that woulde, to appeale vnto his seate. And to ẏ end that he might obtayne that which he demaunded, did committe falshode, in alledging a decree of his owne inuenting, the which sayd that it was made in the counsell of Nice: After that the lye of the Pope was knowen, through the doublenesse of the Councelles

celles, brought from Constantinople, the request of the Pope was refused & denied.

The counsell of Ariminum or Rimino, which was holden by.60. Byshops was generall, condemned the counsell of Nice. And did erre with Arius, who was before condemned, by the word of God in the said counsell. In like manner the.2. counsell of Ephesus hath erred, with Eutyches, and Dioscorus.

The Councell of Ariminũ hath erred, neuerthelesse it vvas general.

The counsell of Carthage in which that holy man Cyprian was present, with.86. Byshoppes, that is to saye almost all the Byshoppes of Africa, Numidia, and of Mauritania, decreed that Baptisme ministred by the Heritickes, ought not to take place, but that those which haue bene baptised by them should be baptised agayne: The whiche sentence was afterwardes condemned, as it appeareth in the.5. distinction, chapter, *Quare*.

The Councell of Carthage in vvhich Saint Cyprian vvas present hath erred.

S. Augustine writing against Maximian bishop of the Arians. Lib.3. Chapter.14.

I ought not to preferre the Councell of Nice, nor of Ariminum, as though I shoulde preferre them before the Scrip-

VVe are not holden by the authoritie of Coũcels, but by holy scripture.

 tures,

tures. For by the authoritie of the same, I am not bounde, neyther thou likewise by the other: But by the authorities of the holy Scriptures, and not of men what soeuer they be. But witnesse vnto both a lyke, as the thing with the thing, the cause with the cause, reason with reason. &c.

We ought also to obserue the decrees of Pope Alexander the 3. of Gelasius, of Nicholas the 2. of the Councell of Illyberis, of Toledo, of Carthage, of Chalons, of Calcedonia, & the Lateran, the which haue forbidden to take money and gyftes for the satisfaction of sinnes, for baptisme, for the temples, for the sacramentes and giftes of God. And haue ordayned that none shoulde be promoted and ordained in the Church by money and rewardes, and that he shoulde be holden for an Apostate, and not for an Apostolike, which shall obtayne the seate of Rome, eyther with money or fauour.

The Councell of Orleans hath determined, that the poore, the sicke, and the weake, shoulde bee nourished and clothed by the Bishoppes, and that the Monkes shoulde possesse nothing of their owne.

Iohn Gerson in his first part of the examination of doctrines.

The first veritie shoulde be so sure, that euery simple man not authorised, might be so well instructed in the holy Scriptures, that one ought rather to beleeue his assertion in the cause of teaching, than the doctrine of the Pope. For it appeareth that rather we should beleeue the Gospell than the Pope. If then such a man doe teache any veritie which is contayned in the Gospell, there where the Pope cannot greatly erre, it is manifest of whether one ought to preferre the iudgement. By and by afterwardes he sayth: If it shoulde happen that there shoulde be a generall Counsell assembled, in which such a man were present which is well instructed, in case the greatest part should declyne through malice or ignorance, to the opposition of the Gospell, such a lay man may be obiected agaynst the sayde generall Counsell.

A lay man vvell instructed in the Scriptures, may be obiected against the Councell, or the Pope, if they erre.

Panormitan in his Chapter, Significasti, extra de electionibus, who was present at the Counsell of Basill, and of Constance.

In matters which concerne the fayth, the

the saying of a lay man ought to be preferred before that of the Pope, if his saying be more probable, by better authoritie eyther of the olde or newe Testament, than that of the Pope.

Thomas of Aquino in the somme, 3.parte.46. addition 6.article.

Bicause that the church is buylded upon faith and the Sacramentes, it appertayneth not unto the ministers of the church to make new articles of the faith, or to make newe Sacramentes, or to chaunge or take awaye those that are made: for that is the excellency and puissance which appertayneth onely unto Jesus Christe, which is the foundation of the churche.

Articles of the faith not to be altred.

The counsell of Gangres in Galatia, doth curse those which abide not in the faith of the Lorde, and which doe make euery day newe constitutions.

The Canons and Decretals of the Popes in the.9.distinction chapter Noli, and chap.Ego, and chap.Negare, and.24.Q.1.chapter. Non afferamus.

We must holde our selues unto the holy Scrip-

Scripture, and not vnto the sayinges of men how holy soeuer they be.

Origene vpon the Prophet Ieremy, in the first homilye.

It is necessary for vs to call to witnesse the holy Scriptures: for vnto our senses and allegations, without those, one ought not to beleeue.

S. Ierome vpon S. Mathewe.

That which is spoken without authority of the Scriptures through the like facilitie may be despised as it is saide.

Saint Augustine vpon S. Iohn. 46. treatise. Chap. 10.

Verily in sitting vpon Moyses seate, if they doe teache the lawe of God, it followeth that God teacheth by them: but if they will teach that which is theirs, heare them not, neyther do them. For truly such people do seeke the things which are their owne, and not of Iesus Christ. VVhat it is to sit vpon Moyses seat.

S. Cyprian vnto Cecill, 2. booke of his Epistles. 3. Epistle.

If you doe whatsoeuer I commaunde you, I will not call you seruauntes, but frendes: and also that Christ ought to be onely hearde, the father hath witnessed it *Iohn. 15.*

Mat. 17. from heauen, saying: this is my deare sonne, in whome I delite, heare him. Wherefore if it bee so that Christ alone ought to be hearde, we ought not to haue regarde what that is that others before vs haue thought good to be done: but that which Christ which is before all hath don. For we must not followe the custome of men, but the veritie of God, forasmuch as the Lorde speaketh by Esaye the Prophet, saying: They doe prayse me highly with their lippes, teaching the commaundements and doctrine of men. And againe in the Gospell, ye haue made that the commaundement of God is without effecte, through your tradition. And therfore, dere brethren, if any of our predecessors either through ignorance, or through simplenesse, hath not obserued and kept that which the Lorde hath taught vs to doe by his example, or doctrine, the same maye be left of through the simplicitie therof, and it may be pardoned him, through the mercie of the Lorde. But it cannot be pardoned vs which are now admonished and instructed of the Lorde. And also we must wryte letters vnto our companions that the lawe of

Christ alone ought to be hearde.

Esay. 29.

Mat. 15.

Those vvhiche doe reiecte the vvorde of God, haue none excuse

the

the Gospell and the doctrine of the Lorde be kept of euery one, and that wee doe not goe backe from that ỷ Christ hath taught and done.&c.

Afterwardes he saithe: If wee bee the priestes of God and of Christe, I doe not finde that we ought to followe any other than God and Christ. Forasmuch as especially he saith in the Gospell: I am the *Iohn.8.* light of the worlde, he that followeth mee shal not walke in darkenesse, but shal haue the light of life.

Lactantius Firmianus in the.6.booke of his godly institutions 8.Chapter.

We ought not to follow men but God.

S. Augustine writing vnto Fortunatus.198. Epistle.

We ought not to holde or esteeme all the disputations of men as canonicall scriptures, although they haue bene made by learned men, insomuch that it is lawefull for vs (sauing the honor of men which is due vnto them) to gainesay or reproue some thinges in their writinges, if peraduenture we doe finde that they sauor otherwyse then the veritie conteyneth, vnder-stoode

The vvritings of holy men are not to be preferred before the canonicall scriptures.

stoode by others, or of vs through the help of God. I am such a one in other mens writings, as I woulde that they shoulde be which doe vnderstand mine.

S. Augustine in his Prologue of the.3. booke of the trinitie.

Augustine vvoulde not that vvee should obey his vvritings as canonical

Obey not my writinges as if they were the canonicall Scriptures, but all that which thou shalt finde in them, beleeue the same without doubting: But giue no farther credit vnto myne than they do accorde and agree with them.

In the same booke.

I cannot denie, but aswell in my greate workes as in my small workes there are many thinges, which iustly and without any temeritie might be blamed.

S. Augustine in his Epistle vnto S. Ierome.19.Epistle.3.Tome. folio.161.

There is no fault in the canonicall scriptures.

I doe confesse thorowe thy loue, that I haue learned to beare that honor and reuerence only vnto the bookes of the holy Scriptures which are called canonicall. And I doe beleeue most surely that no Authors of them, writing them haue erred: but if any thinges are found in them

the

the which do seeme to be repugnant to the truth: I doe esteeme it none otherwyse, but that eyther the booke is euill written, or that the interpreter hath euil vnderstode that which is saide therein, or els that I doe vnderstande it nothing at all. And as for others, I doe reade them in such sort, that with whatsoeuer holinesse or doctrine they be set and paynted forth, yet I do not thinke that to be true which they saye, bicause that they haue such an opinion, but so farre as they coulde persuade me, eyther by those canonical authors, or by probable reasons which are not disagreeing from the truth. And as for thee, my brother, I doe thinke that thou thinkest none otherwise. Yea, I doe esteeme truly that thou wouldest not that we shoulde reade thy bookes, as the bookes of the Prophetes and Apostles, which haue written so certainly, that it shoulde be a wicked thing to thinke that they haue erred or fayled in their wryting. Augustines opinion.

S. Augustine in the. 112. *Epistle written vnto Paulinus.*

I woulde not that thou shouldest follow mine authoritie, thereby to thinke that it is is necessary for thee to beleue it, bicause I haue spoken it: but to the ende that thou beleeue the canonicall scriptures. &c.

Saint Ierome vpon the Epistle vnto Titus. 1. Chapter.

Without authoritie of the Scriptures, babling and scoffing ought not to be beleeued.

Tertullian in his prescriptions agaynst the heretikes.

It is not in our desire or free will, lawfully to bring in, to chose, or to alledge for witnesse, that that another shall bring in or alledge, for his will and pleasure. For we haue the Apostles of the Lord for authors, who haue brought in nothing for their pleasure, neyther no newe thing, but they haue faythfully taught vnto the people, the discipline & knowledge which they haue receyued of God.

S. Augustine of one onely Baptisme in the Epistle vnto Vincent.

What is hee that knoweth not the holy scriptures? &c. My brother meddle not against so great & heauenly things. For the places are knowen by the Canon lawe of the Bishops.

Saint Augustine writing vnto Vincent, in the.48.Epistle.

Gather not togither false accusations agaynst the brethren, of the writings of the Bishops, or of ours: as of Hilarie, or of that vnitie (before that the part of Donatus be deuided or seperated) as of Cyprian, or Agrippin, agaynst the heauenlye witnesses, which are in so great number, so cleare, and not to be doubted. First of al, bicause that such kynde of letters ought to be discerned from the authoritie of the canonicall Scriptures. For we do not read them after that sort, as for to take witnes, to whiche it is by no meanes lawfull to speake agaynst, except peraduenture they haue perceyued any thing otherwyse than the truth requireth. Immediatlye afterwarde he sayeth: But neuerthelesse let vs walke in that in which we are come vnto, (that is to saye) in that waye whiche is Christ. For the integritie and the knowledge of letters, of any Bishop (howe noble and vertuous so euer he be) cannot bee kept as the canonicall Scripture is kept, through or by so many letters, orders, and tongues, and through the susception of the

VVe ought not to bring the faults of the auncient doctors againste so great number of vvitnesses of the holy scriptures.

the ecclesiasticall celebration. Against the which, there are some notwithstanding, who vnder the name of the Apostles, haue inuented and imagined many things: neuerthelesse, it hath bene in vayne, bicause that it is to well proued, celebrated, and knowen. &c.

S. Augustine in his. 2. booke of Baptisme against the Donatistes 3. Chapter.

You haue accustomed to put before vs the letters of Cyprian, the sentence of Cyprian, wherefore doe you take the authoritie of Cyprian, for your schisme, and do repeale and keepe backe his example for to trouble the churche? And what is he but that he knoweth that the holy canonicall scripture, aswel of the olde testament as of the newe, is kept within his limits which are certaine, and that the same is to bee preferred before all the writinges of the Byshoppes that are past, insomuch that we must nothing doubt thereof neyther dispute, to wete, whither that all that which is written in the same be true. But it is lawefull to rebuke the writinges of the byshops which haue bene written or whiche they haue written sithence the confirmation of the canonicall scriptures, or by word, peraduenture more full of wisedome of euery one better instructed in such things, or by greater authoritie of other byshops: or through the wisedome of the wyse, or by the counsels, if peraduenture they haue swarued in any thinge from the truth, and also the counsels which are done, through out euery region or prouince, without all doubtes ought to giue place vnto the authoritye of the first counselles whiche are made through out all Christendome, and the first & generall determinations, ought often times to be amended by those that follow after, when through any experience of thinges that which was secrete is declared, and that which is hid is made knowen, without any kinde of pryde, which is no sacriledge, not hauing a necke puffed vp with pride, without any contention or enuye, with holynesse, humilitie, with the catholicke peace, with christian charitie.

Irenæus in his. 3. booke. 4. chap.

What would it be if there were any disputation or debate moued, of anye lighte question, must wee not haue our recourse

vnto

vnto the moste auncient churches, which were in the time of the Apostles, and to take of them that which is cleare and certayne, for to resolue the debate or question put foorth?

S. Augustine of baptisme against the Donatistes. 3. booke. 9. Chapter.

Honoratus Attuca hath saide, forasmuch as Christe is the truth, we ought rather to followe the truth, then custome.

The Byshop Castus in the 5. Chapter.

Custome ought not to be followed.

He that presumeth to follow custome, in condemning the truth, eyther he is enuyous or wicked towardes the brethren, vnto whom the truth is reueled, or he is ingratefull towardes God, through whose inspiration the church is instructed.

Iere. 7.

Trust not in false lying wordes, saying: here is the Temple of the Lorde, here is the Temple of the Lorde, here is the temple of the Lorde. &c But take heede howe ye doe trust in cousels that beguile you and doe you no good.

Mat. 17. *2. Pet. 1.*

God hath witnessed of his sonne saying: This is my deare sonne, in whome I delight

light here him.

The Lorde hath saide: But the prophet which shall presume to speake ought in my name, whiche I commaunded not to speake, and he that speaketh in the name of strange Gods, the same prophet shall dye. *Deut. 18.* *Deut. 17.*

Moyses saide, ye shall doe after nothing that we doe here this daye, euery man what seemeth him good in his owne eyes. *Deut. 12.*

Ye shall put nothing vnto ẏ word which I commaunde you, neyther doe oughte there from, that ye may keepe the commaundementes of the Lorde your God which I commaunde you. Beholde I haue taught you ordinances and lawes such as the Lorde my God commaunded me. *Deut. 4.* *Apoc. 22.*

S. Augustine writing vnto Orosius against the Priscillanistes and Originistes. 11. Chapter.

The doctrine of man seemeth to haue reason so long as it is not compared vnto the heauenly knowledge: but when the lye approcheth to the truth, it is by and by deuoured and destroyed, as a sparke of fire, and all the teachinges of faulshod and lyinges the whiche nowe are called Idolles.

Mans doctrine hath great apparance in it selfe, but compared to the truth, is confounded.

Forasmuch as they are made, they shal be altogither broken.

He that commeth from an hie, is aboue all: he that is of the earth is earthly, and speaketh of the earthe: he that commeth from heauen is aboue all. And what hee hath seene and heard, that he testifieth: but no man receiueth his testimony, howbeit he that hath receiued his testimonye, hath sealed that God is true. For he whom God hath sent, speaketh ẏ words of God.

Iesus Christ saith. And his wordes haue ye not abiding in you: for whom hee hath sent, him ye beleeue not. Search the scriptures, for in them ye thinke ye haue eternall life: and they are they which testifie of me.

My doctrine is not mine but his that sent me. If anye man will doe his will, hee shall knowe of the doctrine, whither it be of God, or whither I speake of my selfe. He that speaketh of him selfe seeketh his owne prayse: but he that speaketh his prayse that sent him, the same is true, and no unrighteousnesse is in him.

He that sent me is true: and I speake in the world, those thinges which I haue heard hearde of him.

If ye continue in my wordes, then are ye my disciples, and shall know the truth, & the truth shall restore you to libertie. &c. I speake that I haue seene with my father: and ye doe that which ye haue seene with your father. Verily, verily, I saye vnto you, if a man keepe my saying, hee shall neuer see death. *Iohn.8.*

My sheepe heare my voyce, and I know them, and they followe me. *Iohn.10.*

I haue not spoken of my selfe: but the father which sent me, gaue me a commaundement what I shoulde saye, and what I shoulde speake. And I knowe that this commaundemente is lyfe euerlasting. Whatsoeuer I speake therefore, euen as the father bade me, so I speake. *Iohn.12.*

The wordes that I speake vnto you, I speake not of my selfe. If ye loue me, kepe my commaundements. He that hath my commaundements and keepeth them, the same is he that loueth me. He that loueth me not, keepeth not my sayings, and the wordes which ye heare, are not mine, but the father which sent me. *Iohn.14.*

Many other signes also did Iesus in ẏ pre- *Iohn.20.*

sence of his disciples, which are not written in this booke. These are written that
ye might beleeue that Iesus is Christ the
sonne of God, and that in beleeuing yee
might haue lyfe through his name.

Galat.1. Though that wee, or an aungell from
heauen, preach vnto you other wayes than
that whiche we haue preached vnto you,
holde him as accursed. As we sayd before,
so say I nowe agayne, if any man preache
vnto you other wayes than that yee haue
receyued, holde him accursed.

Iohn.4. The woman that was a Samaritane,
sayde vnto Iesus, I wote well Messias
shall come, which is called Christ: when
he is come, he will tell vs all things.

Act.20. I haue kept nothing backe, but haue
shewed you all the counsell of God.

Chrysostome in the first homilie vpon the Epistle vnto Titus.

The Gospell doth contayne all things,
the things present, and things to come,
honor, pietie, and fayth. &c.

Saint Hilarie vpon Saint Mathew. 14. Canon.

Mat.15. Euery plant which my heauenly father
hath not planted, shall be plucked vp by
the

the rootes, that is to say: all mans traditions ought to be plucked vp, by the fauor of the whiche they haue transgressed the commaundement of the lawe. And therefore he called them the blinde leaders, promising the waye of euerlasting lyfe, the which they see not themselues: and sayth that the falling hedlong of those blind leaders and their conductors, is common. All mans traditions ought to be plucked vp by the rotes.

S. Augustine vpon S. Iohn. 49. treatise. 9. Chapter.

Although that the Lorde Iesus Christe hath done many things which haue not bene written, as also his owne Euangelistes doe witnesse it, that the Lord Iesus Christ hath sayde and done many things whiche are not written, neuerthelesse, the things haue bene chosen to be written, whiche were thought sufficient for the saluation of the beleeuers.

Of the holy scripture, and howe it is lawfull for all men to reade it.

Happie is he that readeth, and happie are they that heare the wordes of this *Apoca. I.*

Prophecie, and keepe those things which are written therein: for the tyme is at hande.

Luk.11. Jesus Christ sayeth: Happie are they that heare the worde of God, and kepe it.

Psal.119. Thy worde is a lanterne unto my feete, and a light unto my pathes.

Eccle.1. Gods worde in the heygth is the well of wisedome, and the euerlasting commaundements are the entrance of hir.

Iere.15. When I had founde thy wordes, I did eate them up greedilye: they haue made my heart joyfull and glad.

Ephes.6. Take the helmet of saluation, and the sworde of the spirite, which is the worde of God.

S. Augustine of the Citie of God. 19. booke. 19. Chapter.

VVe ought not to forbid any man to knovve the truth.

It is forbidden no man to knowe the truth, that which he ought to doe through honest repast and recreation: howe much time doe men and women lose daylye, in going and comming, playing and scoffing, in detracting and beholding playes and follies.

Chry-

Chrysostome vpon S. Iohn in the end of the.16. homilye.

I praye you marke well one thing which is true, is it not a thing full of absurdite that a surgian,a shoomaker, a weauer and generally all men of occupation,euery one of them doe striue for the profession of their arte and science, and that a christian knoweth not howe to make an account or a reason of his religion? It is very true that when the occupation is not knowen it is but a losse of mony, but the despising of christian religion bringeth with it the losse of the soule, and yet neuerthelesse we doe trauayle through so greate misery and through so great madnesse, that we doe put therein all our heart and cogitation: but the thinges which are necessary for vs, and which are as most strong holdes of our saluation, we esteeme them nothing at all. That same is that which letteth the Gentils to knowe their error. Forasmuch then as they doe ground them selues vpon lyinges, for to doe all that, that they doe, and for to defend the ignominye and sclander of their teachinges, we which doe obey and serue the truth, dare not open the

The ignorance of the Christians is the cause that the infidels doe not acknowvlege their error.

mouth for to defend that which is oures. What letteth them that they cannot condemne our great imbecillitie and weakenesse, and that they should not suspect vs of some discept and follye? That they doe not speake euill of Christe, as of a lyar, whiche by his fraude and discept hath abused a great multitude? we are the cause of that blasphemy: This is commaunded

1.Pet.3. vs of Saint Peter. For he saith, let vs be ready alwayes to giue an answere to euery man that asketh vs a reason of the hope that is in vs.

VVe ought to be readie to giue a reason of our fayth vnto those that aske vs.

Colos.3. Let the word of Christ dwel in you plenteously. But what do they which are more fooles then madde answere vnto the same, blessed be euery simple soule, and he that

Prou.10. walketh surely. But this is the cause of all euilles, that many knowe not to bring witnesses of the Scriptures in due time: for we must not vnderstand in this place here the simple for the foole, and for him that dothe vnderstande nothing, but for him which is not crafty and malitious. For if we should vnderstand it so, it should be superfluous to say, be wyse as serpents and

Common vvordes to be simple.

Mat.10. innocent as doues.

S. Ierom in his Prologue vpon the Prophet Sophony.

If they had knowen that Huldah did prophecie when men held their peace, and that Debora did iudge and prophecy, who ouercame the enemies of Israell when Barack was a frayde, and that Iudith and Hester (in figure of the church) killed the aduersaryes and deliuered Israell whiche were like to perishe, they would neuer haue played the noddyes behinde my back (that is to saye) they would not mocke me behind my backe. And a little after he saith, it suffiseth me to saye in the ende of the prologue that our Lorde Iesus Christ appeared first vnto the women, and they were Apostles of the Apostles, to that end that the men should be ashamed that they haue not sought that, which that same britle or frayle kinde hath already founde.

4. *Reg.* 22
Iudges. 4.
Iudith. 13
Hester. 7.

Chrysostome vpon S. Iohn. 3. homilie. 4. Chapter.

Let vs then bee ashamed, that the wyfe that had fiue husbandes, and a Samaritane, was so diligent to learne, who neyther for the time of the day, nor for any other businesse coulde not be drawne from the

The slothfulnesse of Christians in not reading diligentlye the vvorde of God.

the doctrine of Christ. But as for vs, we are not only far of frō enquiring any thing of that which appertayneth vnto the erudition of heauēly things, but also we are, as it were assured in all things, & we do care no more of the one, than of the other, and therefore wee are ignorant of all things. What is he among vs, I pray you, who being come into his house, doth go about to doe anye worke appertayning vnto a Christian? What is he that will declare the sense and meaning of the scriptures? Trulye none. Wee doe finde oftentimes Dyce and Cardes, but verye seldome tymes bookes: and if any haue them, they doe keepe them sure in their chambers, as though they had none. Or else all their delyte and studie is to haue fayre and pleasāt couerings, & painted or goodly figures of letters, not for to read them, nor vse thē, but for to shewe forth their riches and ambition, and studie none other thing. Vaine glorie is so great, as I doe not heare any ambitious persons to vnderstād any boke, but onely to esteme letters of golde. What gayne commeth thereof I pray you? The Scriptures are not giuen vnto vs, for to haue

A great number of those vvhich doe cal them selues christians, haue oftener the tables and dyce in their hands, than holy bokes.

aue them only in bookes, but to that ende *Prou.7.*
ve shoulde print and engraue them in our
eartes. Wherefore such hauing and kee- Scriptures to be grauen in our harts, and the bokes diligently read ouer.
ing of bookes, is of the ambition of the
Iewes, vnto whom the commandements
vere giuen in letters. But vnto vs it is
ot so, vnto whome they are giuen in the
ables of the heart of charitie. I doe not *Iere.31.*
nbyd to haue bokes, but I doe admo-
ishe them, and instantly pray them, that
e may so haue them, that neuerthelesse,
s wee maye rehearse often times in oure
ryndes, both the letters and the sense,
n such sort that thereby we may be cleane.
For if the diuell dare not enter into an
ouse where the Gospell is, muche lesse
hall he touch his soule, which by continu-
ll reading hath that doctrine familiar
nd common.

Sanctifie then the soule and the bodye, *Psal.1.*
nd that shall come if thou haue alwayes
e Gospell in thy heart, and in thy tong.

S. Ierome in his Proheme vpon the first booke of his Exposition vnto the Ephesians. 9. Tome.

All wordes and all reasons are conteined
n the holy bookes, by the which also wee
knowe

knowe God, and forgette not the cause, wherefore wee are created. I doe muche maruayle, that some haue bene giuen so muche vnto foolishnesse, and to slothfulnesse, not willing to learne the most excellent things, yea, they haue esteemed and doe esteeme worthie of rebuke and blame all those whiche haue such a studie: vnto whome although I coulde aunswere more straitly and briefely, leauing them eyther angrie or appeased. I doe say that it is a great deale better to reade the scriptures, than to giue themselues after riches, for to gather and heape them vp. *1.Tim.6.*

Chrysostome vpon Genesis.6.Tome. 5.Homilie.1.Chapter.

Neighbours ought to take holye scripture in their handes to sprinkle their soules.

I desire you that wee bee not negligent vnto our owne saluation, yea rather that our worde be of spirituall things, and let vs take in our handes Gods bookes, and calling togither our neyghbors, sprinkle with heauenlye wordes oure owne selues, and of the assistentes, that thereby we may chase and driue away the treasons and assaultes of the diuell.

S. Ierome in his first Tome vnto Marcellus, perswading him to goe to Bethleem.

In the towne where Iesus was borne, there are none but rusticall people, where ye shal here nothing but singing of psalms in euery place: the ploughman holding the plough by the tayle singeth *Alleluya*: The mower to passe away the time singeth psalmes, the Vine dresser with his hooke cutting the vine, singeth some thing of Dauid, these are the songes of this prouince, these are (as we say commonly) the songes of loue.

Athanasius vpon the Epistle vnto the Ephesians. 6. Chapter.

Ye fathers moue not your children to wrathe. &c. he addeth the cause of the obeying of the fathers commaundement, and sheweth vnto the parents how they should make their children obedient and ready to doe that that they are bydde. If thou wylt (saith he) that thy children doe obey thee, accustome them vnto heauenly wordes, and saye not that it belongeth vnto the Monkes to vnderstand holy letters: For truely it is the office rather of euery christian, *Ephes. 6*

stian, and chefelye of him which medleth and hath to doe with the affayres and businesse of this worlde. And the more that he hath neede of the greater healpes, the greater neede hath he to vnderstand it: for he is more prouoked with the assaults of this world. This then is greatly for thy profite, that thy children may heare & read holy Scriptures, for thereby they shall learne to honor father and mother: But thou doest the contrary, thou bringest vp thy children in the doctrine of panims and gentiles, of whiche they shall learne moste wicked thinges, the which shall not be so when they are instructed in the heauenlye Scriptures.

Reading of the scriptures maketh children obedient.

Primasius (Byshop of Vtica in Africa, disciple of S. Augustine) vpon the Epistle to the Collos. 3. chapter.

Collos. 3.

Let the worde of Christ dwell in you plenteously. &c. Here is most amply declared, that the laye people ought also to haue the word of God, not only simply, but also aboundantly and plenteously, and they ought also to admonishe and teach the one the other.

The lay people ought to haue the holy scriptures.

Atha-

Athanasius vpon the.3. Chapter of the Collossians.

Let the worde of Christe dwell in you plenteously in all wisedome: He declareth the way by the which we may giue thanks in all things. For if the worde of God (sayth he) dwell in you, that is to say, the doctrine or heauenly commaundementes and admonitions, by the which he instructeth vs to despyse this lyfe, we cannot greatly esteeme earthly riches. Truly we shoulde not fall or bee ouercome with to grieuous things, but to beare all things stoutly and manfully rendring thankes vnto God, although there happen aduersities. For he hath not sayde, let the word of God be in you simply, but let it dwell in you plenteously. For if we doe abound in the knowledge of the holy Scriptures, we shall easly beare trybulations, paines and calamities, and all other manner of euill.

Collos.3.

The holy scriptures cause vs to beare all tribulations paciently.

Theophilacte vpon the.6.chap.to the Ephesians.

If thou wylt (saith he) that thy children should obey thee, instruct them in the word of our Lorde, and saye not that it dooth belong onely unto the Monkes to reade the Scriptures. For it belongeth aswell unto euery christian, and cheefely unto all those which haue to doe in this worlde.

S. Ierome vpon the.6.chap.vnto the Ephesians.

Little children ought to be taught the holye scriptures.

If he doe commaund the Ephesians being laye men, and unto many that are occupyed in the businesse and affaires of this life (as we see among the people) to teach their children in all discipline, and admonition of the Lorde: what oughte wee to thinke or iudge of the priestes? of whose order he hath written unto his disciple Timothe saying, hauing children subiect in all reuerence.&c.

S. Ambrose vpon the.2.Epistle vnto Timothe.3.chapter.

2.*Tim*.3.

All scripture giuen by inspiration of God.&c. It is manifeste that all scripture of which God is said to be the author, to be profitable: For it is giuen to that ende that it may profite the ignorant and amend the disformed creatures, drawing the wicked into all good workes: For in profitting a little and little to the newe man, it will make him the man of God.

Chry-

Chrysostome vpon the.2.Epistle vnto Timothe.3.chapter.

Thou hast (saith he) through me the Scriptures, if thou doest desire to learne any thing, of them thou mayest learne it: If he did write those thinges vnto Timothe who was full of the holy ghoste, howe much more ought we to thinke that it is spoken vnto vs.

Lactantius Firmianus in the Proeme of his heauenly institutions.

We which haue receiued the Sacrament of true religion, for asmuch as the truthe is reueled vnto vs, and that we may followe God the doctor of sappyence and wysedome, let vs call vnto that heauenlye banket all men vniuersally without anye difference eyther of kinde or age: for there is no meate sweeter and more delectable vnto the soule, then the knowledge of the truthe.

S. Augustine in the.6.chapter of the vtilitie and profyte of beleeuing.

Euery one may dravve out of the holy scriptures that vvhich is needefull for his soules health.

All that which is in the Scriptures is high and heauenly, all is truth and moste fitte and holsome doctrine (beleeue me) for to fill and satisfie the spirites, in such sorte that euery one may drawe out that which is sufficient for him, so that he drawe it deuoutly and holily, according as true religion requireth.

Augustine of true religion.51.chapt. about the letter E.

In forsaking (sayeth he) the open and Poeticall trifles and foolishnesse, let vs feede and comfort our spirite, in treating and considering of holy scriptures. The which spirite being wearye and to muche ouercome with the heate, hunger, and thirst of vayne curiositie, and things to no purpose, desireth to bee refreshed and comforted with vain fantasies, as of goodly and daintie meates.

Chrysostome vpon S. Iohn 5. Tome. 10. Homilie, first Chapter.

VVe ought to teach one another in Gods vvord.

Before I doe come to intreate of the wordes of the Gospell, I would request of you one thing, which I woulde not haue you to despyse. For I doe not demaunde of you heauie things, nor such as are hard to be done, neyther that which is onely profitable to me, but a great deale more to you. What is then the request that I demaunde?

maunde? That one day in the weeke, or at the least vpon the Sundayes and Festiuall dayes ye be diligent to haue in youre handes before the preaching the Gospell, which we doe reade vnto you, and to repeate them often in your houses, searching diligently the vnderstanding thereof, and noting that which is easie or obscure and harde in them, and that which seemeth to haue contrarietie, yet notwithstanding hath not: and after that ye haue throughly examined it, bee very attentiue to those Sermons, by whiche meane shall come great profite both to you and to me. For I shall haue no great labor to declare vnto you the vertue and efficacie of the gospell, so that the sentence before be made easy by you in your house. And you shal be a great deale more wyse, not onely to heare and vnderstande, but to teach others. For there are a great manye that heare, and take great payne to keepe all the wordes of the Gospell, and all that wee doe interprete vpon them, yet neuerthelesse they profite not very much, although wee shoulde remayne there with them a yeare. Wherefore? Bicause they giue not themselues

VVhat is the cause that manye doe profite so little in the scriptures.

vnto our sermons but a small time, & that onely in the Churche. And if anye excuse themselues by reason of their businesse, and occupations of publike and particular things: First of all, they erre very much, chiefly in that they vnderstande so manye things, and are so much giuen vnto temporall affayres and businesse, as they doe nothing at all studie on the things whiche are moste necessarie, and doe alledge a vayne excuse, and of no force. For one may rather accuse in this matter, the long conuersation of frendes, the long sitting in the theaters and gasing places, the long time that men spende in beholding the running of horses, in which vayne things they consume and spende manye times a whole daye, and the which neuerthelesse, they excuse not themselues by reason of their occupations. Furthermore, ye are to diligent in things that are vyle, and nothing worth. But when ye muste vnderstande heauenly things, ye esteeme them vnprofitable, and of no price: insomuch as yee make none account to bestowe on them anye little care and diligence. And howe are they worthie of victuals, and to

No excuse from reading of scripture.

see

see the sunne, which make so small account of it. The negligent people haue yet another excuse, but very euill, ẏ is to say, that they haue no bokes. That should be a ridiculous thing to answere here for the rich, but bicause I doe thinke that many poore men doe vse manye times that excuse, I will a little speake vnto them, and aske them whether they haue not all the instruments and tooles that belong to their arts and sciences. Although that pouertie letteth or hindreth them greatlye to buye them: It is then a foolishe thing to excuse themselues through pouertie, and to be diligent in lacking nothing necessarie for their occupations and sciences, yet to excuse themselues vppon their occupations and pouertie, in things whereof commeth vnto them so great vtilitie and profite.

An admonition vnto the poore people to haue the holy bookes.

Augustine in the.56.Sermon vnto the brethren being in sorrowe and care.

He which maketh none account to reade the holy Scriptures, sent from paradise, ought to feare, ẏ he do not only peraduenture receiue eternall retributions and rewardes, but also that he escape not eternall paines.

He ought to feare vvhich vvill not reade the Scriptures, to be tormẽted vvith eternall paynes.

paines. For it is so dangerous not to reade
the heauenly precepts, that the Prophet
Esay.5. with great mourning doth crye, therefore
commeth my folke into captiuitie bicause
they haue no vnderstanding: for he that is
1.Cor.14. ignorant shall be ignorante still. Without
doubt he whiche maketh none accounte in
this world to seeke God by heauenly reading, God will scorne to knowe him in the
eternall and euerlasting blessednesse: We
ought greatly to feare with the fiue foolish
virgines (who came after the gates were
Math.25. shutte) when Christe saide vnto them, I
knowe you not, depart from me ye workers of iniquitie. What is that to saye, I
knowe you not, I knowe you not? Howe
doth he not knowe those whom he sendeth
to the fire? not without cause both of them.
For as he saide not long sithence, those
whiche will not vnderstande in reading in
this worlde, God will not knowe them in
the daye of iudgement. We ought also to
heare not negligently, but diligently, and
with great feare that which is written in
Pro.28. the prouerbes of Salomon, hee that turneth (saith he) awaye his eare from hearing the lawe, his prayer shal be abhorred.

He that woulde be hearde of God, oughte first to heare God: for howe would he that God should heare him, considering that he dispiseth so much as he maketh none account to reade his holy commaundements And that, what is it my brethren? Some christians yea and which is worse some of the clergye, when they would bring them into the right waye doe ordaine that bread wine and oyle and other necessarye things of coste be prepared for them. And forasmuche as euery one prepareth so manye thinges for his terrestriall iorney, for to nurrishe his fleshe, wherefore hath he no care or desyre to reade so excellent a booke of whiche his soule shoulde be refreshed here eternally.

Hee that vvoulde be hearde of God, ought first to heare God.

What soeuer thinges are written afore time are written for our learning, that we through pacience, and comfort of the scriptures, might haue hope. Rom. 15.

To all you that be at Rome: he hath written vnto all, that that he did write. Rom. 1.

These thinges were written to put vs in remembrance, whom the endes of ŷ world are come vpon. 1. Cor. 10.

Saint Ierome writing vnto Cælantia a gentlewoman of Rome.

You demaund and redemand very carefully and earnestly, that I should describe for you a certayne rule of the holy Scriptures, to whiche you shoulde addresse and leade the course of your life, to the end that knowing the will of the Lorde, among the honors of this worlde, and the pleasure of riches, you should rather haue a heape and great store of good manners. And to that end that you being maryed may please not onely your husbande, but also him whiche hath permitted maryage. And againe, first of all that the authority of the husband be kept, and that all his family doe learne of you, how greatly they ought to honor him, the Lorde declareth through seruice and great obedience by humilitie, for the more you honor him, the more you shalt be honored: for the Apostle saith: The husband is the wiues heade. For the bodie hath more ornaments vpon the head, than all the residue of the whole parts.

The maried vvife ought to be an example to all those of hir house, in holynesse of life and conuersation.

Ephe.5.

1.Cor.11.

Againe S. Ierome writing vnto the sayde Cælantia.

Let all excuse of error cease, the filthie

the filthie and dishonest reioycing in sinne, let them be put awaye : for if we will excuse and defende our selues by the example of the multitude, reciting many times the vices of others for our consolation and comfort, & saying that we haue none whō we may followe, we doe nothing. We are sent to the example of him, who, we doe all confesse, ought to be followed. And therefore the chiefest care is to knowe the heauenly lawe, by the which thou mayest see the examples of the saints, as if they were present: Learne by the counsell of the same what we ought to do, & what to auoid. For he helpeth greatly to iustice (that is to say increaseth vertues) that filleth his spirite and mynde with heauenly wordes, and whiche hath alwayes in his heart that which he desireth to fulfill by works. &c.

The vvicked lyfe of another to couer ours, ought not to be alledged.

Immediatly after he sayth : Let the holye Scriptures bee then alwayes in thy handes, and continually in thy thought, and thinke it not sufficient for thee to remember, or to haue in mynde the commaundementes of God, and not fulfilling them by workes. But knowe them, to the ende you may learne that which ought to be done. For before God they are not righteous which heare the lawe: but the doers of the lawe shall be iustified. Truly the fielde of the heauenly lawe is muche, and without measure enlarged, the which doth shyne with many witnesses of truth, and as with a certayne heauenlye flower feedeth and nourisheth the spirite of him that readeth it, with a marueylous delite: All which things you shall knowe to be very good to keepe iustice.

Rom. 2.

S. Ierome writing vnto the Ladie Gaudentia, of the bringing vp of hir daughter Pacantull.

Howe we ought to bring vp the yong daughters in reading.

When the little & yong damsel shal come vnto seauen yeares of age, and that she beginneth to be shamefast, to knowe when she woulde keepe silence, and to doubt of that that she ought to speake. Let hir then learne by heart the Psalmes, and vnto twelue yeares, that shee doe make a treasure in hir hart of the bokes of Salomon, of the Gospels, of the Apostles and Prophetes.

Agayne, writing vnto another good Ladie called Leta, exhorting hir to instruct hir daughter from the cradle in the holy

oly scriptures, he willeth hir to loue the
godly bookes, in steade of precious stones
and silke, in which bookes, let not the co=
uers being embroderied with diuers co=
lours please hir, but the erudition distinct
and corrected according to fayth: Let hir
learne first the Psalter, and through such
songs, that shee doe withdrawe hir selfe
from the worlde: Let hir be taught to liue
vertuously in the Prouerbes of Salomon.
And that shee doe accustome hirselfe to de=
spyse and contemne worldlye things in Ecclesiasticus. That she doe followe the
example of vertue and pacience in Job.
That she doe learne the Gospell, not let=
ing it go out of hir handes. That she wil=
linglye learne the Actes and Epistles of
the Apostles. And when she hath enriched
hir heart with suche riches, to learne by
heart the Prophetes, and the bookes of
Moyses, the bookes of the Kings, Para=
lipomenon, Esdras, also Hester, and last
of all the Canticles of Salomon, called
Cantica canticorum. For if she should read
them at the beginning, it might hurt hir,
vnderstanding not the holye songs of the
spirituall mariages, vnder carnall words.

The canonicall bokes

That

That she doe auoide all bookes that are apocrypha or hidden. That shee haue alwayes in hir handes the workes of Cyprian, Athanasius, and Hilary.

S. Ierome in his Proeme of his commentaries vpon Esay vnto Eustachius.

I giue vnto thee that which I doe owe thee, obeying the commaundementes of Christe, whiche saithe, seeke diligently the Scriptures, seeke and you shall finde, that it be not sayde vnto me as it was said vnto the Iewes, you doe erre knowing not the Scriptures and the vertue of God and the wysedome of God, and hee that knoweth not the Scriptures, knoweth not the vertue of God, nor his wisedome. Ignorance of the Scriptures, is ignorance of God.

Iohn.5.

Christ is the vertue of God.

Chrysostome in his.3. Sermon of Lazarus.

I haue tolde you many times, before nowe whereof we ought to speake, to the ende that in the meane season you maye take the booke, and consider it diligently, and after that you haue vnderstoode that whiche shall be saide, and that whiche shall remayne to be declared, you shall

make

make your spirites more instructed & redy to heare the thing spoken of. I doe exhort you and wil not cease to exhort you alwais to be attentife, not only to that which shall be spoken here: but also when you shall be in your houses, alwayes giue good eare to the holy Scriptures, which I haue not ceased to pricke forwarde cheefely those which haue bene with me, and that none say vnto me his wordes are colde, there are many things finally to be esteemed: I am an aduocate: I am let with publicke affaires: I haue an occupation: I haue a wyfe: I doe bring vp my children: I haue charge of my familie: I am a temporall man, it belongeth not to me to reade the Scriptures, but for those that haue forsaken the worlde, whiche dwell aboue the mountaynes, which chastly leade a solitary life. What saiest thou O thou man? doth it not belong vnto thee to reade the Scriptures, bicause thou art let and hindred with businesse and innumerable cares? Therefore the more thou haddeste neede to reade them then they.

The excuses that the temporall people doe make, to auoyde from reading the holy Scriptures.

For those haue not so much neede of the ayde and helpe of the Scriptures as thou which art tossed through the middes of the waues of businesse troubles, and cares: for truely the Monkes and those that dwell in solitary places which liue without sute of lawe and other businesse, and which dwell in the desertes, haue none acquaintance with any man, but studye philosophy in moste peaceable tranquillitie with safetie, and haue the fruition of most safe thinges. On the contrary we (as in the middest of the sea) tossed with innumerable sinnes, haue alwayes neede of the perpetuall and continuall solace and comfort of the scriptures. They are very farre of from the combat, and therefore they doe not receiue many strokes and woundes, but thou bicause thou art still in the battayle, and that thou doest receiue many woundes, thou hast the greater neede of remedy.

Monkes vvere solitarie people, vvho notvvithstanding did lead a common life, not as the Monkes at this day.

For thy wyfe doth prouoke thee, and thy sonne doth make thee sad, and doth styrre thee vp to anger, and thy enemy goeth aboute to circumuent and deceiue thee, and thy freende doth beare thee enuye and hatred, & thy neighbour doth persecute thee, and thy companion doth deceiue thee, and many times the Judge doth threaten thee,

and

and pouertie doth molest and greeue thee, the losse of the thinges in thy house dooth make thee sorowfull, and prosperitie maketh thee proude, and aduersitie draweth thee awaye: to conclude diuers occasions and necessitie of cares, troubles, sorrowe, boasting, pride, doe compasse and inuirone thee on euery side, and rounde about innumerable dartes doe flye, for whiche thinges it is necessary to take incessantly the weapons and armor of the Scripture. Acknowledge thē that thou walke through the pinnacles (that is to say the most high places) of the citie. For the concupiscences of the fleshe doe eleuate them selues more sharply against those which liue amongest the multitude of men, whom the beauty of the face and the comlynesse of the bodye conceiued through looking on and dishonest wordes which entre in at the eares, doe trouble muche. And the harmonious and pleasant songes doe weaken often times the constancy of the spirite. But to what ende doe I recyte this? The sauor of the sweete smelles (which seemeth to be a thing more vile then all that) comming from those women whiche dwell at the

stewes

stewes for gayne in playing the whores, doth leade vs captife and ouercommeth vs by only meeting them: so many things there be which doe assayle our soule: And therefore we haue neede of heauenly remedyes, not aswell to heale the hurtes wee receiued, as for to keepe vs from them, that they doe not assault and afflict vs againe, but to auoyde and giue the repoulse through the continual reading of the scriptures, to the darts of the diuell comming a farre. For if we be alwayes hurt & take no remedy, what hope of health shall we haue? Doest thou not see the workers of mettal, goldsmythes, coyners, and all those which doe exercise any occupacion, to haue all the instrumentes of their occupacion readye and to lacke none? Although that honger constrayneth them, and pouertie doth afflict them, they had rather to suffer all thinges then to sel any instrument of their occupacion for to nurrish them, yea many had rather to borrowe mony vpon vsurye, then to lay to gage any little instrument of their science or occupacion, and for a good cause, for they doe knowe that after that they haue solde it, the occupacion should shoulde be vnprofitable, and all the foundation of their gayne taken away: but in hauing them, it may be that in time they will paye that they haue borowed of another, in vsing alwayes their occupation: But if they doe sell them to other before they haue payde that they doe owe, they haue not whereby to excogitate or inuent any thing to helpe their hunger and pouertie. Truly it behoueth vs to be of such courage: for euen as to them the Hammers, Anuiles, and Tongs, are instruments of their Artes, euen so the bookes of the Apostles and Prophets, are instruments of the Arte and waye of saluation, and all Scripture being heauenly inspired, is profitable. And euen as they finishe all that they doe take in hande to doe by those instruments, euen so truly by those bookes, we frame our soule, and amende and correct it when it is wicked, and renue it when it is waxen olde. For those can but onely by their Arte giue formes and fashions to things, for they cannot chaunge nor alter the substaunce of the mettall, neyther make golde of siluer, but onely giue them their figures to be like.

Euen as the instruments of arte for to gayne the lyfe, euen so are the bookes of the Apostles for the lyfe of our soules.

But it is not so with thee, but thou mayst doe more, for thou mayest sometime of a vessell of wood make a vessell of golde: of which thing S. Paule is witnesse, speaking after this maner: In a great house are not onely vessels of gold, and of siluer, but also of woode, and of earth, some for honour, and some for dishonour. But if a man purge himselfe from such fellowes, he shall be a vessell sanctified vnto honor, meete for the Lord, and prepared vnto all good works. Wherfore let vs not be negligent to buye vs bookes, that we receyue not woundes in our heartes, and let vs not lay vp our gold in the earth, but let vs furnishe our selues with a treasure of spirituall bookes. Truly when that golde aboundeth greatly, then it deceyueth greatly those which possesse it: but great store of bookes gotten togither, doe bring great vtilitie vnto those that haue them, euen as weapons in the roial assemblies: although that none doe vse them, yet neuerthelesse they giue great assurance vnto them which dwell in the house where they are, when neyther theeues, nor breakers of wals, nor anye wicked persons, dare not assayle the house.

2. Tim. 2.

house. Euen so in any house where these spirituall bokes shall be, from them all the force of the deuill is driuen awaye, and great consolation and comfort commeth vnto those that dwell there: for the onely beholding of bookes maketh vs the slower to sinne. And although that we haue done some things that are prohibited, and haue defiled our selues: the conscience doth condemne vs more sharplye, when wee are come vnto the house, and haue beheld the bookes, and are made slower to committe at another time such things agayne. If we doe persist in holynesse, wee are made surer and stronger by the bookes. For as soone as any hath touched the Gospell, he hath by and by withdrawne his spirite from worldly things, by the beholding of them: and if he reade diligently, the soule is by such meanes purged & made better, no otherwise thā being in ẏ holy secrets, it imploieth it selfe to holy things, God speaking vnto it by such scriptures. What thē (say they) if we vnderstand not ẏ which is contayned in ẏ bokes: truly although thou vnderstād not ẏ which is hid, yet neuerthelesse, great holines cōmeth of such reding:

The profite that commeth vnto vs of the holy bookes.

Although that many doe not vnderstand all the scripture, they must not therefore leaue of to profit in it.

For it cannot be that thou be ignoraunt o it altogither. For trulye the grace of the holy spirite hath so dispenced and moderated it, to the ende that the Publicanes and sinners, makers of Tabernacles, Pastors, and Apostles, Idiotes, and the unlearned shoulde be saued by those bookes. And to the ende that none of those Idiotes might excuse themselues, alledging the difficultye thereof, he woulde that those things whiche are spoken, shoulde be easie at the first sight, and that the labourers, seruants, women, wydowes, and the most ignorante of all men should receiue some gaine and profite of the reading that they did heare. For those whom God hath reputed from the beginning worthy of the grace of the holy spirite, haue not done all these things through vayne glorie as gentilles, but to the saluacion and healthe of the hearers. Truely the Philosophers being ignorant of Christe, good orators, and composers o bookes, not seeking that which profiteth all men, but tending to make them selues esteemed, although they haue saide some thing that is profitable, yet notwithstanding obscuritie hath kept it hid, as in a certayne

The Philosophers haue not searched that vvhich profiteth, but to make themselues esteemed.

ayne kinde of foolish wysedome: but the Apostles and the Prophets, haue done altogither therwyse, expounding vnto all men the bookes clearly and manyfestlye that they haue written, as publicke doctors of the worlde, in such sort that euerye one may learne the thinges which are spoken by the onely reading: That whiche the Prophet did pronounce, saying al shall be taught of God: and from thence foorth shall no man teache his neighbour or his brother, and say: know the Lorde: But they shall all knowe me, from the lowest vnto the hyest.

The Apostles and Prophetes haue vvritten clearely and plainly.

Iere. 31. Heb. 8.

I brethren when I came vnto you, came not in gloriousnesse of wordes or of wysedome, shewing vnto you the testimonye of God: And agayne, my wordes and my preachinges was not with entising words of mans wysedome: but in shewing of the spirite and of power. And againe: That which we spake is not the wisedome of this worlde, neyther of the rulers of this worlde whiche goe to noughte. For vnto whome are not all the thinges that are in the gospell manyfest? who would haue a maister for to learne, hearing any of these

1. Cor. 2.

wordes? Blessed are the meeke, blessed are the mercifull, blessed are the pure in heart and such other thinges: The signes, miracles and historyes are not they knowen and manyfest vnto euery one? That is a colour and a cloked excuse of their slothfulnesse, to saye thou vnderstandest not the thinges which are there, how canst thou athing at all vnderstand when thou wilt not but with great paine lightly see it? Take the bookes in thy handes, reade all the hystory, and keeping in memory the thinges that are playne and knowen, let passe the harde and obscure thinges. And if thou canst not with continuall reading find out that whiche is there spoken, goe vnto one that is wyser then thy selfe, or vnto a doctor, declare vnto him the thinges that ar written, declare vnto him thy feruent desire: And if God would giue vnto thee s great promptitude of corage, he will no dispise thy diligence and carefulnesse. Bu yet although that no man will teache the that whiche thou desirest to knowe, ye without doubt he will declare it vnto thee Remember the Eunuch of the Queene o the Ethiopians, who although he were

barbarous

barbarous and rude man, letted and hindred with innumerable cares, and on euery side enuironed with worldly affaires and troubles, and that he did not vnderstande that which he reade, neuerthelesse he did reade it sitting in his charret. If all the time as he went in the way, he ceased not to reade, much lesse when he was at rest in his house: if he did reade vnderstanding not that which he reade, and hath not ceased to reade: muche lesse after that he hath learned: Now to the ende that thou know that he did not vnderstande that which he did reade, heare what Philip sayde vnto him. Doest thou vnderstande (sayth he) that which thou readest? And he hearing his wordes, was not ashamed, but confessed his ignorance, and sayde: Howe can I vnderstande except I had a guyde. When there was none that coulde shewe him the way, neuerthelesse he did reade, and therefore he had immediatly a guyde. God knowing his prompt and ready courage, and louing his diligence, incontinently did sende him a doctor: but we haue not Philip ready. Let vs not despyse my brethren and frendes, our health and sal-

The diligence of the Eunuch reading the scriptures, not vnderstanding them.

Act. 8.

uation, all thinges are written for the loue of vs, for our correction vnto whome the endes of the ages are come vpon. The reading of the Scriptures is a great munition against sinne, the ignorance of the Scriptures is a greate perill of falling headlong into hell: to know nothing of the heauenly lawes is a great perdition of saluation. This thing hath engendred heresyes, this hath made vs lead a naughty life, and hath mingled all thinges bothe high and lowe. Truely it can not be that he shoulde be sent awaye without fruite which taketh pleasure in continuall and attentiue reading of the Scriptures.

1. Cor. 10.

S. Ierome in his. 6. Tome vpon Ieremie. Chapter. 9.

VVe ought not to follovve the error of oure forefathers.

The error of our forefathers ought not to be followed, but the authoritie of the Scriptures, and the commaundement of God which he teacheth vs. And agayne, truly through the ignoraunce of the lawe, they receyue Antichrist for Christ.

Chrysostome in the 29. homilie vpon Genesis.

There is neither the passion of the body nor of the soule in mans nature, but that it it maye take medicine of the holy Scripture. Afterwarde he sayth: Therefore I pray you come often hither, and marke diligently the reading of the holy scripture, not onely when you doe come hither, but also in your houses, take in your handes the holy Byble, and receyue with greate diligence and care the vtilitie that lyeth therein hid, for thereby you shall get great profite: First trulye that by the reading your tongue bee reformed: afterwarde your soule taketh wings, and eleuateth hir selfe, and is illuminated through the splendor and brightnesse of the sunne of righteousnesse. And in the meane time it is deliuered from the inticementes and allurements of filthie and vncleane thoughtes, reioicing with great rest and tranquillitie. And furthermore, that whiche the corporall meate doth vnto the body, for to augment & increase strength, ẏ same doth the reading of the holy scriptures vnto ẏ soule.

The Canon lawe in the Chapter, Prælatum, de consecratione. 3. Distinction.

That whiche the Scripture doth vnto the readers, the same doth the Paynter

vnto

vnto the Idiotes and ignoraunt in beholding it: for in the same the ignorant people doe see that whiche they ought to followe: in the same they doe reade whiche knowe not the letters. The Emperor Iustinian in his newe Constitutions autentike, in the 146. Constitution of the Hebrues, sayth thus: It was expedient that the Hebrues shoulde take great pleasure, not of the hystorie onely, when they gyue eare vnto the holy bookes, but that they shoulde marke and beholde the sense hidde in them, by the whiche they shewe forth the great God, Jesus Christ, sauiour of mankinde. But although that by the interpretation among them dreamed, they doe debate and reason it among them selues vnto this day: neuerthelesse they haue erred from the right sentence. And bicause we haue knowen that they haue amongst themselues debates, we woulde not leaue them in such dissentions. For wee haue known by the interpellation and reports, whiche haue bene tolde vs, that some of them would not receiue but the Hebrewe tongue onely, and would that we shoulde vse them in the reading of holy bookes, other

This constitution in the bodie of the lavve is imprinted at Paris at the signe of the golden sunne.

ther doe holde an opinion that wee muste haue the Greeke tongue, and there hathe bene for this thing of long time sedition among them. We then hauing understode this debate, haue iudged those better whiche desire to haue the Greeke tongue in the reading of holy bookes, and for to be short, such a tongue as the place requireth moste fitte and meetest for the hearers, we then doe ordayne that in what so euer place the Hebrewes are, it shall be lawefull for them in their assemblies to reade the holy Scriptures in the Greeke tongue, and in the Italian tongue, or translated and changed into any other tongue, as the place shall require, to the ende that all the continuation and order of that whiche is sayde, be manifested unto those which shal understand the holy boks, by the reading of them. And according to these thinges, they doe direct their lyfe and study, and their interpretors (whiche doe use only the Hebrewe tongue) may not after their owne fancie maliciously entreate and expounde them, hiding and cloking their wickednesse by the ignorance of the people.

The holye ordinaunce that Iustinian made touching the holy bokes, to haue thē in al tōgues, to the ende they should be reade of all men.

And

And a little after he saith, let vs altogither forbyd that, which they doe call *Deuteros*, as the second tradition, not contayned in the holy bookes, not giuen from aboue by the Prophets, but conteyning a certayne extracte of men, whiche speake not but of earthly and terrestriall things, not hauing in it any thinge of the heauenly spirite. But truly we desire that they reade the holy sayinges, when they declare the holy books, not hiding the things that are therein contayned, and not heape togither vaine wordes that are not written, but excogitated and inuented by them, to the destruction of the simple people, which licence by vs giuen shall not turne to any mans hurt or dammage, of those that receiue the Greeke tongue & other tongues: and that shall not be prohibited nor forbidden them by no man what soeuer he bee: And ouer and besides those which are cal: Archpharasies or Auncients, or maisters shall not haue licence to prohibite through their cautelous inuentions, or anathematisations, if they will not be chastised nor corrected with corporall punishment, and after confiscation of their goodes, malgre

their

their heades to consent unto us, who doe will and commaunde thinges better agreable unto God. And againe a little after he saith: For our will is that by this and other tongues, those which giue good eare unto the holy bookes, ought to be ware of the malice of the interpretors, and that they doe not onely understand the letters, but also taste well the thinges therein contayned, and receiue it throughly, and understande the moste holy sentences, to the ende they may learne better that which is best, and be no more deceiued, erring and fayling in the ende. For there is nothing so excellent as for to haue affiance & truste in God: Therefore we haue opened unto them all tongues, for the reading the holy bookes: to that ende that if all by order, do embrace the science and knowledge of them, they may be the more diligent to learne that which is the best: Forasmuche as it is most euident that he whiche hathe ben and is nourished and instructed in the reading of holy bookes, is more prompte and ready to discerne and receiue that which is the best, to receiue correction and to be conducted and leade into goodnesse, then

VVe oughe to take hede of the malice of the interpreters.

The Emperour Iustinian giueth libertie vnto all men to read the holy scriptures, and the reason vvherfore.

then he that understandeth none of all this, depending of the only name of religion: and staying him selfe as to the anker of respecte and soueraigne refuge, thinking that the scyence and true knowledge of God, is in the only calling of the secte.

This then whiche hath pleased vs, and which is declared by this holy lawe, shall keepe aswell thy glorye as those whiche are vnder thy obedience: And also shall keepe and obserue them which shall succeede in the honor of thy magistrate and ruler. And shall not suffer that the Jewes doe contrary or against those thinges: but shall vtterly put to exile and banish al those that shall resiste, or attempt to let this ordinance, punishing them first by corporall punishment, afterward confiscating theyr goodes, to the ende they may not eleuate them selues against God and the imperial maiestie, more insolently through a foolishe and rashe boldnesse, and vse their Edictes towardes the presidentes of the prouinces, considering our law, to that end that knowing those thinges, they may set them foorth in euery towne and village, and that they may knowe that they ought necessarily

Those whiche woulde not suffer the scripture in all languages and tõgues, wer punished through the confiscation of their goodes.

necessarily to obserue these thinges, by them whiche doe feare our indignation and displeasure.

S. Ierome in his Proeme of the Prophete Ieremie.

What other lyfe can there be without the knowledge of the Scriptures, by the which Christ also is knowen, who is also the lyfe of the beleeuers.

Saint Ambrose in his. 35. Sermon.

The Lorde doth witnesse that the reading of the Scriptures is lyfe, saying: The wordes that I speake unto you, are spirite and lyfe. *Iohn. 6.*

Moyses sayde: What is he that causeth that all the Lordes people doe prophecie, and that the Lorde doth giue them his holy spirite. &c. *Num. 11.* Moyses enuyed not those vvhich had the gift of God.

As for me, I am no Prophete, nor Prophetes sonne, but a keeper of cattell. &c. *Amos. 7.*

Eusebius bishop of Cæsaria in his Ecclesiasticall historie: lib. 6.

Chapter. 11.

Alledging the Epistle of Alexander bishop of Ierusalem agaynst Demetrius, and rebuking him thus, sayeth: That which thou hast added in thy letters, thou

sayest,

The Priestes doe say that it appertayneth not vnto the laye people to dispute in the Church: behold diligently the contrarie.

sayest, that it was neuer seene that the lay and secular people shoulde dispute of the fayth in the presence of the Bishoppes. I maruayle what moued thee to affirme a lye so euident. Inasmuch that as often as there is founde any man that is sufficient and apt for to giue good counsayle, and to instruct the people, the Byshops haue accustomed to desire him to doe it, as oure brother the Byshop Neon did vnto Euelpius in the Citie of Laranda, and the Bishop Celsus vnto Paulinus in the Citie of Iconium, and the Byshop Atticus vnto Theodosius in the Citie of Sinnas. And there is no doubt but that the other Byshops may doe the lyke in their diocesses, when they finde any one whiche is a man for to profite the people.

Chrysostome vpon the first Chapter of Genesis. 8. homilie.

Chrysostom vvould that all vvere doctors.

I desire most earnestlye, and doe praye that ye may be all in the order of doctors, and not only to be hearers of our wordes, but also that ye woulde report and declare vnto others our doctrine, and that ye wold correct those that doe erre and go astraye, to the ende they may returne into the way of of truth, as S. Paule sayeth: Exhort one another, and edifie one another. &c. 1. Thes. 5.

And a little after he sayth: God would not that the Christian shoulde bee onely content with himselfe, but that he do also edifie others, and not only with doctrine, but also with good lyfe & conuersation. &c.

Chrysostome vpon the. 2. Chapter of Genesis. 10. Homilie.

He which hath the care to teach and instruct his neyghbour, doth not so muche good vnto his neighbor, as he getteth gret gayne vnto him selfe, when hee shall receyue double rewarde, and obtayneth of God great retribution. &c.

In the same place he sayeth moreouer: If we do vnderstand rightly those things, we may being at home in our houses, and taking the holy Scriptures after we haue well dyned or supped, to take the profite and giue spirituall meate vnto the soule. For as the bodie hath to doe with sensible meates, in lyke maner also hath the soule neede to refreshe it selfe dayly with spirituall meates, to the ende that the same be corroborated and made strong agaynst the assaultes of the flesh, and agaynst the continuall battayle, by the which we are constrayned, that it may resist it. And it is to be feared least the soule should be brought into seruitude and bondage, if we will be slothfull any thing at all.

Chrysostome vpon the first Chapter of Saint Mathew. 1. Tome, 2. Homilie.

You that are here present, aunswere me I pray you, what is he among you, who if one demaunde of him a Psalme, can say it without booke, or any other parcell of the holye Scripture? There is not one, and yet this euill is not only here, but for bicause you are slothfull and negligent in spirituall things, so much do you surmount through feruentnesse the fire vnto diuelish things. For if any man will demaunde or aske you foolishe, or (as men call them) merye songs, or songs of bawdrie, they shall finde many which moste diligentlye haue learned them, which they will sing very willingly.

Many doe learne sooner foolish and baudie songs than spirituall.

But yet they would defend such crimes, saying: I am not a Monke, I am maried, and haue care of children & of my house keeping. Truely it cometh thereby, that you

The excuse of many.

you doe corrupt and marre all thinges togither, as a plague, bicause that you doe thinke the reading of holy Scriptures to belong only unto the Monkes, where it is a great deale more necessary and needefull for you then for them: For those whiche are in the middest of the battayle, and which doe receiue continually woundes upon woundes, suche people haue more neede of Gods medicine or helpe. &c.

Chrysostome vpon the. 21. Chapter of S. Mathewe. 39 homily.

And when he was come into the temple, the cheefe priestes and the elders of the people came unto him as he was teaching, and sayde: By what authoritie doest thou these thinges? and who gaue thee this power? They declared that there was some which did giue power unto men, be it corporall or spirituall: As if they had said thus, thou art not engendred of the sacerdotall family, the Senat hath not permitted thee to doe this, Ceasar hath not giuen it thee, but if they had beleeued that all power is from God, they woulde neuer haue asked, who hath giuen thee this power, knowing that euery good gift and eue- *Math. 21* *Rom. 13.*

ry perfect gifte is from aboue, and commeth downe from the father of lightes, and that a man can receiue nothing at all, except it be giuen him from heauen.

Of the assemblies and congregations of the faithfull.

Saint Hilary against Auxentius.

I Praye you O ye Byshoppes, whiche doe thinke your selues to be so, what suffrages haue the Apostles vsed for to preach the gospell? with what power were they ayded for to preache Christ, and as it were to change all Gentils from images to God? haue they taken any dignitie of the palace, in singing of Himmes & Psalmes vnto God in prison, being in yrons and chaynes? and afterwarde to be whipped and scourged? Did Paule assemble the Churche of Christ by the Kings Edicte, when he was as a spectacle in the theater? He did defende himselfe (as I beleeue) by Nero, or Vespasian, or Decius, through whose hatred and malice the confession of the

the heauenly preaching hath flourished: they nourishing and keeping themselues with their owne handie labour, in assembling themselues togither within chambers and secret places, and by the stretes, and villages, did enuiron and compasse about almost all people, by lande and by water, against the decrees and ordinaunces of the Senators, and Edictes of the Kings.

Tertullian in his Apologie against the Gentiles. 29. Chapter.

This assemblie of the Christians should be very vnlawfull, if it were like or equall vnto the vnlawfull things, it shoulde bee worthilye condemned, if it were complayned of as of a faction or sect. But whome haue we endammaged or hurt by our assembling and meeting togither, wee are the very same as when we were all dispersed asunder, euerye one by himselfe, not hurting any man. When wyse men, and good and faythfull people doe assemble themselues togither, we must not call that a faction or sect, but rather a court. And on the contrary, we must applye the name of faction, vnto those which hate good mẽ, that

The Christians neuer assembled themselues to the hurt of any man.

that crie agaynste the bloude of the innocents, vnder colour of their vnitie, and for defence of their hatred, forasmuche as they doe esteme and iudge that the Christians are the causes of all losses and common mishaps. If the riuer Tyber mounteth or swelleth aboue the walles: If the riuer Nylus doe not descende vppon the fieldes: If the heauen doe stande still: If the earth tremble: If there be famine or pestilence: by and by they crie after the Christians, for to cast them into the lyons denne.

If there happeneth any euill vnto the vvorlde, the vvorldlings doe say that it is bicause of the faithfull.

Saint Luke declareth in the Actes, the order of the primitiue Church, that the faythfull assembled themselues oftentimes in the fieldes, saying thus: On the Saboth day we went out of the citie, besides a ryuer where they were wont to praye: and wee sate downe and spake vnto the women which resorted thither. &c.

Act.16.

They assembled themselues togither in the night, within chambers, for to preach the word, & celebrate the Lords supper, as it appeareth by that which is written: And the first day after the Saboth, ye disciples being come togither so to breake breade,

Act.20.

Paule

Paule preached vnto them, redy to depart on the morowe, and continued the preaching vnto midnight. And there were many lightes in an vpper chamber where we were gathered togither. &c. *Act. 2.* *Act. 1.*

And when the dayes were ended, we departed, and went our wayes, and they all brought vs on our way, with their wyues and children, till we were come out of the citie, and we kneeling downe on the shore, prayed. &c. *Act. 21.*

Tertullian in his Apologie.
39 Chapter.

We coming and assembling our selues togither, doe pray for the Emperors, for their seruants, and for the magistrates, for the estate of the worlde, for peace. &c. We are assembled to make commemoration of the diuine scriptures, we doe feede and nourishe the fayth with voyce and holye wordes, we hope well, we plant and graffe most stronglye our fayth, and doe trauayle much to imprint in the hearts the discipline of the commaundements. &c.

In the auncient assemblies they prayed for the Emperors and magistrates.

Tertullian in his Apologie
30. Chap.

We christians haue our eyes eleuated

vnto heauen, and our handes streched out, bicause they are innocente, and the heade bare and vncouered bicause we are not ashamed, and we doe it without bydding. For we doe pray with the hearte, we pray alwayes, for all the Emperors, that God would giue them long life, and assured empyre and a trusty and sure house, mightye in battayle, a faithfull counsell, good people, a quiet worlde, and all that man and the Emperour can desire. I may not demaunde and aske these thinges but of him of whom I doe know I shal obtaine them: for it is he onely that will giue it, and I am he that ought to require it, that is to say his seruant, which doe honor him, and which haue in reuerence him only: which am killed for his doctrine and discipline and whiche doe offer the best and greatest sacrifice that he hath commaunded, that is to saye the prayer that proceedeth from a chast body and from the innocent soule and from the holy ghoste. Not with little graines of incence of small balew, nor also with the teares of the tree of Arabie, nor those two drops of wine, neither the bloud of a wicked man that desireth his owne deathe.

Praier is the best sacrifice that one can offer vnto God.

deathe.&c.

Plinie in the.10. booke of his Epistles 317. Epistle.

The Emperor Traianus did sende him a commaundement, commaunding him to make enquirye of the faithfull, and of their manner of liuing: and afterward to persecute them. Plinie did write againe vnto the Emperor, that after he had throughly enquired, yea with most cruelty and tormentes, vntill suche time as he deliuered them into the handes of the hangmen to see them executed, he neuer did finde anye other thing, but that the faithfull haue accustomed to assemble them selues togither at certayne times in the morning, before daye, and when they were come togither, they did sing prayses and psalmes vnto Christe as vnto God.&c.

Plinie vvriteth vnto the Emperor of the lyfe and maner of the faithfull in their assemblies.

If any wyll see more amplye these thinges, let him reade the ecclesiasticall historY and there he shall finde howe the faithfull did assemble them selues in the mountaines, in caues and dennes for feare of persecutions. As it is declared in the historye of Theodorite, after this manner. When that the faithfull were driuen awaye

Eusebius Cæsariensis in the ecclesiasticall historie, lib.1x. Chap.4.

Theodorite lib.4.cha.24.

Historie tripartite, lib. 10. chap. 20. waye (by Ualentius) they assembled them selues togither at the foote of the mountaine, and there gaue prayses and thankes vnto God, reioysing of the heauenly scriptures, suffring there the impetuositie and violence of the cõtrarietie of the ayre, some time raines, snowes and coldes, and other times moste extreame heates. Ualentius not suffering them to vse this most laborious and paynfull commoditie: sent men of war who draue away and scattred that assemblye euery where.

Ievves burned in a caue. The Jewes being in captiuitie were not suffered to liue after the lawes of God. They went and assembled them selues togither in the next caues, for to celebrate secretly the saboth: But being accused vn-
2. *Mac*. 5. to Philippe the gouernor, he caused them all to be burned

Psal. 133. Behold, how good and ioyfull a thing it is brethren to dwell togither in vnitie. &c.

Math. 18. Jesus Christ saith in the Gospel, where two or three be gathered togither in my name, there am I in the middest of them.

That

That no man oughte to bee compelled to beleeue by force.

Lactantius Firmianus in his diuine institutions. Li.5. chap.20.

Those whiche kyll theyr owne soules and the souls of others, let them learne and know that they haue committed a faulte that will not be forgiuen. &c.

O meruaylous and blinde foolishnesse, they thinke that those who endeuor them selues to keepe the faithe haue wicked thoughtes, and that the tyrants and hang men haue good. Haue those wicked thoughtes, who against the right of humanitie, and agaynst all heauenly or godly right, are torne and pulled in peeces: It should be rather those that doe such things vnto the bodyes of the innocentes: The which the most cruell theeues, nor the cruellest ennemyes, nor barbarous people neuer did? Doe not they deceiue them selues in turning and chaunging the name of

In this latter time the vvicked are called good, & the good vvicked.

of euill into good, and good into euil? wherfore then doe they not call the daye, night, and the night daye, the sunne darkenesse: otherwyse it is the like impudency to giue the name of euill unto good, and of fooles unto wyse men, and of the wicked unto the iuste and righteous. If they haue anye beleefe or trust in Philosophy, or in eloquence, let them arme them selues with their disputacions, let them ouercome or vanquishe us if they can with the wordes that wee speake: let them approche for to fight togither, and to examine particulerly euery poynt: let them defend their gods, to the end they be not forsaken with theyr temples, tromperies, and disceptes worthy to be mocked. Nowe bicause they can doe nothing by force and violence (forasmuch as Gods religion the more it is oppressed the more it augmēteth and encreaseth) let them proceede rather by prayer, and exhortations. Let the Byshoppes and Priestes of their religion call us unto their Sermons and disputations: let them exhort us to receiue the adorations of their gods: let them tell us that there are a greate many whiche take a greate care to

gouerne

gouerne, and to mayntaine all thinges by their puissances and powers: Let them declare vnto vs the originall and beginning of their ceremonies, of their sacrifices, and of their goddes, and howe they were giuen vnto men: let them declare the beginning of them, and the cause wherfore. Let them declare vnto vs and tell vs what reward those shall haue which shall adore and worship them, and what payne they shall haue that shall dispise them. &c. Let them proue and confirme all these thinges, not with their owne opinions, (for the oppynion of mortall men is nothing worth or auaylable) but that it be by some witnesses of holy Scriptures, as we doe. It is no neede to vse any force, nor iniuries, forasmuche as religion cannot bee compelled, they ought rather to proceede by faire wordes, then by stripes, for to cause vs to be willing. Let them display all the puissance and subtiltie of their spirites: And if their reason be good, let it be brought forth, and we are ready to heare it. But if they doe hold their peace and be dumme, we will not beleeue them, nor any more we wil giue them the victory, through

Mortal man is vvoorth nothing.

their

their crueltye. Let them followe vs, or els tell vs the reason of all the doinges: For wee drawe none vnto vs throughe fayre wordes (as they say) but we doe teache, proue and declare: And so we compell none by force, for he is vnprofitable vnto God which hath neyther fayth nor deuotion, and yet neuerthelesse none departeth from vs, bicause the truth holdeth them. If they haue any confidence or truste of the truthe, let them speake and open their mouth, and let them dispute with vs, vpon any matter.

Truth and force inseperable, and righteousnes and crueltie.

Trulye their error and their foolishnesse is nowe mocked at of the olde men whom they despised & set nought by, and by our children, wherefore then are they so incensed and mad that where they would diminishe their follye and foolishnesse they augmente it? There is greate difference betweene crueltye and pitie, and truthe can not be ioyned with force, or righteousnesse with cruelty, but it is not without cause that they dare not teache any thing of heauenly thinges, for they feare to be mocked at of our people, and forsaken of their people, &c. Religion ought to be defended, not

in

in putting to death, but in suffering hir selfe to be killed: not through cruelty, but by patience, not through wickednesse, but through faith: For to kill and exercise cruelty, is wickednesse, and belongeth unto the wicked: And to suffer death and to haue patience and faith, belongeth unto the good. There is no question but the good is in religion, and not the euill, forasmuche as if thou wilt defende religion, throughe sheading of bloude, throughe torments & cruelty, it shall not be then defended, but polluted and defiled: For there is nothing more franke and free then religion. The reason is then good and righte, if thou defendest religion throughe patience, and by suffring death, in the whiche the faithe kepte and preserued, is agreeable unto God.

To kill and exercise crueltie belongeth not vnto the good, but to the euill.

Saint Jerome saithe: He followeth Christe, which is persecuted, he followeth Antechrist which persecuteth.

Rubert or Robert writing vpon the. 13. Chap. of the Apocalyps.

Beholde the signe and token whereby you shall knowe those that are of God, from the euill and wicked: Those are the

The signe of the good and the euill.

wicked

wicked, which doe kill and leade into captiuitie, the which thing all those that are of God, haue not done nor doe.

Lactantius Firmianus in his diuine Institutions. Lib. 5. Chap. 21.

I woulde demaunde this question, vnto whome do they thinke chiefly to doe pleasure in compelling men, agaynst their will to doe sacrifice: Is it vnto them whome they compel? But that which is in charge vnto him that refuseth, that is no benefite vnto him. But we must also giue counsell vnto him that refuseth when they knowe not that which is good: Wherefore then doe they torment and vexe them so cruelly, if they desire to haue them saued? Or frō whence commeth the pietie so vnfaythfully, and most miserablye to destroy, lame, and make impotent them vnto whom they shoulde prouide and giue remedie? Is it vnto the Gods they doe suche pleasure? No, for that whiche a man doth by compulsion is not a sacrifice, forasmuch as if it be not done voluntarlye and with the heart, it is most execrable and accursed. Forasmuch as there are but they whiche are constrayned and compelled throughe banish-

Compulsion auayleth not

banishments, iniuries, imprisonmentes, and tormentes which doe it: If they bee Gods which are so honored, truly for that only cause they ought not to be honored, in as much as they woulde be so adored and worshipped: they are worthye to be detested of men, unto whome sacrifice is made with teares and sighings, and with bloud running downe all their bodie. But we to the contrarie, require not that any will he, nill he, shoulde adore and worship our God, which is the Creator of all things: nor we are not angry if they doe not worship him. For we doe trust in his maiestie, that he hath also great power to auenge as well those that doe contemne and despyse him, as the iniuries and troubles of hys seruants: and therefore when we suffer such things so wicked and execrable, wee doe not therefore repugne agaynst the worde, but we referre the vengeance unto God.

God vvill auenge the griefes of his seruants.

The Prophete Esay sayeth: Truth is fallen downe in the streete, and the thing that is playne and open may not be shewed, yea, the truth is layde in prison, and he that refrayneth himselfe from euil, must

Esay. 59.

be spoyled. When the Lorde sawe this, it displeased him sore.&c.

Ezec.34. The Lorde sayde by the Prophet Ezechel: I will deliuer my sheepe from their mouth, so that they shall no more be spoyled.&c.

Lactantius Firmianus in his diuine Institutions.Lib.5.Chap.22.

Veritas odium parit.

They are not then madde or angry with vs, bicause we adore not or worship their Gods. For there are many people that do not worship thẽ, but it is bicause the truth is with vs, the which, as the Prouerbe is, getteth hatred.&c.

Lactantius Firmianus.Lib.5. Chapter.23.

VVhat patience is.

Pacience is a principall vertue, the which is by the common voyce of the people, and of the Philosophers and Orators exalted with great prayse. If no man wil denie but that pacience is a soueraine vertue: It is necessary that the righteous & wise man be in the power of the vnrighteous mã, for to haue that pacience: for pacience is a volũtary suffring of euils which are done vnto any man, or which doe happen vnto him, whereby the righteous and the wyse man, hath in himselfe pacience, bicause that he receyueth the vertue of the which he shall be altogither depriued, if he suffer nothing to the contrarie: Although that he do no iniurie vnto anye man, nor that he coueteth his neyghbors goodes, and though he defende not his own goods if they be taken from him by force and violence, forasmuche as he can quietlye ynough suffer the iniurie that is done vnto him, bicause that he is garnished with vertue. It is necessarye that the righteous man be subiect vnto the vnrighteous mã. And the wyse be despised of the foole, to the ende that the one doe sinne, bicause he is vnrighteous, and that the other be in seruitude and bondage, bicause he is righteous. For howe can a Captaine prooue and trie his souldiers, if he haue no enimie? And yet neuerthelesse the aduersarie eleuateth and exalteth himselfe maugre him, bicause that he is mortall and maye be vanquished and ouercome: but bicause we cannot repugne and striue agaynste God, he himselfe moueth and stirreth vp the aduersaries agaynst his name, not for to striue and fight against him, but against

It is necessary that the righteous man be afflicted of the wicked, to the ende he haue pacience.

gainst his souldiars, to that ende he maye proue and trye the faithe and deuotion of his: untill suche time as he doth correcte and amend in pressing and beating the discypline whiche was become colde. There is also an other cause wherefore hee dooth permitte and suffer that we should be persecuted that is to the ende that the people of God shoulde bee augmented. Some desire to know what that goodnesse is which is defended euen unto death, which is preferred aboue all the pleasant thinges and best loued and set by in this world: of which goodnesse, nothing can drawe them from it, neyther the losse of their goodes, nor the losse of their sight, dolor of body, nor anye other tormentes whatsoeuer they be: all thinges are much worth, but the greatest causes which followed, haue alwayes augmented our number. The people being rounde about the good christians, hearde them saye in their tormentes, that they should not do sacrifice nor offer unto stons made and hewen with mans handes, but unto the liuing God which is in heauen: many doe heare that the same is good and true, they receiue it in their minds and understandinges

The cause vvhy aduersaries are stirred vp.

Through persecutions a great nūber is ioined to the gospell.

verstandinges. Afterwarde (as men haue accustomed or vsed to doe in vncertayne thinges) when they demaund and enquire within them selues, what may be the cause of that perseuerance and constancie, many things belonging vnto religion are spread abroade and knowen, and declared from the one to the other, by the report that they make: And by ỹ meanes they are taught, who for asmuche as they are good, it is necessary that they please. Furthermore, the vengeance that followeth (as it happeneth often) hath a greate vehemence to make them beleeue: All these causes put togither, haue gotten and drawen vnto God, a maruelous great company of people.

S. Hilary in his booke against Auxentius.

Ambition doth ayde it selfe by the name of Christe: The Churche doth feare and compell the people through banishements and imprisonmentes to beleeue hir, the which they haue beleeued through banishmentes and prisons: Shee dependeth vpon those that doe disdayne to communicate with hir: She which is consecrated and made holy by the terror of the persecutors, driueth awaye the prestes. Shee which hath bene engendred by the running away of priestes, doth glory and extoll hir selfe to be beloued of the worlde, Shee whiche coulde not be beloued of Christe, if the worlde had not hated hir: Experience cryeth in all mens mouthes and declareth and sheweth the comparison of the church, the which of late hath bene giuen vnto vs, and neuer shall be destroyed.

Rom.14. All that which is not of faith is sinne.

Chrysostome in his first Tome vpon S. Mathewe.47.homily

Chapter .13.

Math.13 Let them both growe togither till haruest come, the Lorde did forbid them least while they wente aboute to weede out the tares they should plucke vp the wheate also: whiche thing he spake to forbidde the sheading of bloude. For if the Heritickes were put to deathe without alliance of peace, warre shoulde bee without truce. Wherefore he doth forbyd it for two causes, the one bicause they shoulde hurte and hinder a little the corne. The other is that if they doe not heale them selues, they shal neuer

Iesus Christ doth not require shedding of blud

neuer escape the eternall and euerlasting punishmentes and tormentes: wherefore if thou wouldest amend and in no wyse hurte the corne, you must attend and tarry the time conuenient and that is meete for the same. But he doth not forbyd to deuide breake vp and put asunder the consistories of the Heritickes, with their counsels, and to stoppe their mouthes and to restrayne them of their libertie to speake, but he forbyddeth to kill them, and to put them to deathe.

S. Augustine in the.58. Epistle of the catholike clarkes of the citie of Hipona, vnto Ianuarius, and Donatus.

This is then our desire, whiche wee doe alledge by these letters vnto your reuerence, and also by the brethren whome we haue sente. Firste if it may bee, that you would conferre with our Byshoppes peaceably and quietly, to the ende that the error be taken away from those in whom it shall be founde, and not that the men be taken awaye, nor punished but gently corrected.

In the history tripartite.Lib.6.Chap.22.

Athanasius in the satisfaction of his fleing saith. Behold the presumption of the infidelles, which doe such thinges, and are without shame, of whiche, firste they haue imagined euilles and discept against vs. And vnto this present time they accuse vs that we flee from them, being ready to kill vs. But whiche is more they doe sighe and mourne most bitterly, bicause they cannot altogither destroy vs. And doe rebuke vs bicause that we feare: And when they murmure of the thing, the more doe they cause the euil to returne vpon them selues. For if it be euill done to flee, to persecute is a great deale worse. For the one hideth himselfe, to the ende he turne not & change his opinion, & the other persecuteth for to kill. But it is commaunded to flie, and he that demaundeth to kill transgresseth the lawe, and giueth vnto vs greater occasion to flie. Then if the persecutors doe rebuke vs bicause that we doe flee, let them rather be ashamed in them selues, and let them cease and leaue of to lye in wayte, and incontinently those whiche did flie will flie no more: but they will not cease from their

malyce

malice, but haste themselues as much as in them lyeth to take them, knowing that the fleeing of those which suffer persecution, is a great signe of those which persecute them.

For none did euer flee from the meeke and gentle, but rather from the cruell and deceyptfull: euerye man that sighed and which was vexed of Saule, went for refuge vnto Dauid, and fled from Saule: But therefore these here desire to put to death those that are hidde, fearing that their malice shoulde not be by them stopped. Who are not blinded in that matter. Forasmuch as the more the fleeing is manifested and knowne, the more are they knowne by their slaughters, murders, and banishments: For although they kill, their death crieth dayly against them: Againe, although they threaten to banishe, it is knowne all about, that they establish a memorial or remembrance of euil against thẽ.

The persecutors do seke to put to death, for feare that their malice shoulde bee vncouered and knowne

If they were wyse and had any vnderstanding in them, they shoulde see themselues stopped and let in such things, & they themselues fayle in their counsayles: but bicause they haue no vnderstanding, therfore

fore are they deceyued through their persecutions, and in seeking to kill, they consider not their infidelitie: for if they rebuke those which flie, when they seeke to kill them: What will they say that Iacob did flee from Esau his brother, and that Moyses went downe to Madian for feare of Pharao? What will they say of Dauid which fled from Saul, who sent into his house to kill him, when he hid himselfe in the caue, and that he chaunged his face untill he was come to Abimelech? By which meanes he escaped the watchings and vayne deceytes of his enimies. What will those here say, which rashly vtter and speake all things, seing the worthie man Helias which throughe his prayer had raysed vp one that was deade, and yet neuerthelesse hid himself for feare of Achab, and fled for feare of the snares of Iezabel? yea, then the children of the Prophetes which were sought for to be put to death, were hid in ditches and holes by Abdias: but if they haue not reade those auncient histories, at the least let them remember the Gospels. For the Disciples for feare of the Iewes, did withdrawe and hid them selues

Genes. 27. *Exod. 2.*

The holye men haue fled from the handes of the persecutors.

1. Reg. 21. *3. Reg. 19.* *3. Reg. 18* *Iohn. 20.*

selues. And when Paule was sought for *Act.9.*
by the Prince of the countrie at Damas-
cus, the Disciples put him out of the
wall, and let him downe in a basket, and
so hee escaped their handes that sought
for him. Wherefore in as much as the
scripture telleth such things of holy men,
what excuse doest thou think that they can
find to excuse their madnesse? If then they
rebuke their feare, they speake as men
madde and incensed agaynst themselues,
and if they say that it is done agaynst the
will of God, they shewe themselues altogither ignorant of the holy scriptures: for *Num.35.*
in the lawe it was commaunded, that aun- *Iosua.20.*
cient cities were deputed and appoynted
for refuge, to the ende that they whome
men did seeke for to put to death, myght
there saue themselues. And in the latter
time of the worlde, when the worde of the
father (which was spoken vnto Moyses)
is come, he hath giuen agayne a commaundement, saying: When they perse- *Mat.10.*
cute you in one citie, flie into another.
And a little after he sayth: When ye therfore shall see the abhomination of desola- *Mat.24.*
tion spoken of by Daniel the Prophete,
stan-

standing in the holye place : let him that readeth it, take hede. Then let them which be in Iurie, flie into the mountaynes, and let him which is on the house top, not come downe to fet any thing out of his house : neyther let him which is in the fielde returne backe to fetch his clothes. Wherefore in knowing these things they are so gouerned : For that which the Lord hath commaunded, the very same hath he spoken by his saintes, before he tooke on him our fleshe. And this is the ende that leadeth to perfection, that we doe that which the Lorde hath commaunded. Therefore also the very same worde being made man
Iohn.8. for vs, did hyde himselfe when they did
Iohn.12. seeke for him (as also wee doe.) And agayne, when he suffred persecution, he did flie and hyde himselfe from the treasons, for it was couenable & nedefull for him to suffer such things, as hunger & thirst, and after such sort to shew himselfe to be man.

Yea also at the beginning when he was made man, being yet but a little childe, it
Math.2. was commaunded by the angell vnto Ioseph saying, arise and take the childe and his mother, and flye into Egypte, and bee

there

there tyll I bring thee worde. For it wyll come to passe, that Herode will seeke the babe to destroy him. Also when Herode was dead and that he had hearde that Archelaus raigned in his fathers steade, hee fledde into Nazareth.

Also when Jesus shewed him selfe as God, and had healed the hande that was dryed, and that the Phariseys went out, and consulted against him, how they might destroy him, Jesus knowing the same departed from thence. *Mat.* 12.

Also when Jesus raysed Lazarus from death, from that day foorth (sayth he) they consulted togither to put him to death. Jesus therefore walked no more openlye among the Jewes: but went thence into a country nye to the wildernesse. *Iohn.* 11.

In like manner when Jesus sayde, yer Abraham was I am. Then tooke the Jewes vp stones to cast at him, but Jesus hidde him selfe, and went out of the temple, and passed euen through the middest of them, and wente his way. Thou doest nowe knowe how that they which see these thinges, or which doe heare them (for they see them not) as it is written, ought not to burne *Iohn.* 8. *Luc.* 4.

Men ought not to burn them that speake otherwise than the truth alloweth.

Mat.14. burne those which speake & thinke things contrary vnto suche as the Lorde hathe made and taught. For when Iohn suffred martyrdome, and that his disciples buryed his body, Iesus hearing thereof departed thence by shippe into a desert place, and euen so the Lorde doth his thinges, and also teach them: But would to God they were so ashamed that they would not declare their furor, but vnto men, and that more and more throughe their madnesse, men should not see them rebuke and check the sauiour, blaspheming agaynst him: But the same the Idiotes and fooles could not suffer, althoughe they are rebuked of them selues, not to knowe onely the gospell: for this is the occasion of our departing and fleeing, of which the euangelistes doth make mention, and of which our sauiour hathe vsed, and we must also thinke suche thinges to haue bene in holy men: For that which is nowe written of the sauiour after the fashion and manner of men, the same is commonly deputed vnto mankinde. He hath taken those thinges that are ours, and hath shewed and declared the passions of our infirmitie, ẏ which

The persecutors them selues are ignorant of the gospell.

Saint

Saint Iohn wryteth thus: They soughte to take him, but no man layde handes on him bicause his houre was not yet come. For before that the same was come hee sayde vnto his mother, woman what haue I to doe with thee myne houre is not yet come. And he sayd vnto those which were called his brethren, my time is not yet come. And agayne at the time of his passion he sayde, sleepe hencefoorth and take your reste, for behold the houre is at hande and the sonne of man is betrayed into the handes of sinners. But he did not suffer him selfe to be taken before the time was come, also he did not hide him selfe, but gaue him selfe vnto his aduersaryes, and enemyes: In like maner the blessed Martyrs, did keepe them selues from temporall persecutions, and when they were sought for they fledde into secrete places. But when they were found out, they gaue them selues to martyrdome: beholde the wordes of Athanasius a Martyre of Iesus Christe.

Iohn.7. *Iohn.2.* *Iohn.7.* *Math.26*

That

That the magistrates that persecute the faithful, vnder coulour of religion, shall be tormented with eternall paines.

Sapien.6. Rom.10.

An admonition vnto Kings, Princes, and Iudges.

HEare therefore (O ye kings) and vnderstande ye therefore ye Iudges of the endes of the earth: Learne and giue eare ye that rule the people, glorifie your selues in the multitude of nations. For the power is giuen you of the Lord, & the strength from the hiest: whiche shall trye your works and search out your imaginations: howe that yee being officers of his kingdome haue not executed true iudgemente, haue not kept the lawe of righteousnesse, nor walked after his will. &c.

Miche.3.

Heare, O ye heades of the house of Iacob, and ye leaders of the house of Israell: Should ye not knowe what were lawefull and right? But ye hate the good and doe that is euill, ye plucke of mens skinnes, and the fleshe from the bones: ye eate the fleshe of my people, and flaye of their skin-

ey

ye breake their bones, ye choppe them in peeces as it were into a cauldron, and as fleshe into a pot.&c.And a little after hee saith, O heare this ye rulers of the house of Jacob, and ye Judges of the house of Israell: ye that abhorre the thing that is lawefull, and wrest aside the thing that is straighte: yee that buylde vp Sion with bloud, and Jerusalem with doing wrong. O ye Judges, ye giue sentence for giftes: O ye priestes yee teache for lucre: O yee Prophetes, ye prophecye for mony.&c.

Lactantius Firmianus in his diuine institutions, Lib.5.Chap.24.writing vnto the Emperour Constantine.

All that whiche the wicked Princes doe against vs, God doth permit and suffer it to be done. And yet neuerthelesse the most wicked persecuters, in whom the name of God hath bene had in derision and mockery, ought not to thinke therefore to scape vnpunished, for they haue bene as ministers of his wrathe agaynst vs: Truelye they shall be punished by the iudgemente of God, bicause that after receiuing power they haue abused it aboue all measure, and by that meanes are waxen & growen

Persecuters cruelly tormented.

into greate pryde agaynst God, and haue vnfaithfully troden vnder their feete his eternall name. Therefore he promiseth that he will with all speede be auenged of them, and roote out of the earth all wicked beastes: But although that he hath accustomed to aduenge the vexations, and tormentes done vnto his people, and especially in this worlde, neuerthelesse he doth commaund vs to attend and tarye patiently in this worlde vntill the celestiall iudgement, at which day he will rewarde or punishe euery one according to theyr workes. Wherefore the wicked people and cōmitters of sacriledge, ought not to hope that those whom they haue so handeled shall be despised & vnreuenged. The reward shal come vnto the rauening wolues, who haue tormented the simple and righteous soules that neuer offended. But as for vs, let vs onely trauayle that nothing be punished in vs by men, but onely righteousnesse, let vs endeuor our selues with all our strength to serue God, and to be auenged of that whiche we suffer, and to receiue our rewarde.

Saint Barnard in his sermon of the conuersion of Saint Paule.

Oh Lorde God, these are the chiefeste and first that persecuted thee, whom men see to loue the hiest seates and romes in thy church, and whiche bare the greateste rule: They haue taken the arke of Sion, they haue occupied and used the castle, and afterwardes haue frankly and by power set al the citie on fire, their conuersation is miserable, the subuersion of thy people is pitifull, and woulde to God that they should not hurt but in that onely part, peraduenture there wilbe some who wilbe aduertised and admonished with the exhortation of the Lorde, who will beware of following their example, and who wyll keepe the commaundements according to that which is sayde, whatsoeuer they byd you obserue, that obserue and doe, but after their workes doe not: But nowe holy orders are giuen for an occasion of moste filthy gayne, and doe esteeme and thinke gayne to be pietie and godlynesse. The Prophet Esay sayth, O Lord our God, though such Lords haue domination vpõ vs as knowe not thee, yet grant, that wee

The despising of the poore people of God is pitifull.

Mat.23

Esay.26.

may hope onely in thee, and keepe thy name in remembrance.

Eze. 22. Thy rulers in thee are like rauishing wolues, to shead bloude, and to destroy soules for their owne couetous lucre.

Miche .7. There is not a godly man vpon earth, there is not one righteous among men, they labour all to shead bloud, and euery man hunteth his brother to death.

Iohn.16. Iesus Christ saith: The time shal come, that whosoeuer killeth you, will thinke that he doth God seruice.

Mat..12. If ye wist what this meaneth, I require mercy and not sacrifice: ye would not haue condemned innocentes.

Psal.116. Right deare in the sight of the Lorde, is the death of his saintes.

Esa. 26. The earth shall discouer the bloud that shee hath deuoured, shee shall neuer hyde them, that shee hath murthered.

Zacha..2. The Lord sayd vnto the faithfull, who so toucheth you, shall touch the aple of his owne eye.

Mat..23. Iesus Christ sayd vnto those that persecuted the faithfull. Fulfill ye likewyse the measure of your fathers, ye Serpentes, ye generation of vipers, how should ye escape

scape the damnation of hell? wherefore, beholde I sende vnto you prophetes and wyse men, and Scrybes, and of them ye shall kill and crucifie: and of them shall ye scourge in your sinagoges and persecute from citie to citie: That vpon you may come all the righteous bloud that was shead vpon the earth, from the bloud of righteous Abel, vnto the bloud of Zacharias the sonne of Barachias, whome yee slewe betweene the Temple and the Aulter. Verily I saie vnto you al these things shall light vpon this generation. Jerusalem, Jerusalem which killest the prophets and stonest them which are sent vnto thee.

Persecution is propheciced to happen vnto the children of God.

The Judges and gouernors willing to please and fulfil the wicked desire of Jezabel, condemned the innocent Naboth to be put to death. 3.Reg 21

Augustine vnto Boniface.

182.*Epistle.*

To doe well, and not to let and forbyd the things which are vnlawfull, is a verye consenting vnto error.

Origen in the 3. Homilie vpon Leuiticus.

Let vs take heede that we doe not consent vnto other mens sinnes, I saye consent, not only in doing the lyke things, but also in holding our peace, or winking at things that are euill done.

Prou.17. *Esay.5.* The Lorde hateth as well him that iustifieth the vngodly, as him that condemneth the innocent.

Prou.29. The righteous considereth the cause of the poore, but the vngodlye regardeth no vnderstanding.

Prou.29. The seate of the king that faythfullye iudgeth the poore, shall continue sure for euermore.

Prou.31. With thy mouth defende the thing that is lawfull and right, and the cause of the poore and helpelesse.

Prou.29. Many there be that seeke the Princes fauor, but euerye mans iudgement commeth from the Lorde.

Moyses hath written what the Magistrates ought to be. They must be (sayth he) vertuous men, fearing God, men of truth, hating auarice and couetousnesse. &c.

Chrysostome in his imperfect worke.

Chapter.23. vpon that text,

And say: if we had bene in our fathers dayes, we woulde not haue bene their cōpanions,

panions, to shead the bloud of the Prophets. When thou shalt heare any man saye, that the doctors of the olde time be blessed, proue and trye, what good will or zeale he hath towardes those doctors, for if he doe honor and reuerence those with whom he liueth, without doubt he would also haue honored the other if he had liued with them.

In the same place he sayth moreouer: the Jewes haue alwayes bene worshippers of the Saintes that be past and dead, and condemners of those that be present and a liue.

S. Ierome in his.4.Tome in the rule of Monkes.

It is very true, that ẏ truth can be kept in and bound, but it cannot be vanquished, whiche is content with hir little number, and is not a frayde of the great number of hir enemies.

Saint Ierome vpon Ieremie.5.Tome. Chapter.26.

When the congregation of the people were assembled togither, the Priestes and false Prophetes accused Jeremie, and the Priestes and false Prophetes would haue

Ierem.26. Ieremy vvas accused by the priests.

destroyed and killed the Prophete, if the Judges had had the power of iudgement: By that we doe vnderstande that they which seeme to be altogither ordayned for religion, being moued with enuie, with the holynesse of the Prophet, were more cruell than they that had the charge of publike necessities.

In the same Chapter he saith moreouer: If at anye time for the commaundement of God, and for the veritie of the fayth, the Priestes, or false Prophetes, or the foolish people, are angry with vs, let vs not esteeme nor make any account of it: but let vs execute the sentence of God, not thinking on the euilles that are presente, but beholding the goodnesse to come.

Wo be vnto you that make vnrighteous lawes, and deuise things which be to hard to keepe: thorow which the poore be oppressed on euery side, and the Innocentes of my people are therewith robbed of iudgement: the wydowes may be your pray, and that ye may rob the fatherlesse. What will ye doe in time of the visitation and destruction that shall come from farre? To whom

whom will ye run for helpe? or to whom will ye giue your honour, that yee maye keepe it: that ye come not among the prisoners, or lye among the deade: After all this shall not the wrath of the Lord cease, but yet shall his hande bee stretched oute styll. The torments of the vvicked princes.

It is verily a righteous thing with God, to recompence tribulation to them that trouble you, and to you whiche are troubled, rest with vs when the Lord Jesus shall shewe himselfe from heauen, with his mighty Angelles, in flaming fire, rendring vengeance vnto them that doe not knowe God, neyther obey vnto the Gospell of our Lorde Jesus Christe. Whiche shall be punished with euerlasting damnation, from the presence of the Lorde, and from the glorye of his power. *2. Thess. 1*

At the daye of iudgement (saythe the booke of wisedome) the righteousnesse shall stand in great stedfastnesse agaynst such as haue dealt extreamely with them, and taken away their labours: when they see it, they shal be vexed with horible feare, and shall wonder at the hastinesse of the sodayne health: Groning for very distresse *Sap. 5.*

The complaint of the persecutors at the day of iudgement.

stresse of minde, and shall say within them selues, hauing inward sorowe and mourning for very anguish of minde. These are they whom we sometime had in derision, and iested vpon. We fooles thought their life very madnesse, and their ende to be without honor. But loe, howe they are counted among the children of God, and their porcion is among the saintes. Therfore we haue erred from the way of truth, the light of righteousnesse hath not shined vnto vs, and the sonne of vnderstanding rose not vp vpon vs. We haue weried our selues in the way of wickednesse and destruction. Tedious wayes haue we gone: But as for the way of the Lord we haue not knowen it. What good hath our pride done vnto vs? or what profite hath the pompe of riches brought vs? all those thinges are passed away like a shadowe. And towardes the ende of the Chapter he sayth: his cruell wrath shall hee sharpen for a speare, and the whole compasse of the worlde shall fight with him against the vnwyse. Then shall the thunder boltes go out of the lightnings, and come out of the rayne bowe of the cloudes to the place appointed:

Sapi.5.

pointed: out of the harde stonie indignation there shall fall thicke hayles, and the water of the sea shall bee wroth agaynst them, and the flouds shall runne roughlye togither, yea, a mihgtie wynde shal stand vp agaynst them, and a storme shall scatter them abroade. &c.

Beholde howe the true christian doctrine is at this day called a new pestilentious doctrine by the worldlinges. Euen as in the old time it was called, and in the Apostles time.

Men haue called before time (as they doe at this day) the doctrine of the Apostles newe doctrine, as it appeareth in the actes of the Apostles where it is sayde: And they tooke Paule, and sayde vnto him, maye we not knowe what this newe doctrine, whereof thou speakest, is? for thou bringest straunge tydings in oure eares. Some called him a babler, and a tidings bringer of newe Gods. The doctrin of the Apostles nevve doctrine. *Act.* 17.

All men did speake agaynst the Apostolicall doctrine, as it appeareth by that which the Iewes sayde vnto Saint Paul when he was come to Rome, saying vnto him: we will heare of thee what thou thinkest: *Act.* 28.

kest: for as concerning this sect, we know that euery where it is spoken against.

Saint Paule being accused and brought before the great gouernor, they accused him after this sort: We haue founde this fellowe, a pestilent fellowe, and a mouer of debate vnto all the Iewes throughout the worlde, and a chiefe mayntayner of the sect of the Nazarites. *Act.24.*

Act.24. Saint Paule answereth vnto the same: This I confesse vnto thee, that after that way (which they call heresye) so worship I the God of my fathers, beleeuing all thinges which are written in the lawe and the Prophets. And haue hope towardes God, that the same resurrection of the deade which they them selues looke for also, shall be both of the iust and vniust: some sayde that the Apostles with their doctrine, did nothing but moue the people to sedition, as it appeareth by the actes of the Apostles: saying, certayne vagabonds which were wicked fellowes did make assault against the house of Iason, and drewe him with certayne brethren vnto ye heades of the citie, crying, these are they whiche haue subuerted the state of the world, and here

The resurrection of the righteous and vnrighteous shall come.

Act.17.

here they are, which Iason hath receiued: and these all doe contrary to the decrees of Ceasar, affirming that there is another king one Iesus.

Therefore we labour and suffer rebuke, bicause we haue sure hope in the liuing God, which is the sauiour of all men, but specially of those that beleeue. 1. Tim. 4.

The Tyrantes shall not escape vnpunished, but often times they them selues that did put to death the children of God, by the handes of the hangmen, haue not that good to be killed of the hangmen, but they them selues are the hangmen or murderers of their owne bodyes. As it appeareth by Saule which persecuted Dauid. It was not needefull that Dauid shoulde haue pursued him, for he was auenged more then he desired. It was not needefull to hang vp Achitophel: nor the Apostles to pursue Iudas that betrayed his maister, for he him selfe was his owne hangman, hanging himselfe by the necke, brast a sunder in the middes, and all his bowelles gusshed out. And Senacherib had for his hangmen his owne sonnes: and it did cost Ezechias nothing for to auenge him selfe

1. Sam. 31

Note the vengeance of God agaynst the vvicked persecutors.

Act. 1.

Esay. 37.

2. Mac. 8

selfe of the tyrannie agaynst him.

*Act.*12. Were Antiochus and Herode left vnpunished for theyr tyrannie vpon the chil-
*Euseb.li.*1 dren of God? It appeareth no. For they
*cap.*9.*li.*2 were consumed and eaten with lyce and
*cap.*10. vermine. God will not leaue the wicked vnpunished as it appeareth
3.*Reg.*22 of Achab, Manasses, Se-
4 *Reg.*15. dechias and many Em-
21.24.25 peroures of
Rome.

1. Timo. 6.

Regi autem seculorum immortali, inuisibili,
soli sapienti deo, honor & gloria
in secula seculorum.
Amen.

FINIS.

A Table to finde oute the principall things contayned in this present booke, and first of the Letter A.

Augu-

B.

C.

D.

F.

G.

H.

I.

Supper.

FINIS.

Lightning Source UK Ltd.
Milton Keynes UK
UKOW05f0629300616
277322UK00001B/96/P